BUREAU FOR PARANORMAL · RESEARCH AND DEFENSE ·

B.P.R.D. HELL ON EARTH:
COUNTY HORROR & OTHERS

created by MIKE MIGNOLA

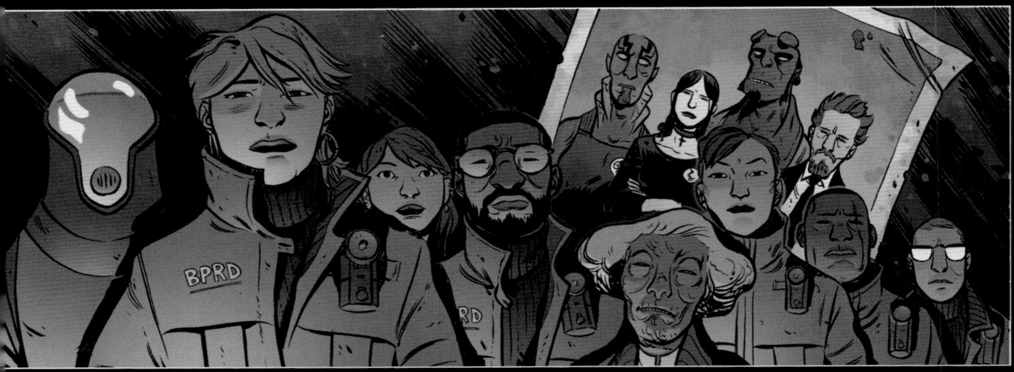
BPRD

Since Liz Sherman destroyed the frog army and the Black Flame in Agartha, the Bureau for Paranormal Research and Defense has seen their charter expanded to oversee international threats, leading to collaborations with Russia's occult bureau. With Liz missing and Abe Sapien on the verge of death, the burden lies upon Kate Corrigan, Johann, and the more conventional agents of the B.P.R.D.

MIKE MIGNOLA'S

B.P.R.D.™
HELL ON EARTH

THE PICKENS COUNTY HORROR & OTHERS

story by **MIKE MIGNOLA** and **SCOTT ALLIE**

art for *The Pickens County Horror* by **JASON LATOUR**

art for *The Transformation of J. H. O'Donnell* by **MAX FIUMARA**

art for *The Abyss of Time* by **JAMES HARREN**

colors by **DAVE STEWART**

letters by **CLEM ROBINS**

cover art by **MIKE MIGNOLA** with **DAVE STEWART**

chapter break art by **BECKY CLOONAN, MAX FIUMARA,** and **JAMES HARREN** with **DAVE STEWART**

editor **SCOTT ALLIE**

assistant editor **DANIEL CHABON**   collection designer **AMY ARENDTS**

publisher **MIKE RICHARDSON**

DARK HORSE BOOKS ®

Special thanks to Jason Hvam

Mike Richardson PRESIDENT AND PUBLISHER · Neil Hankerson EXECUTIVE VICE PRESIDENT
Tom Weddle CHIEF FINANCIAL OFFICER · Randy Stradley VICE PRESIDENT OF PUBLISHING
Michael Martens VICE PRESIDENT OF BOOK TRADE SALES · Anita Nelson VICE PRESIDENT
OF BUSINESS AFFAIRS · Scott Allie EDITOR IN CHIEF · Matt Parkinson VICE PRESIDENT OF
MARKETING · David Scroggy VICE PRESIDENT OF PRODUCT DEVELOPMENT · Dale LaFountain
VICE PRESIDENT OF INFORMATION TECHNOLOGY · Darlene Vogel SENIOR DIRECTOR OF
PRINT, DESIGN, AND PRODUCTION · Ken Lizzi GENERAL COUNSEL · Davey Estrada EDITORIAL
DIRECTOR · Chris Warner SENIOR BOOKS EDITOR · Diana Schutz EXECUTIVE EDITOR · Cary
Grazzini DIRECTOR OF PRINT AND DEVELOPMENT · Lia Ribacchi ART DIRECTOR · Cara Niece
DIRECTOR OF SCHEDULING · Tim Wiesch DIRECTOR OF INTERNATIONAL LICENSING · Mark
Bernardi DIRECTOR OF DIGITAL PUBLISHING

DarkHorse.com   Hellboy.com

This book collects the comic-book series B.P.R.D. Hell on Earth: The Pickens County Horror #1–#2,
B.P.R.D. Hell on Earth: The Transformation of J. H. O'Donnell, and B.P.R.D. Hell on Earth #103–#104,
originally published by Dark Horse Comics.

Published by Dark Horse Books
A division of Dark Horse Comics, Inc.
10956 SE Main Street
Milwaukie, OR 97222

International licensing: (503) 905-2377

First edition: July 2013
ISBN 978-1-61655-140-7

10 9 8 7 6 5 4 3 2 1
Printed in China

THE PICKENS COUNTY HORROR

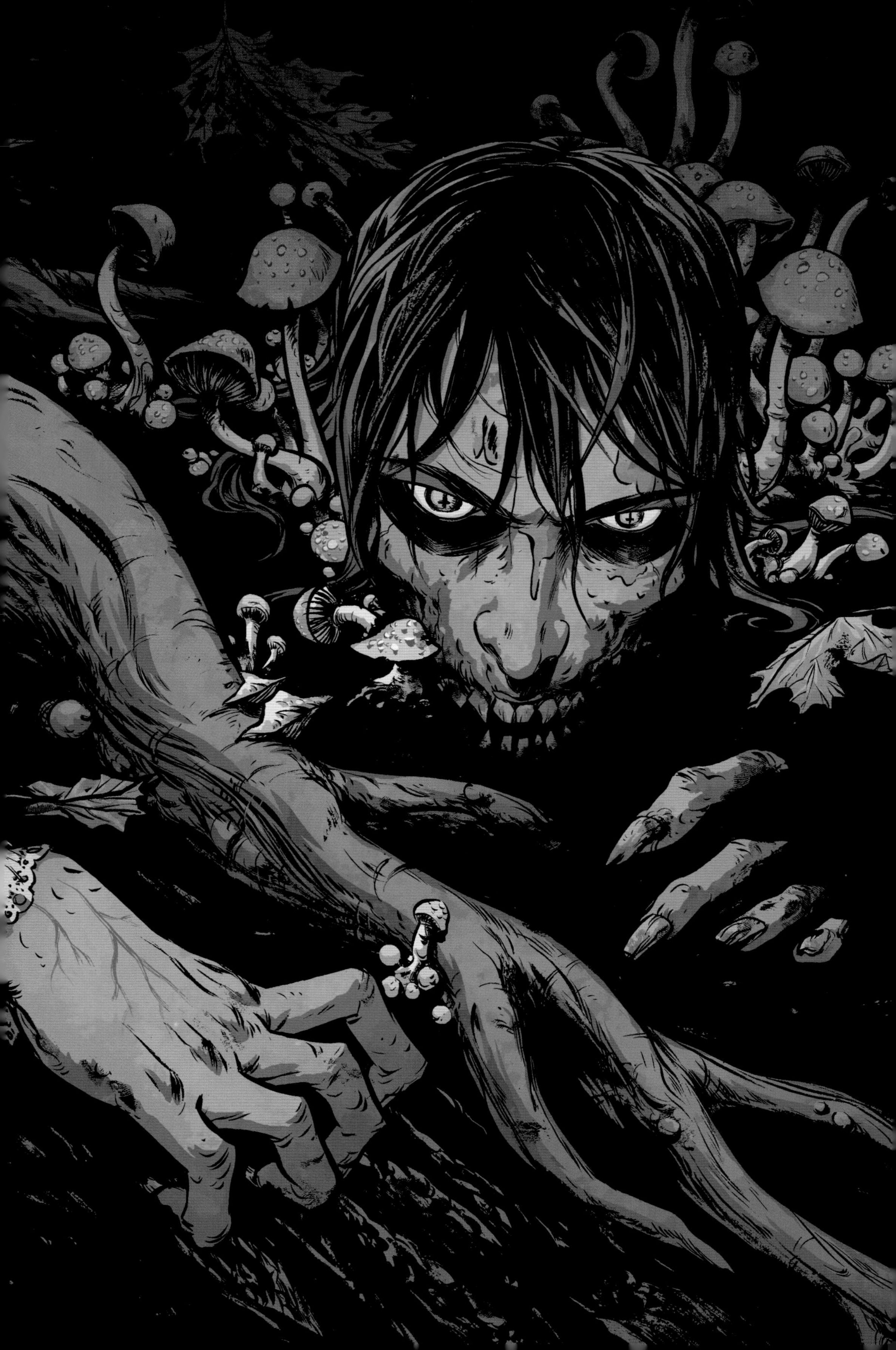

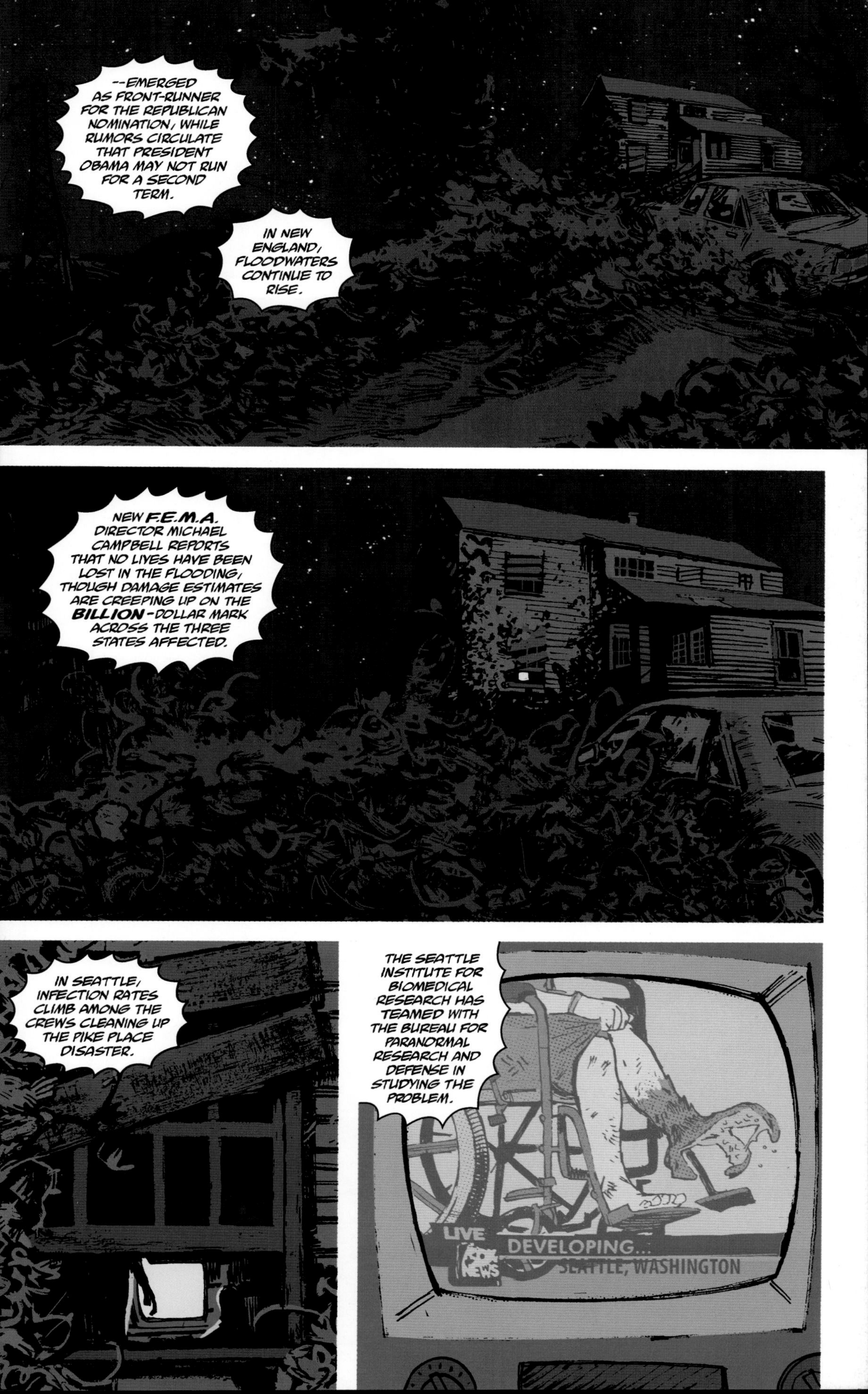
--EMERGED AS FRONT-RUNNER FOR THE REPUBLICAN NOMINATION, WHILE RUMORS CIRCULATE THAT PRESIDENT OBAMA MAY NOT RUN FOR A SECOND TERM.
IN NEW ENGLAND, FLOODWATERS CONTINUE TO RISE.
NEW F.E.M.A. DIRECTOR MICHAEL CAMPBELL REPORTS THAT NO LIVES HAVE BEEN LOST IN THE FLOODING, THOUGH DAMAGE ESTIMATES ARE CREEPING UP ON THE BILLION-DOLLAR MARK ACROSS THE THREE STATES AFFECTED.
IN SEATTLE, INFECTION RATES CLIMB AMONG THE CREWS CLEANING UP THE PIKE PLACE DISASTER.
THE SEATTLE INSTITUTE FOR BIOMEDICAL RESEARCH HAS TEAMED WITH THE BUREAU FOR PARANORMAL RESEARCH AND DEFENSE IN STUDYING THE PROBLEM.
LIVE
NEWS
DEVELOPING...
SEATTLE, WASHINGTON

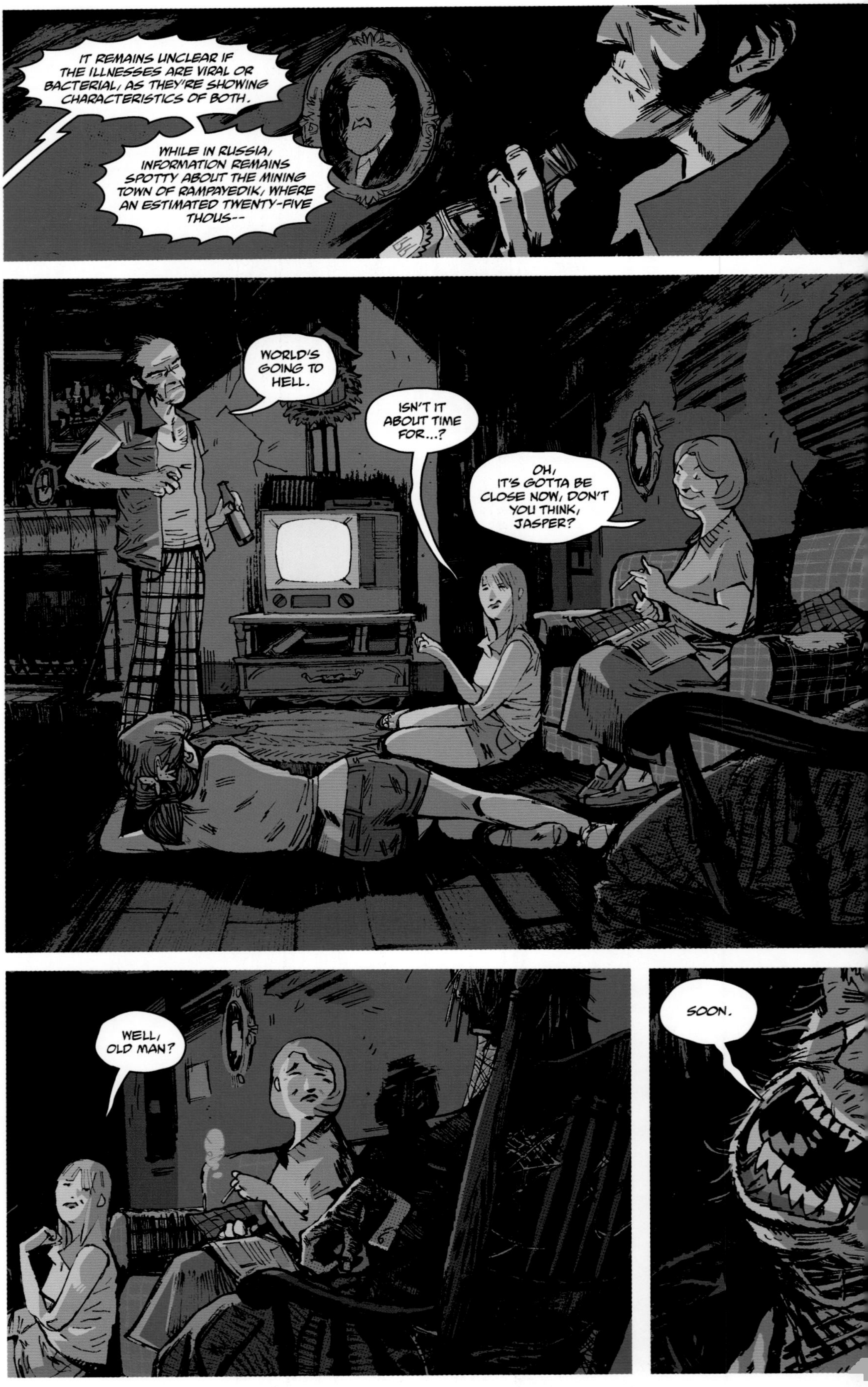
IT REMAINS UNCLEAR IF THE ILLNESSES ARE VIRAL OR BACTERIAL, AS THEY'RE SHOWING CHARACTERISTICS OF BOTH.
WHILE IN RUSSIA, INFORMATION REMAINS SPOTTY ABOUT THE MINING TOWN OF RAMPAYEDIK, WHERE AN ESTIMATED TWENTY-FIVE THOUS--
WORLD'S GOING TO HELL.
ISN'T IT ABOUT TIME FOR...?
OH, IT'S GOTTA BE CLOSE NOW, DON'T YOU THINK, JASPER?
WELL, OLD MAN?
SOON.

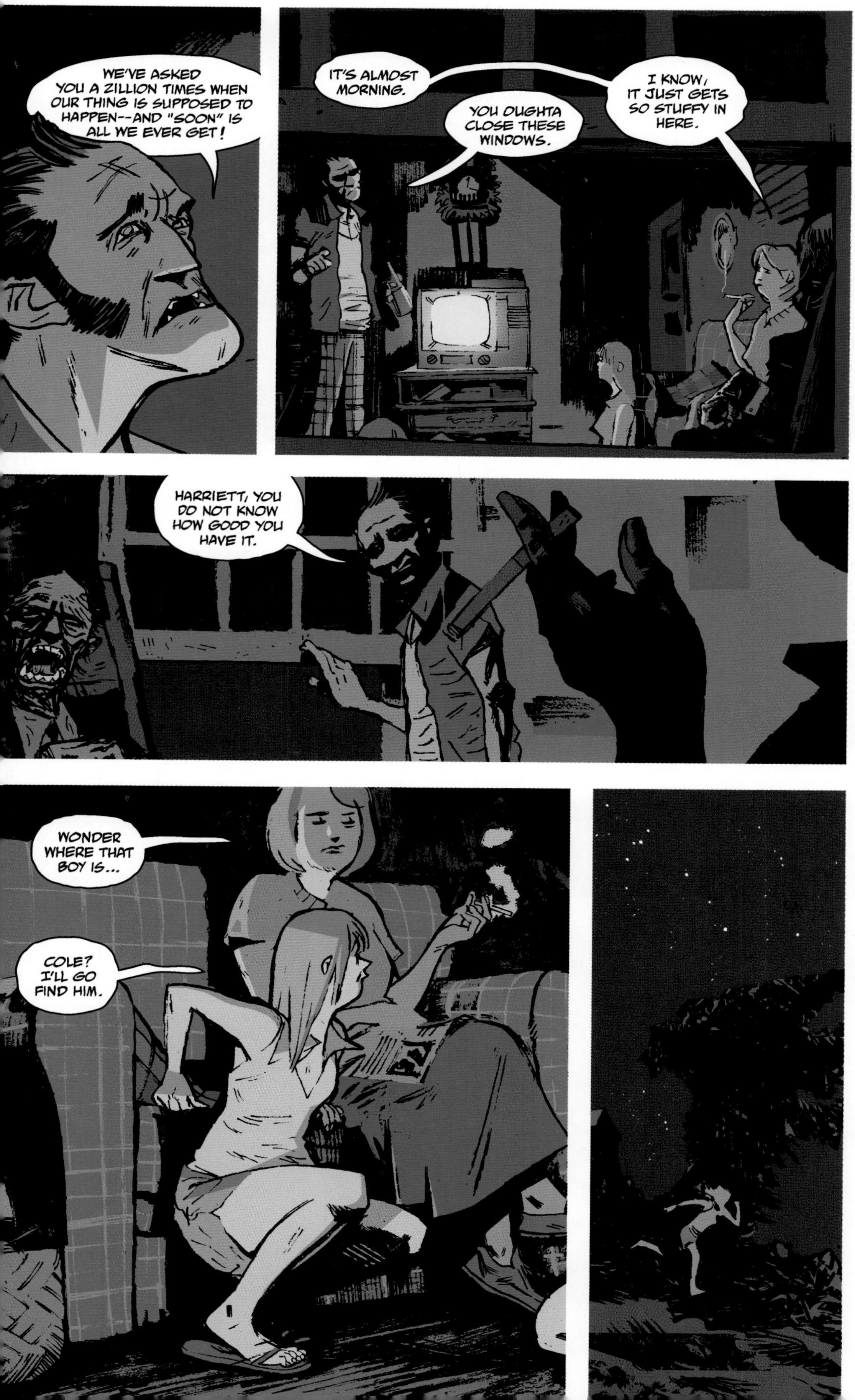
WE'VE ASKED YOU A ZILLION TIMES WHEN OUR THING IS SUPPOSED TO HAPPEN--AND "SOON" IS ALL WE EVER GET!
IT'S ALMOST MORNING.
YOU OUGHTA CLOSE THESE WINDOWS.
I KNOW, IT JUST GETS SO STUFFY IN HERE.
HARRIETT, YOU DO NOT KNOW HOW GOOD YOU HAVE IT.
WONDER WHERE THAT BOY IS...
COLE? I'LL GO FIND HIM.

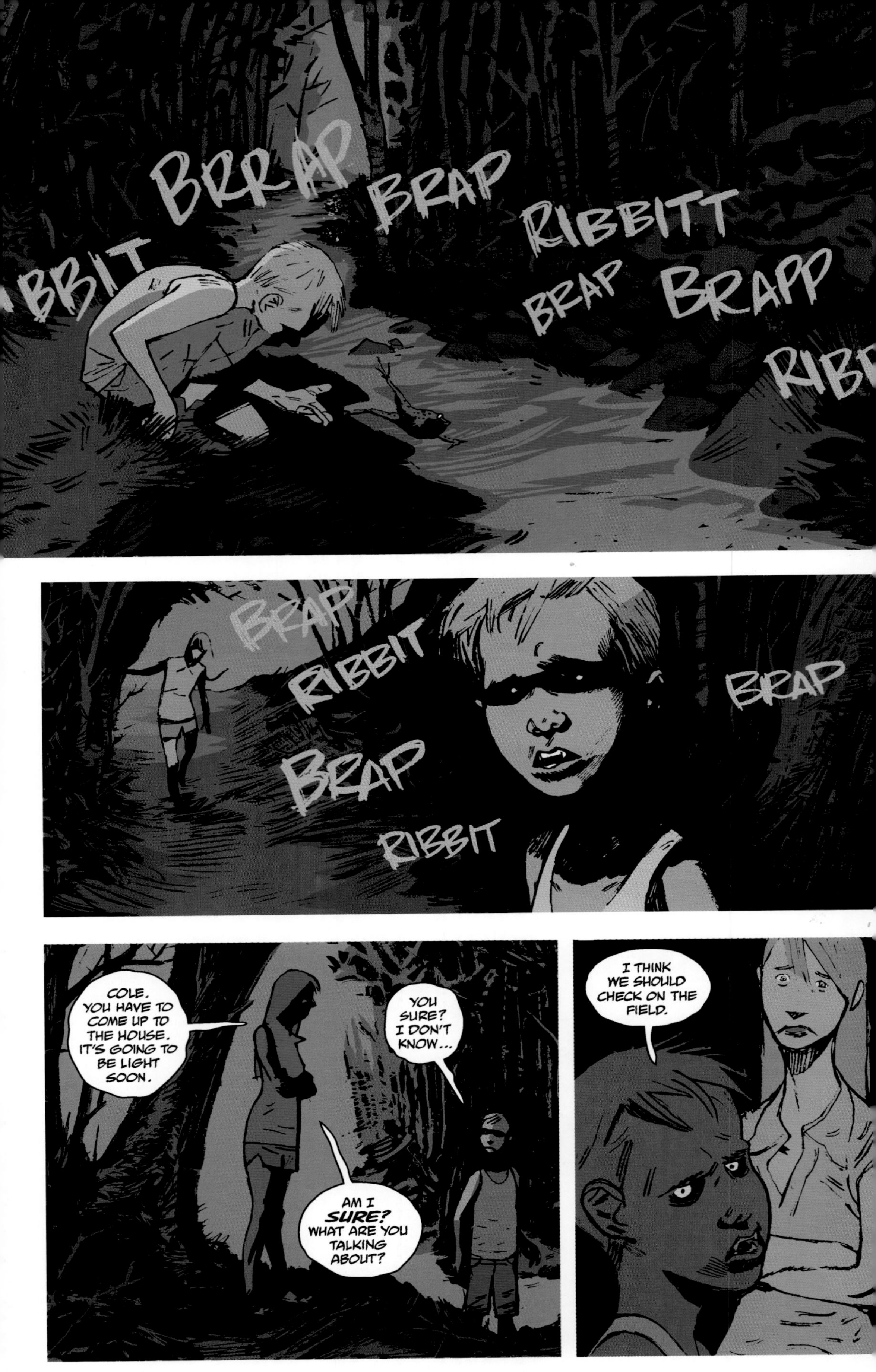
BBIT
BRRAP
BRAP
RIBBITT
BRAP
BRAPP
RIBB
BRAP
RIBBIT
BRAP
BRAP
RIBBIT
COLE. YOU HAVE TO COME UP TO THE HOUSE. IT'S GOING TO BE LIGHT SOON.
YOU SURE? I DON'T KNOW...
AM I *SURE?* WHAT ARE YOU TALKING ABOUT?
I THINK WE SHOULD CHECK ON THE FIELD.

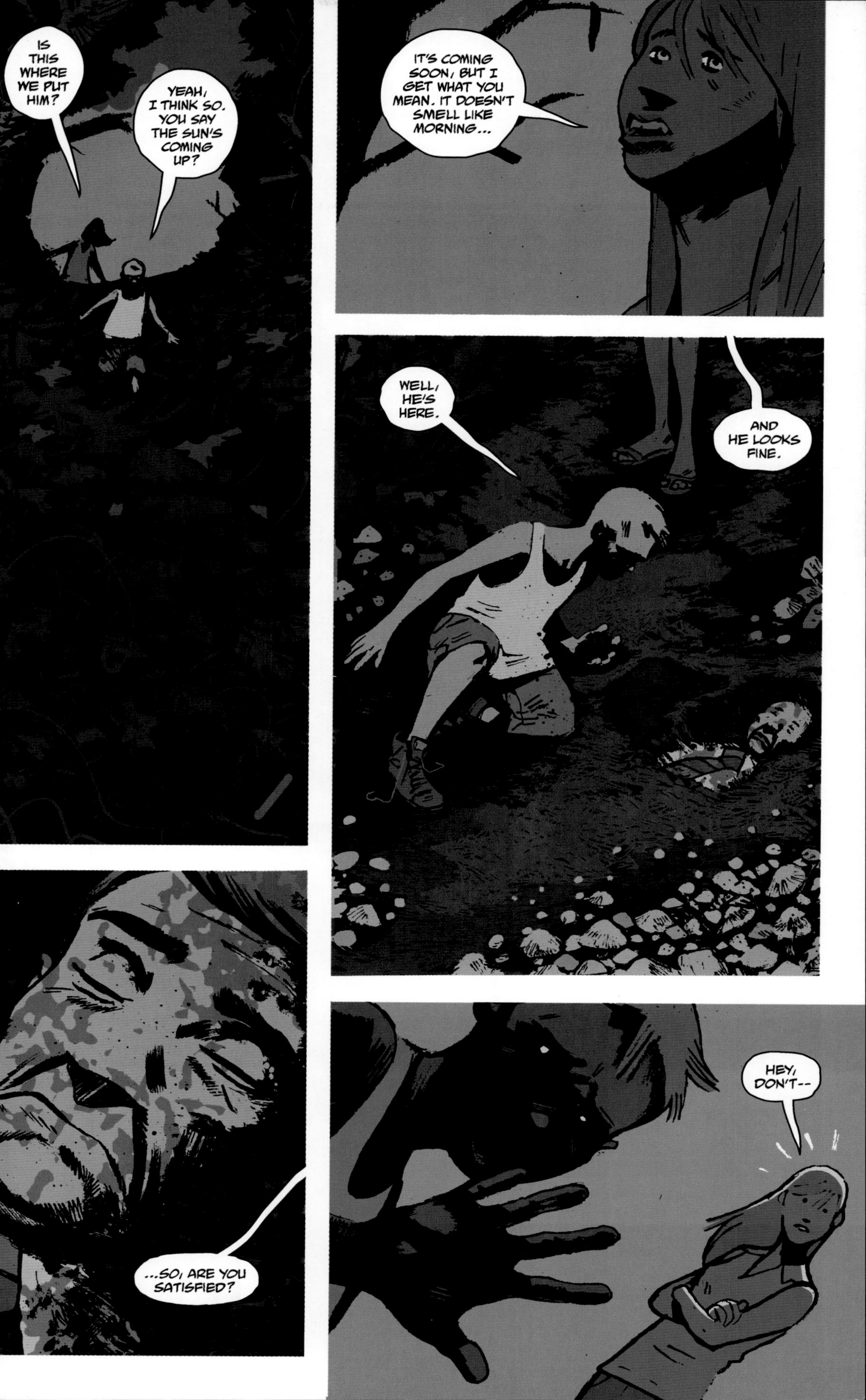

IS THIS WHERE WE PUT HIM?
YEAH, I THINK SO. YOU SAY THE SUN'S COMING UP?
IT'S COMING SOON, BUT I GET WHAT YOU MEAN. IT DOESN'T SMELL LIKE MORNING...
WELL, HE'S HERE.
AND HE LOOKS FINE.
...SO, ARE YOU SATISFIED?
HEY, DON'T--

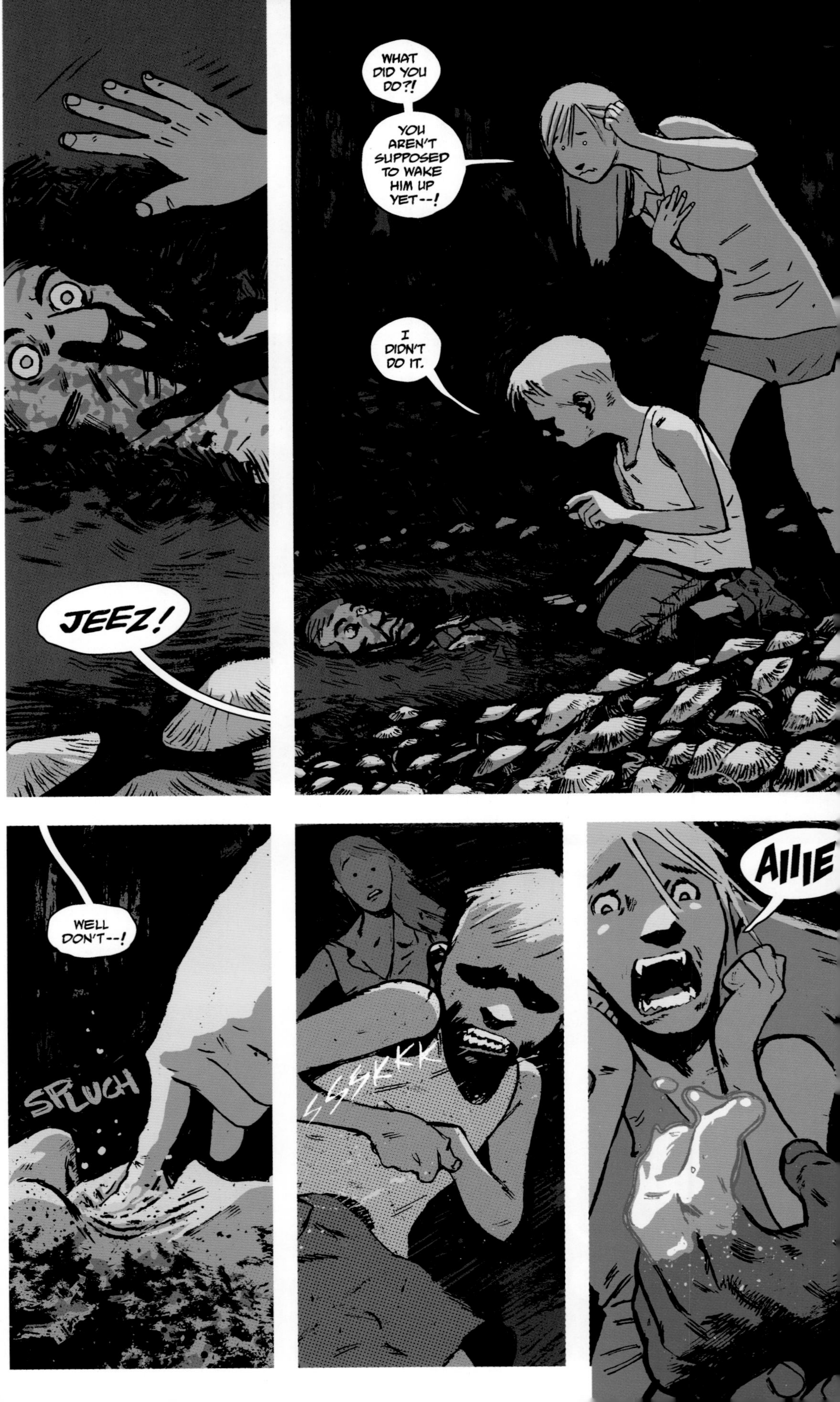
JEEZ!
WHAT DID YOU DO?!
YOU AREN'T SUPPOSED TO WAKE HIM UP YET--!
I DIDN'T DO IT.
WELL DON'T--!
SPLUCH
SSSKKK
AIIIE

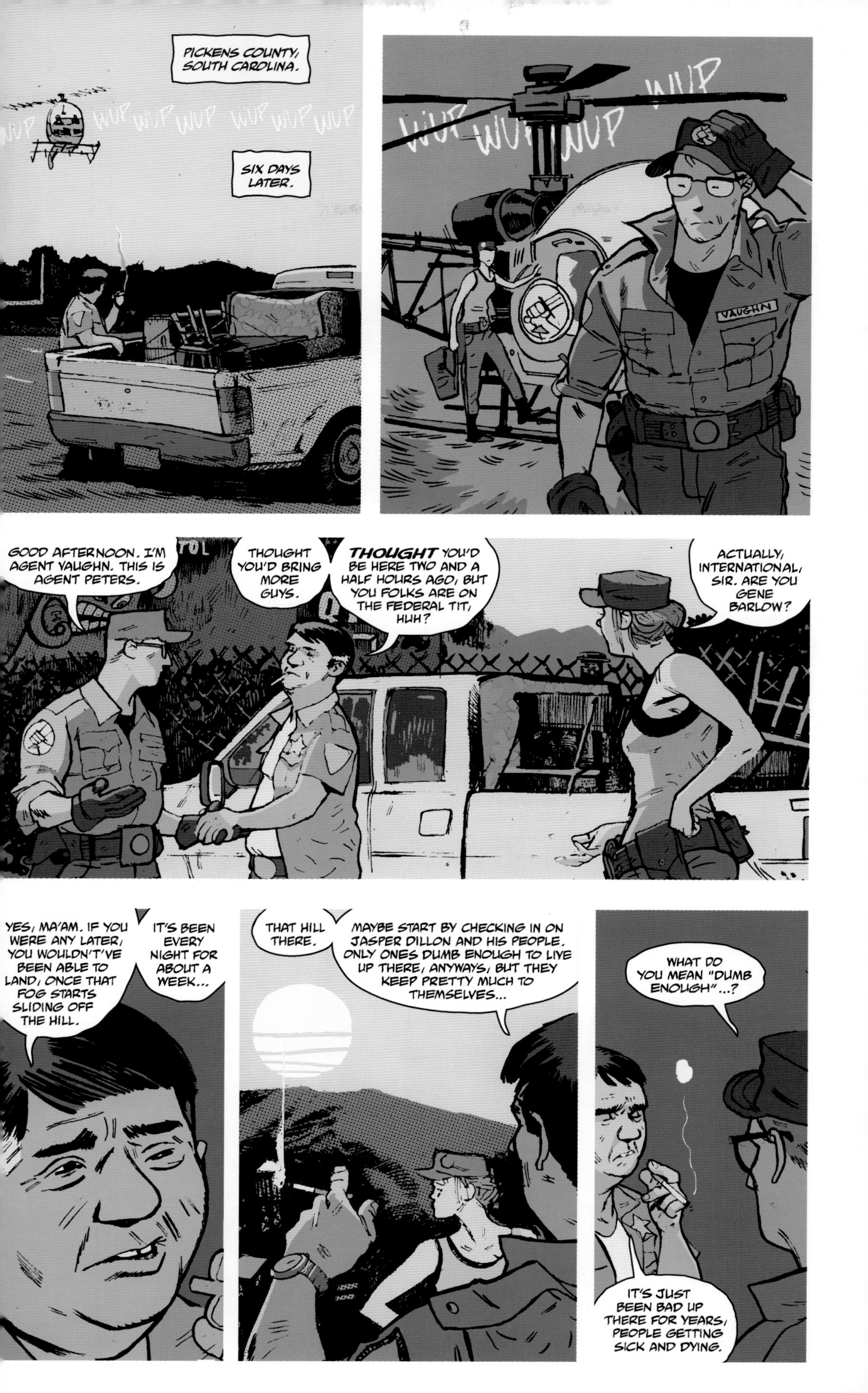
PICKENS COUNTY, SOUTH CAROLINA.
WUP WUP WUP WUP WUP WUP WUP
SIX DAYS LATER.
WUP WUP WUP WUP
VAUGHN
GOOD AFTERNOON. I'M AGENT VAUGHN. THIS IS AGENT PETERS.
THOUGHT YOU'D BRING MORE GUYS.
THOUGHT YOU'D BE HERE TWO AND A HALF HOURS AGO, BUT YOU FOLKS ARE ON THE FEDERAL TIT, HUH?
ACTUALLY, INTERNATIONAL, SIR. ARE YOU GENE BARLOW?
YES, MA'AM. IF YOU WERE ANY LATER, YOU WOULDN'T'VE BEEN ABLE TO LAND, ONCE THAT FOG STARTS SLIDING OFF THE HILL.
IT'S BEEN EVERY NIGHT FOR ABOUT A WEEK...
THAT HILL THERE.
MAYBE START BY CHECKING IN ON JASPER DILLON AND HIS PEOPLE. ONLY ONES DUMB ENOUGH TO LIVE UP THERE, ANYWAYS, BUT THEY KEEP PRETTY MUCH TO THEMSELVES...
WHAT DO YOU MEAN "DUMB ENOUGH"...?
IT'S JUST BEEN BAD UP THERE FOR YEARS, PEOPLE GETTING SICK AND DYING.

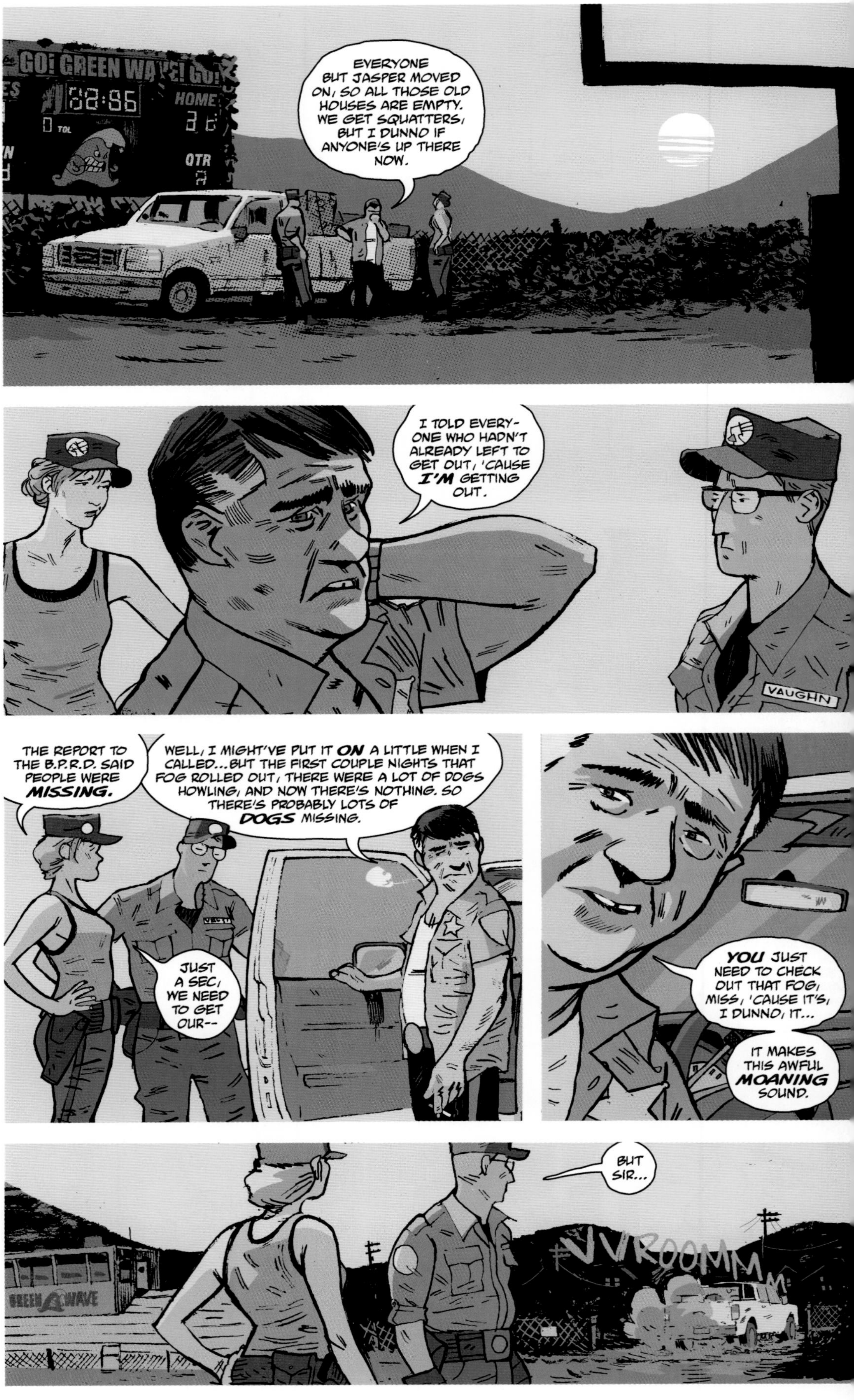
GO! GREEN WAVE! GO!
HOME
QTR
EVERYONE BUT JASPER MOVED ON, SO ALL THOSE OLD HOUSES ARE EMPTY. WE GET SQUATTERS, BUT I DUNNO IF ANYONE'S UP THERE NOW.
I TOLD EVERYONE WHO HADN'T ALREADY LEFT TO GET OUT, 'CAUSE *I'M* GETTING OUT.
VAUGHN
THE REPORT TO THE B.P.R.D. SAID PEOPLE WERE *MISSING.*
WELL, I MIGHT'VE PUT IT *ON* A LITTLE WHEN I CALLED... BUT THE FIRST COUPLE NIGHTS THAT FOG ROLLED OUT, THERE WERE A LOT OF DOGS HOWLING, AND NOW THERE'S NOTHING. SO THERE'S PROBABLY LOTS OF *DOGS* MISSING.
JUST A SEC, WE NEED TO GET OUR--
YOU JUST NEED TO CHECK OUT THAT FOG, MISS, 'CAUSE IT'S, I DUNNO, IT...
IT MAKES THIS AWFUL *MOANING* SOUND.
BUT SIR...
VVROOMM
GREEN WAVE

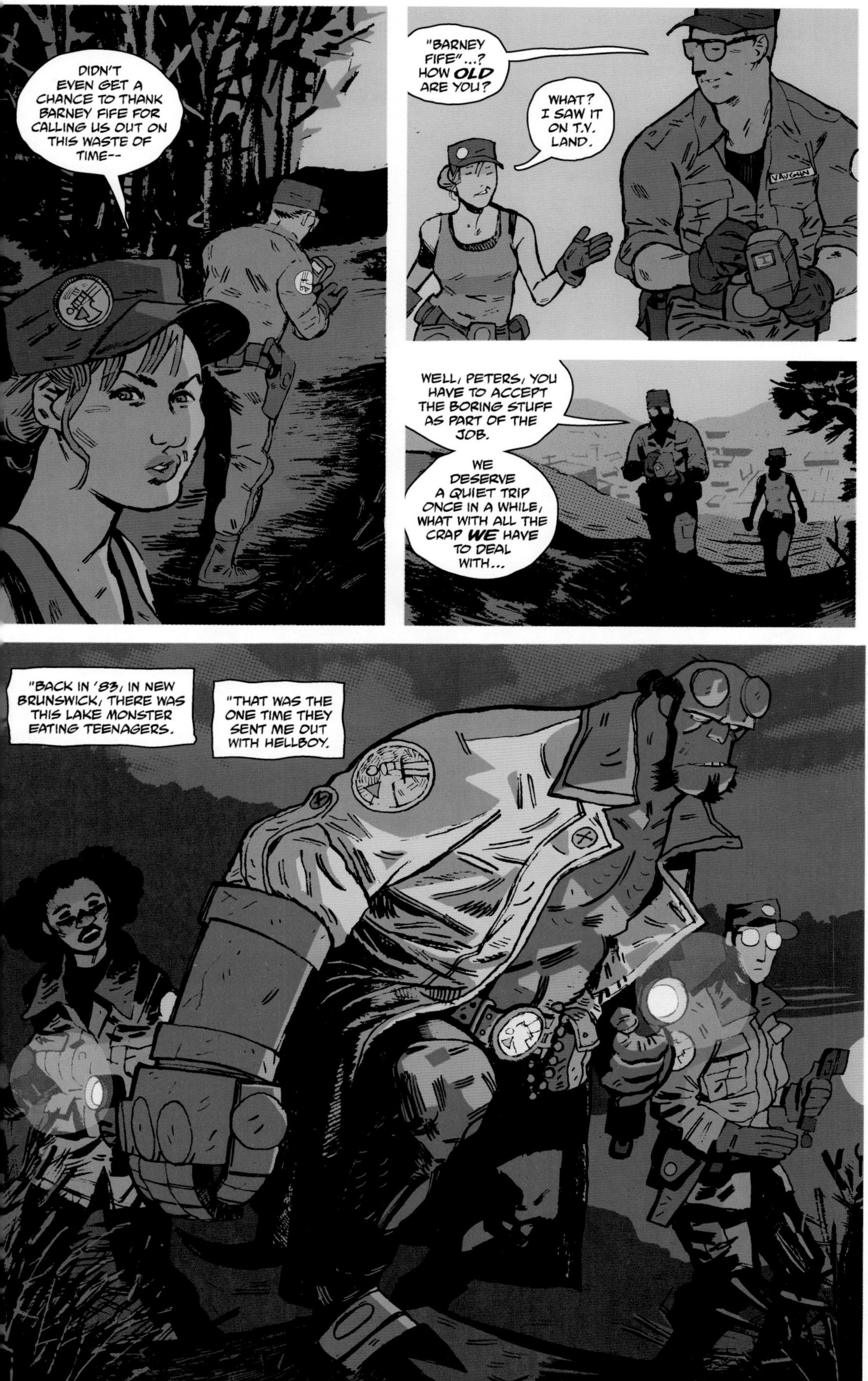
DIDN'T EVEN GET A CHANCE TO THANK BARNEY FIFE FOR CALLING US OUT ON THIS WASTE OF TIME--
"BARNEY FIFE"...? HOW OLD ARE YOU?
WHAT? I SAW IT ON T.V. LAND.
VAUGHN
WELL, PETERS, YOU HAVE TO ACCEPT THE BORING STUFF AS PART OF THE JOB.
WE DESERVE A QUIET TRIP ONCE IN A WHILE, WHAT WITH ALL THE CRAP WE HAVE TO DEAL WITH...
"BACK IN '83, IN NEW BRUNSWICK, THERE WAS THIS LAKE MONSTER EATING TEENAGERS.
"THAT WAS THE ONE TIME THEY SENT ME OUT WITH HELLBOY.

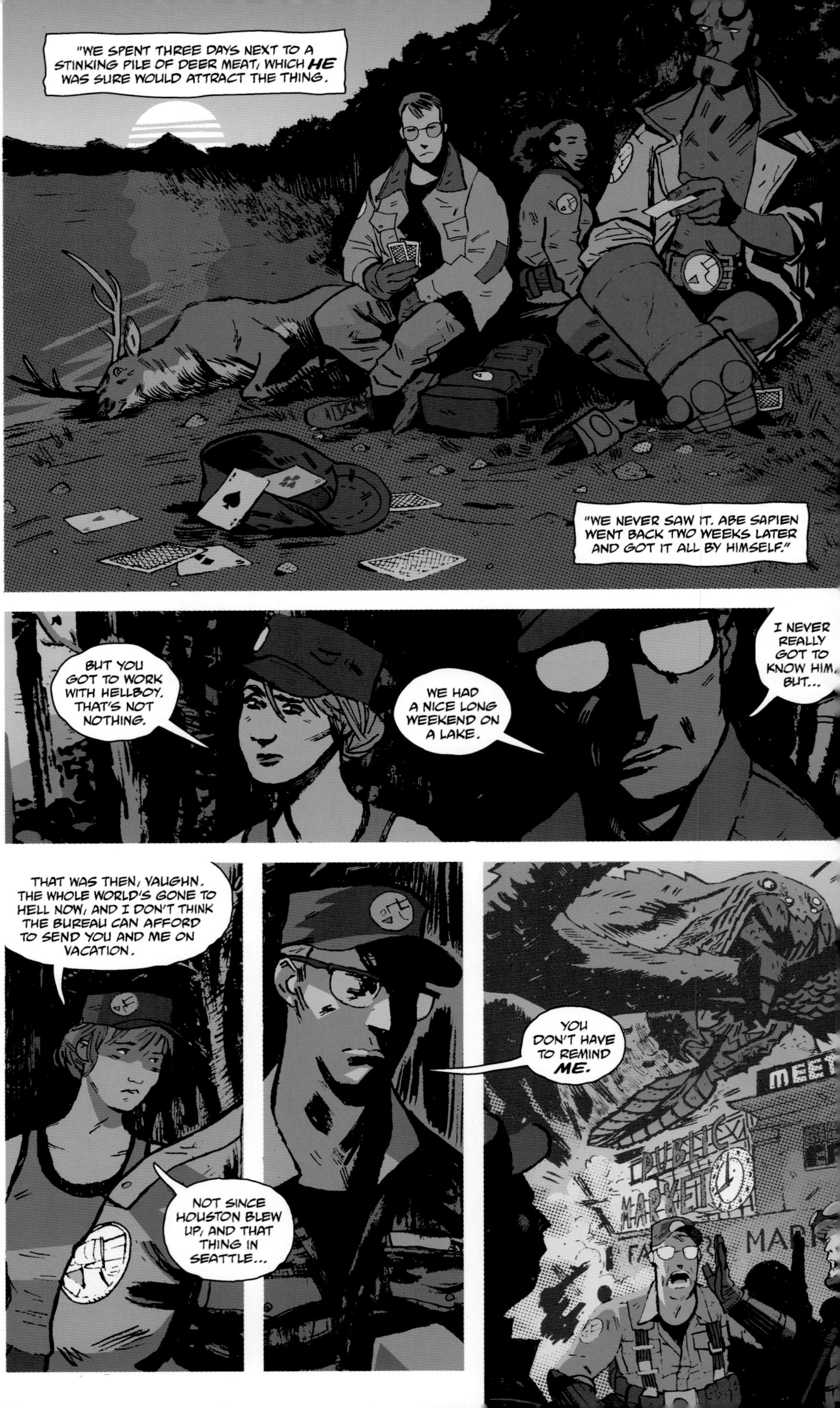
"WE SPENT THREE DAYS NEXT TO A STINKING PILE OF DEER MEAT, WHICH **HE** WAS SURE WOULD ATTRACT THE THING.
"WE NEVER SAW IT. ABE SAPIEN WENT BACK TWO WEEKS LATER AND GOT IT ALL BY HIMSELF."
BUT YOU GOT TO WORK WITH HELLBOY. THAT'S NOT NOTHING.
WE HAD A NICE LONG WEEKEND ON A LAKE.
I NEVER REALLY GOT TO KNOW HIM, BUT...
THAT WAS THEN, VAUGHN. THE WHOLE WORLD'S GONE TO HELL NOW, AND I DON'T THINK THE BUREAU CAN AFFORD TO SEND YOU AND ME ON VACATION.
NOT SINCE HOUSTON BLEW UP, AND THAT THING IN SEATTLE...
YOU DON'T HAVE TO REMIND **ME.**
PUBLIC MARKET

LOOK AT THAT WEED, GROWING ON THE TREES. SOMETHING'S KILLING IT.

IT'S NOT A WEED. IT'S *KUDZU.*

beep

IT'S *INVASIVE* LIKE A WEED. THEY CALL IT "THE VINE THAT ATE THE SOUTH," BECAUSE ONCE IT WAS INTRODUCED, NOTHING THEY COULD DO WOULD STOP IT FROM SPREADING.

BEEP BEEP

VAVGHN

BEEP BEEP BEEP

TINK TINK

PINCH

PETERS.

BEEP BEEP BEEP BEEP

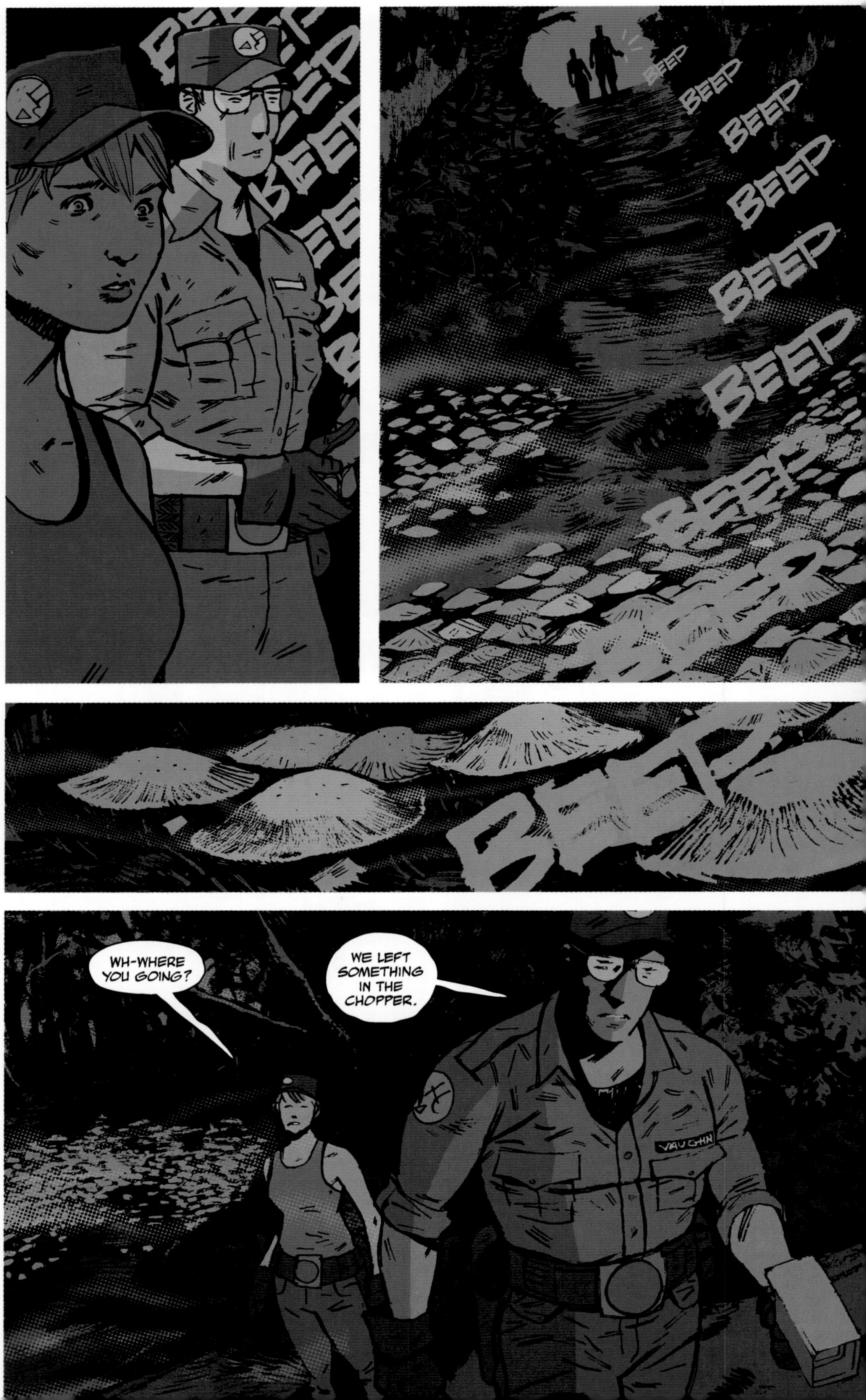

BEEP
BEEP
BEEP
BEEP
BEEP
BEEP
BEEP
WH-WHERE YOU GOING?
WE LEFT SOMETHING IN THE CHOPPER.
VAUGHN

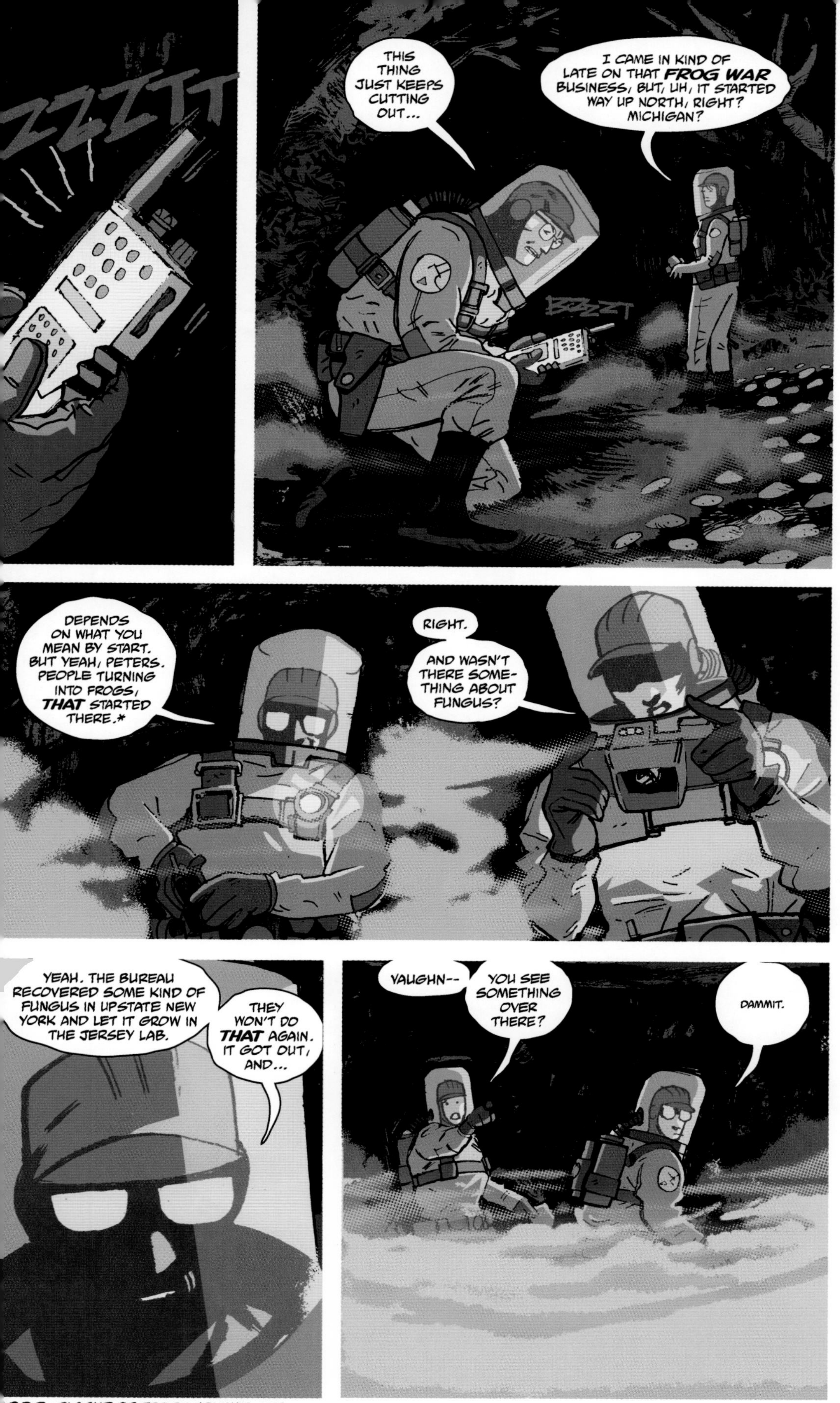
ZZZTT
THIS THING JUST KEEPS CUTTING OUT...
I CAME IN KIND OF LATE ON THAT FROG WAR BUSINESS, BUT, UH, IT STARTED WAY UP NORTH, RIGHT? MICHIGAN?
BZZZT
DEPENDS ON WHAT YOU MEAN BY START. BUT YEAH, PETERS. PEOPLE TURNING INTO FROGS, THAT STARTED THERE.*
RIGHT.
AND WASN'T THERE SOME-THING ABOUT FUNGUS?
YEAH. THE BUREAU RECOVERED SOME KIND OF FUNGUS IN UPSTATE NEW YORK AND LET IT GROW IN THE JERSEY LAB.
THEY WON'T DO THAT AGAIN. IT GOT OUT, AND...
VAUGHN--
YOU SEE SOMETHING OVER THERE?
DAMMIT.

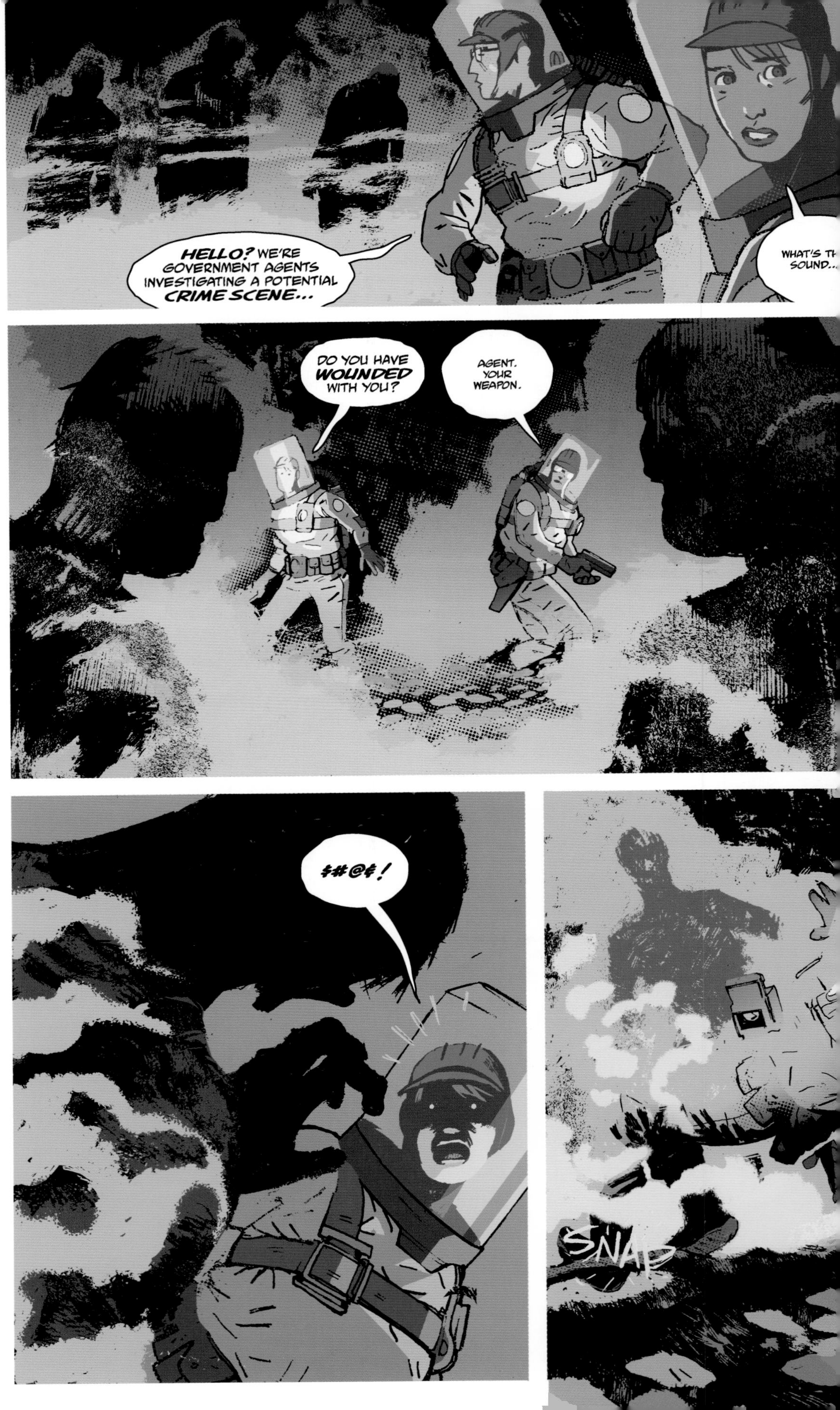
HELLO? WE'RE GOVERNMENT AGENTS INVESTIGATING A POTENTIAL CRIME SCENE...
WHAT'S TH SOUND...
DO YOU HAVE WOUNDED WITH YOU?
AGENT. YOUR WEAPON.
$#@¢!
SNAP

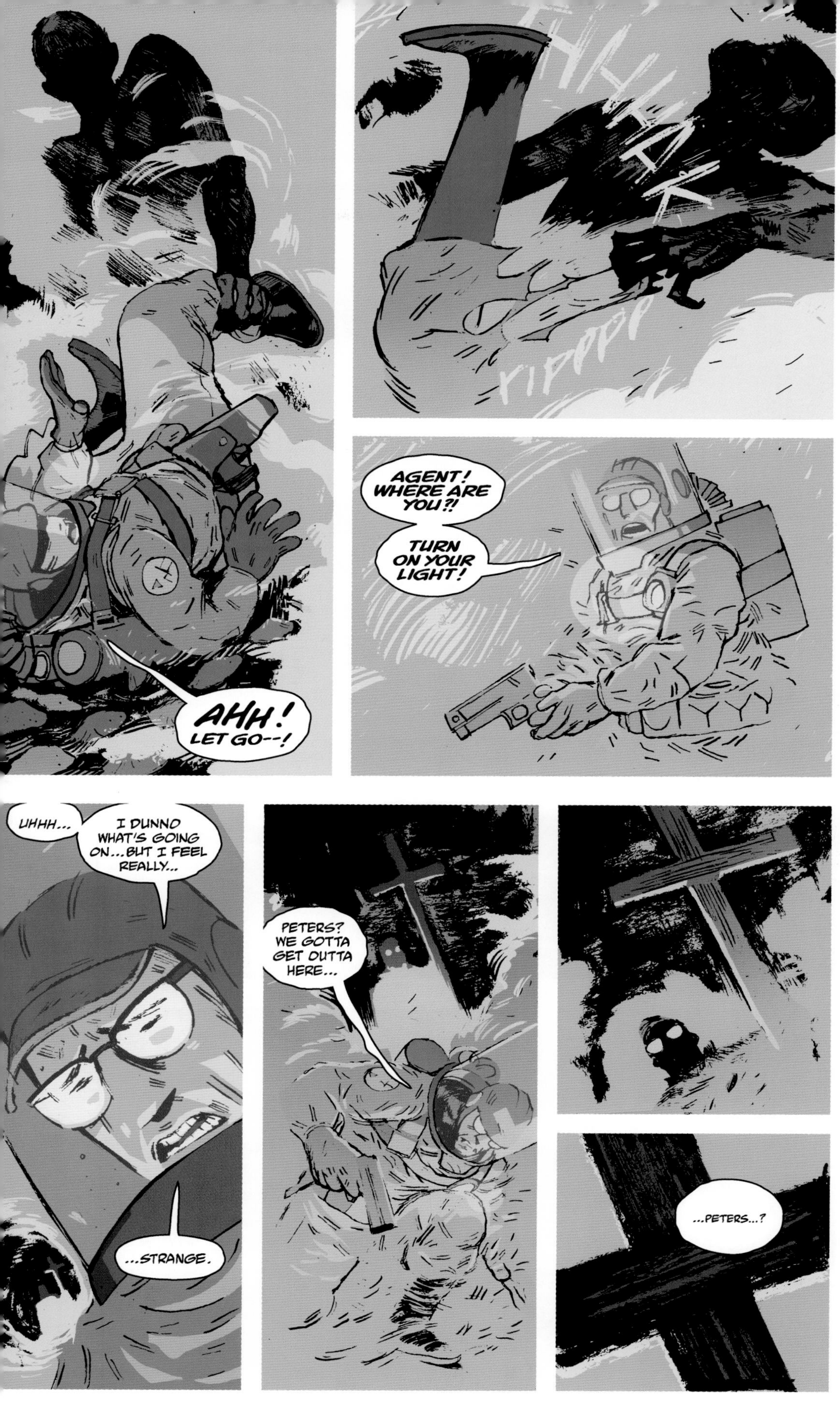
THHAK
RIPPPP
AHH! LET GO--!
AGENT! WHERE ARE YOU?!
TURN ON YOUR LIGHT!
UHHH...
I DUNNO WHAT'S GOING ON...BUT I FEEL REALLY...
...STRANGE.
PETERS? WE GOTTA GET OUTTA HERE...
...PETERS...?

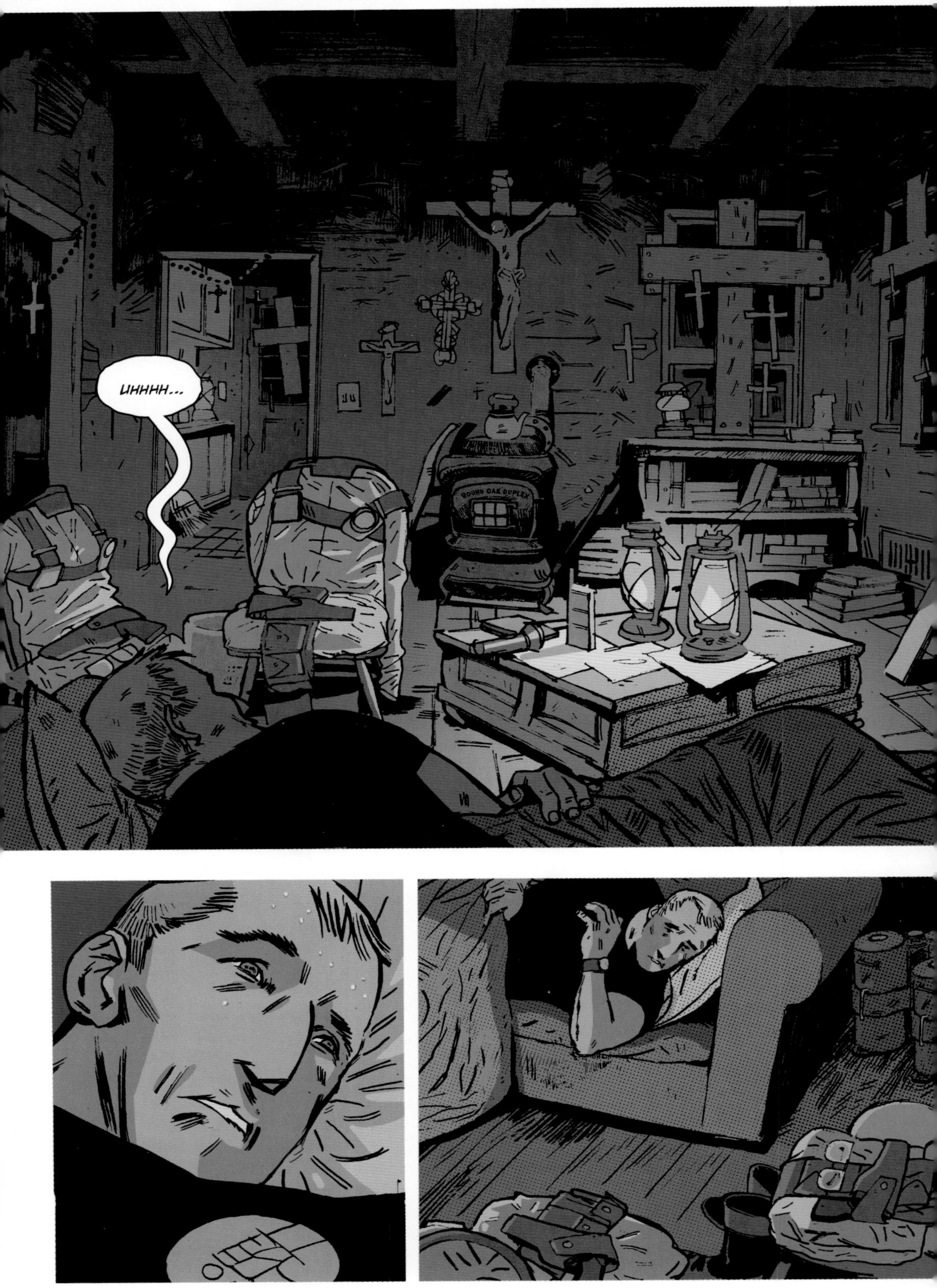
UHHHH...
ROUND OAK DUPLEX

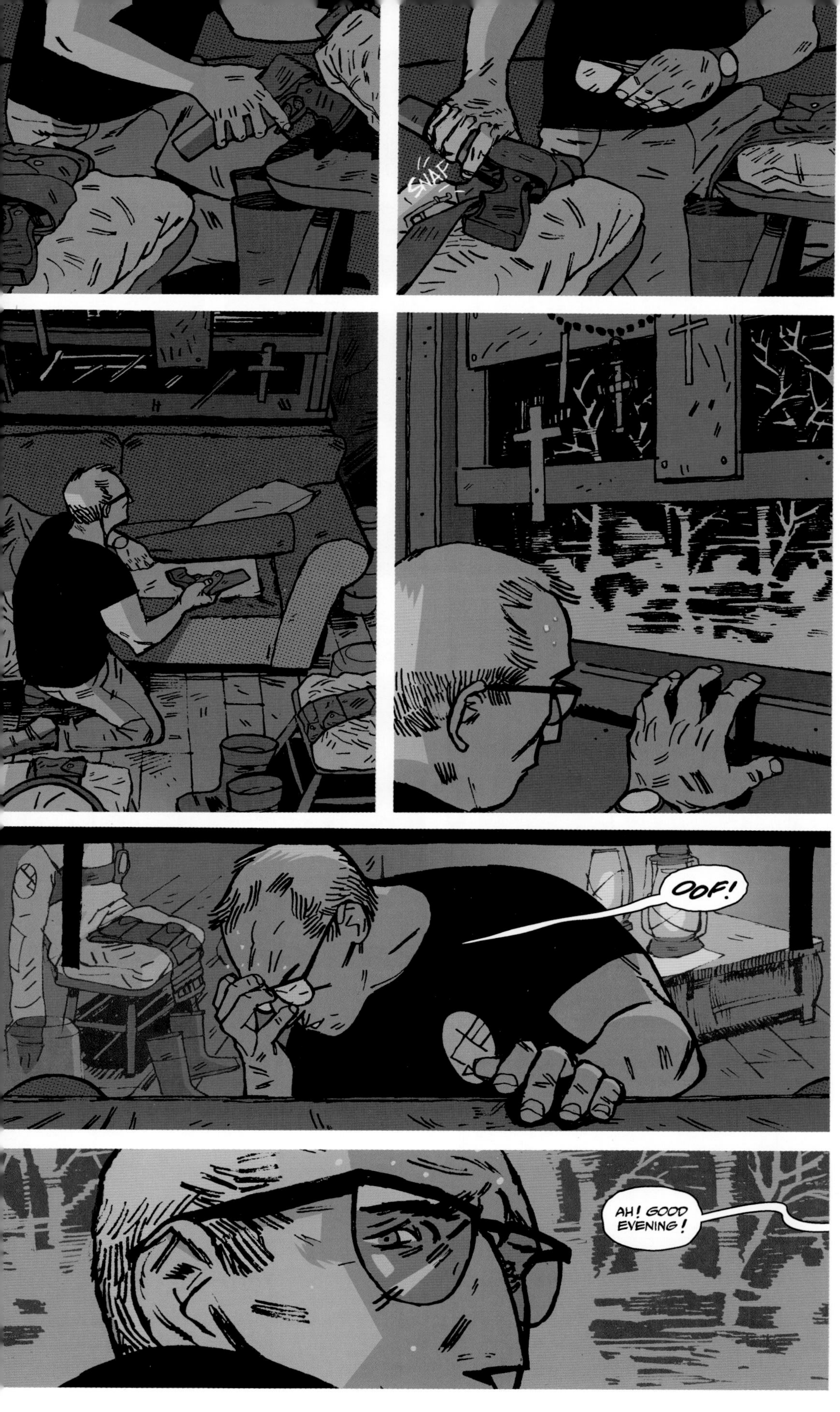
SNAP
OOF!
AH! GOOD EVENING!

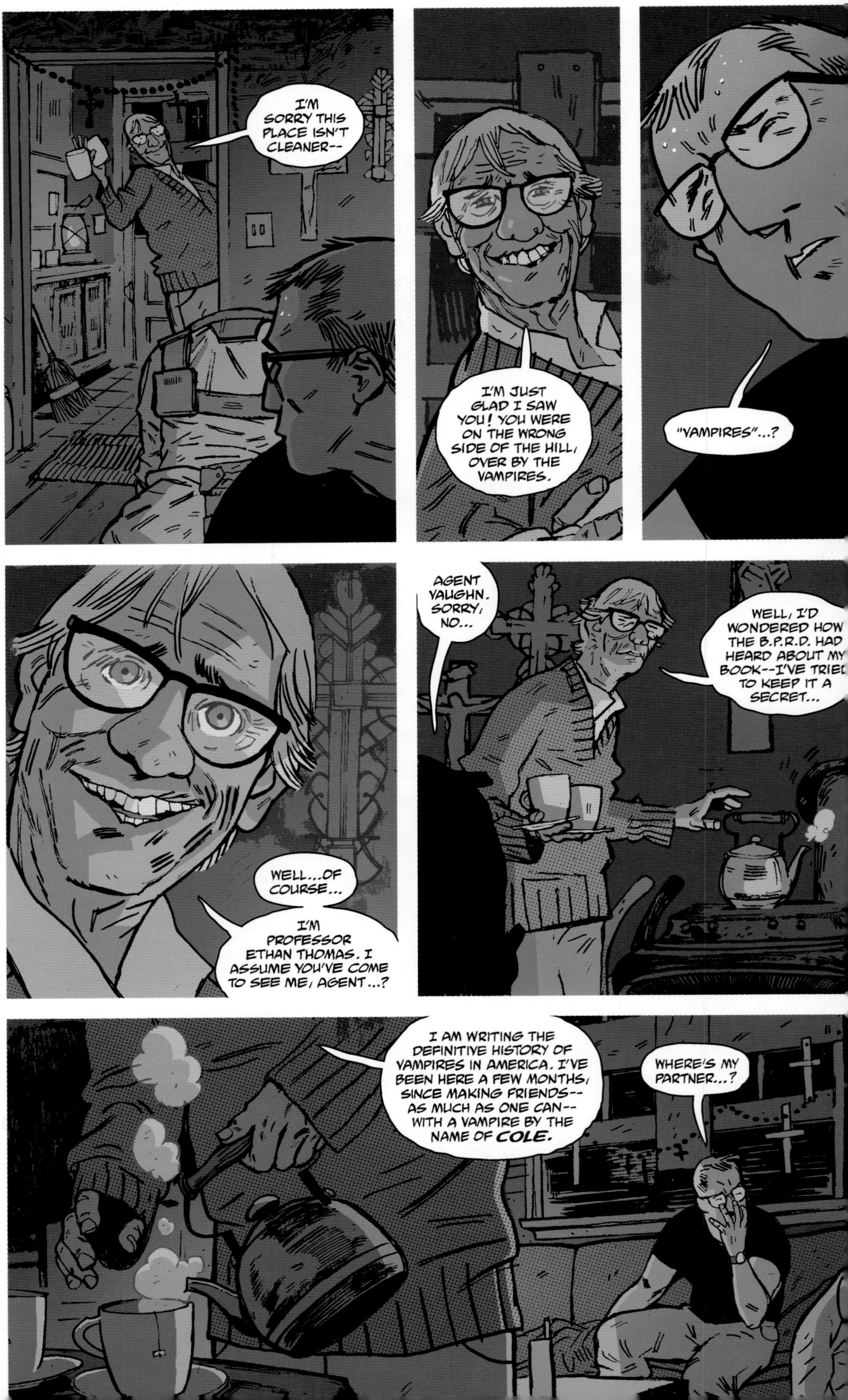
I'M SORRY THIS PLACE ISN'T CLEANER--
I'M JUST GLAD I SAW YOU! YOU WERE ON THE WRONG SIDE OF THE HILL, OVER BY THE VAMPIRES.
"VAMPIRES"...?
WELL...OF COURSE...
I'M PROFESSOR ETHAN THOMAS. I ASSUME YOU'VE COME TO SEE ME, AGENT...?
AGENT VAUGHN. SORRY, NO...
WELL, I'D WONDERED HOW THE B.P.R.D. HAD HEARD ABOUT MY BOOK--I'VE TRIED TO KEEP IT A SECRET...
I AM WRITING THE DEFINITIVE HISTORY OF VAMPIRES IN AMERICA. I'VE BEEN HERE A FEW MONTHS, SINCE MAKING FRIENDS-- AS MUCH AS ONE CAN-- WITH A VAMPIRE BY THE NAME OF **COLE.**
WHERE'S MY PARTNER...?

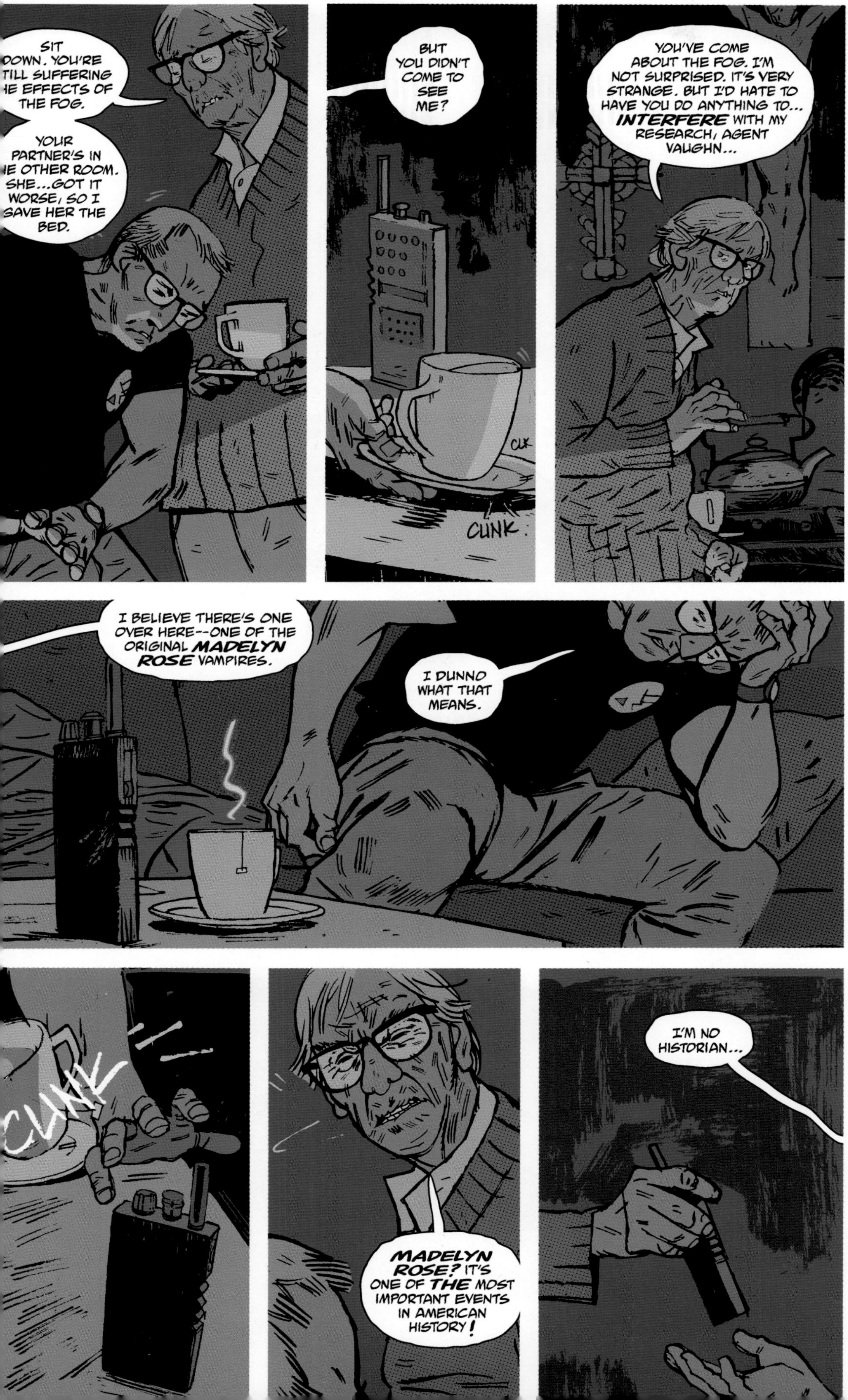
SIT DOWN. YOU'RE STILL SUFFERING THE EFFECTS OF THE FOG.
YOUR PARTNER'S IN THE OTHER ROOM. SHE...GOT IT WORSE, SO I GAVE HER THE BED.
BUT YOU DIDN'T COME TO SEE ME?
CLK
CLINK
YOU'VE COME ABOUT THE FOG. I'M NOT SURPRISED. IT'S VERY STRANGE. BUT I'D HATE TO HAVE YOU DO ANYTHING TO... INTERFERE WITH MY RESEARCH, AGENT VAUGHN...
I BELIEVE THERE'S ONE OVER HERE--ONE OF THE ORIGINAL MADELYN ROSE VAMPIRES.
I DUNNO WHAT THAT MEANS.
CLINK
MADELYN ROSE? IT'S ONE OF THE MOST IMPORTANT EVENTS IN AMERICAN HISTORY!
I'M NO HISTORIAN...

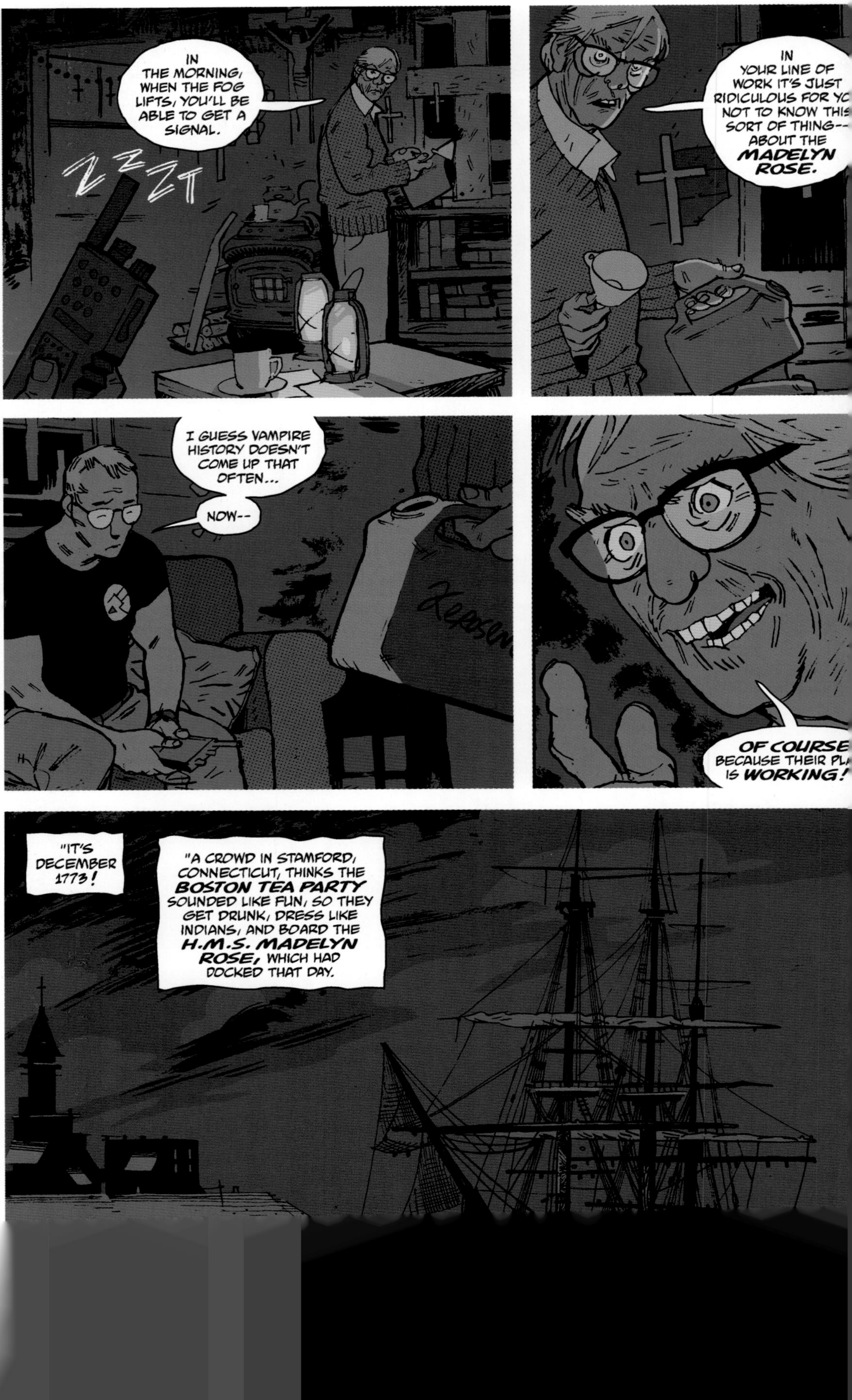
IN THE MORNING, WHEN THE FOG LIFTS, YOU'LL BE ABLE TO GET A SIGNAL.
ZZZT
IN YOUR LINE OF WORK IT'S JUST RIDICULOUS FOR YO NOT TO KNOW THIS SORT OF THING-- ABOUT THE MADELYN ROSE.
I GUESS VAMPIRE HISTORY DOESN'T COME UP THAT OFTEN...
NOW--
OF COURSE BECAUSE THEIR PL IS WORKING!
"IT'S DECEMBER 1773!
"A CROWD IN STAMFORD, CONNECTICUT, THINKS THE BOSTON TEA PARTY SOUNDED LIKE FUN, SO THEY GET DRUNK, DRESS LIKE INDIANS, AND BOARD THE H.M.S. MADELYN ROSE, WHICH HAD DOCKED THAT DAY.

'BUT INSTEAD OF
TEA, THE CRATES
CONTAIN *PRUSSIAN
VAMPIRES*, SENT
BY THE BRITS AS
MERCENARIES TO
SQUASH COLONIAL
REVOLT!

"YOU CAN
IMAGINE THEIR
HORROR...
SHORT LIVED
THOUGH IT WAS.

"THE LONE
SURVIVOR,
SAMUEL ROGERS,
TRIED SPREADING
THE WORD.
ALMOST NO ONE
BELIEVED HIM."

REVEREND TREADWELL AND
THE MATTHIES BROTHERS OF
NEW HAVEN, WHO *DID* BELIEVE
HIM, TRACKED DOWN AND
KILLED A FEW OF THE
VAMPIRES.

THERE'S
DOCUMENTATION FOR
THIS, AGENT VAUGHN,
CONTEMPORARY NEWS-
PAPER ACCOUNTS, BUT
ALSO LETTERS, AND
DIETRICH MATTHIES'S
JOURNALS. I'VE GOT
COPIES HERE...

THE SURVIVING
HALF-DOZEN VAMPIRES--
THERE WEREN'T THAT MANY
TO BEGIN WITH ANYWAY--
WENT INTO HIDING.

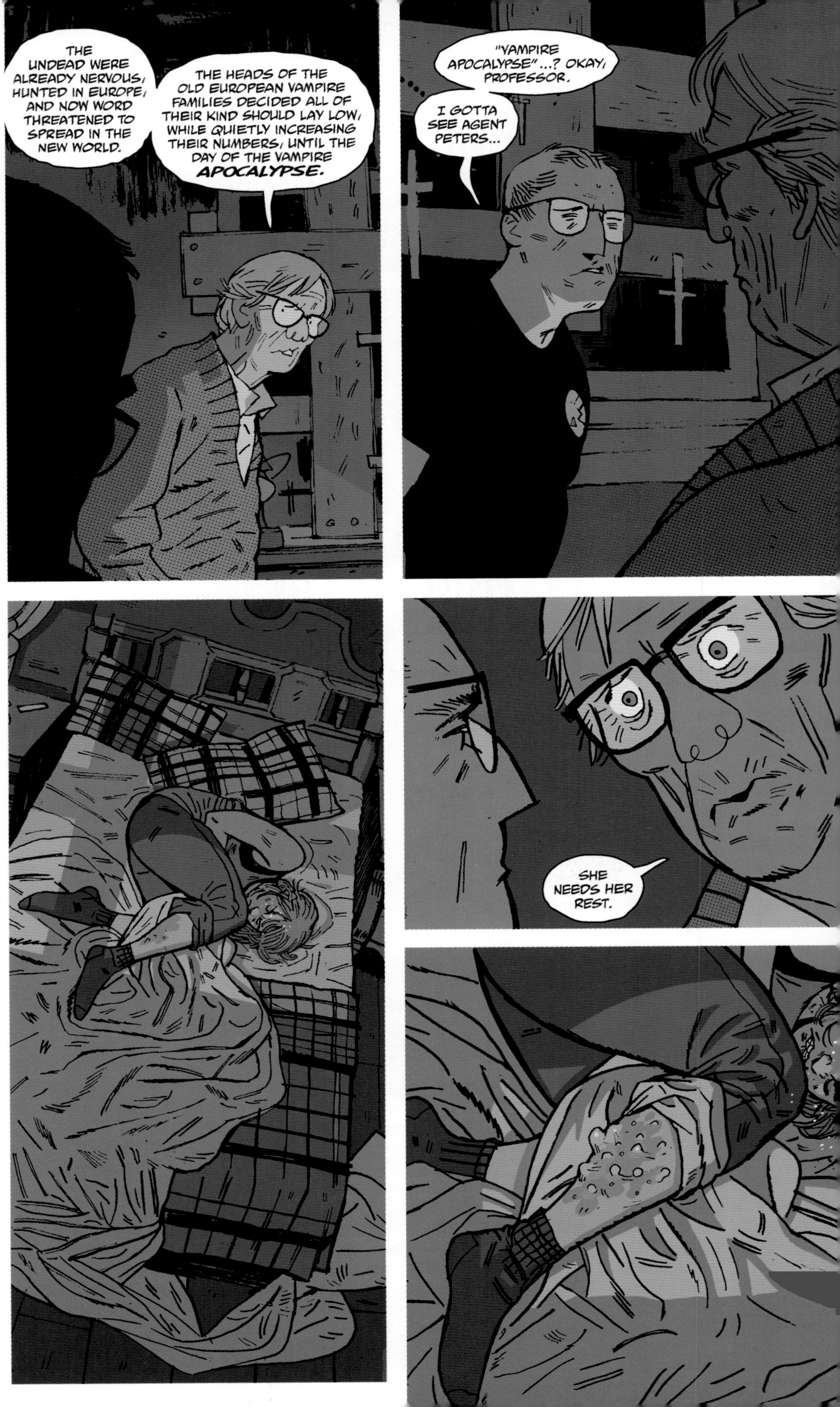
THE UNDEAD WERE ALREADY NERVOUS, HUNTED IN EUROPE, AND NOW WORD THREATENED TO SPREAD IN THE NEW WORLD.
THE HEADS OF THE OLD EUROPEAN VAMPIRE FAMILIES DECIDED ALL OF THEIR KIND SHOULD LAY LOW, WHILE QUIETLY INCREASING THEIR NUMBERS, UNTIL THE DAY OF THE VAMPIRE APOCALYPSE.
"VAMPIRE APOCALYPSE"...? OKAY, PROFESSOR.
I GOTTA SEE AGENT PETERS...
SHE NEEDS HER REST.

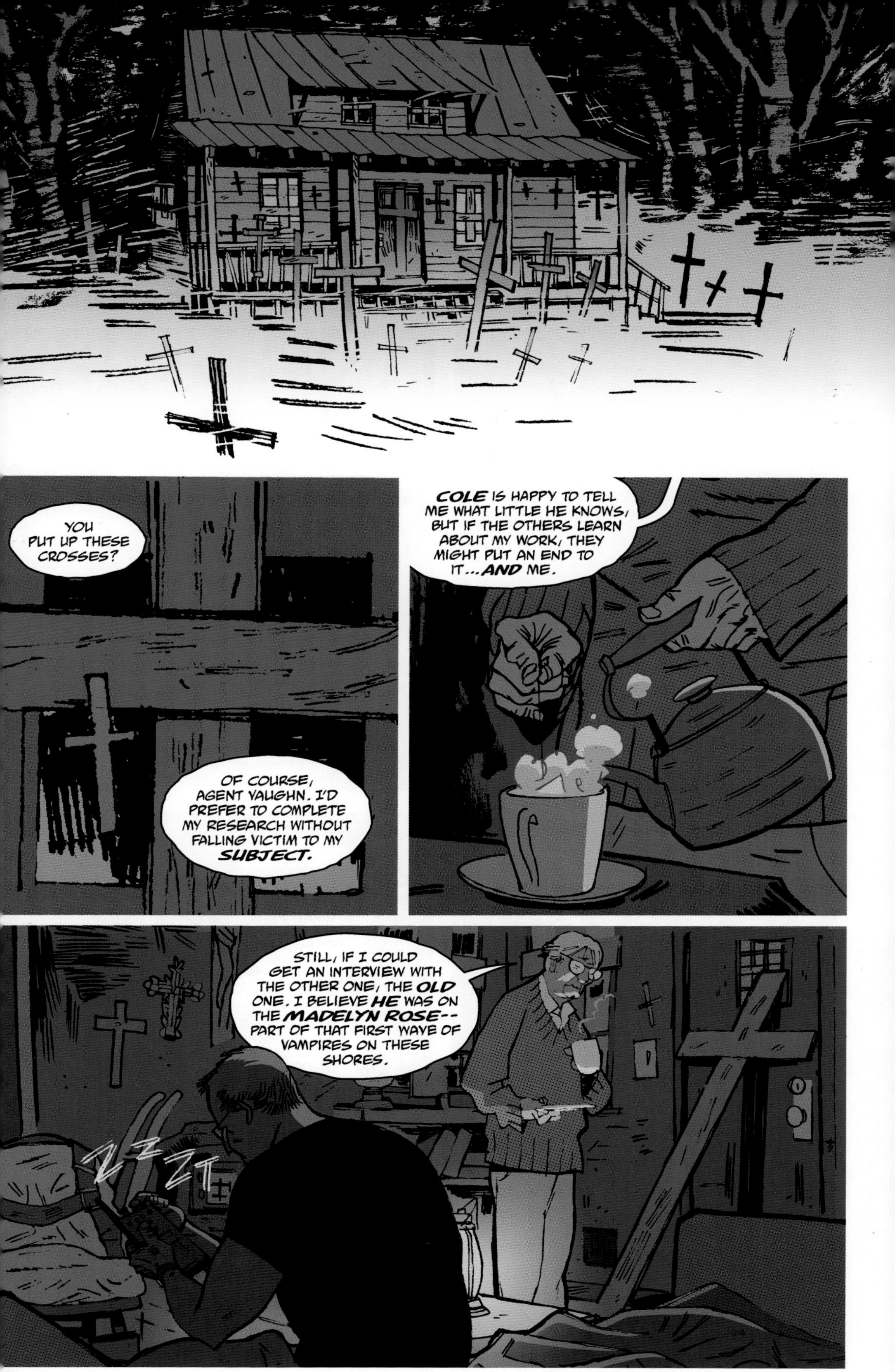
YOU PUT UP THESE CROSSES?
COLE IS HAPPY TO TELL ME WHAT LITTLE HE KNOWS, BUT IF THE OTHERS LEARN ABOUT MY WORK, THEY MIGHT PUT AN END TO IT...AND ME.
OF COURSE, AGENT VAUGHN. I'D PREFER TO COMPLETE MY RESEARCH WITHOUT FALLING VICTIM TO MY SUBJECT.
STILL, IF I COULD GET AN INTERVIEW WITH THE OTHER ONE, THE OLD ONE. I BELIEVE HE WAS ON THE MADELYN ROSE-- PART OF THAT FIRST WAVE OF VAMPIRES ON THESE SHORES.
ZZZT

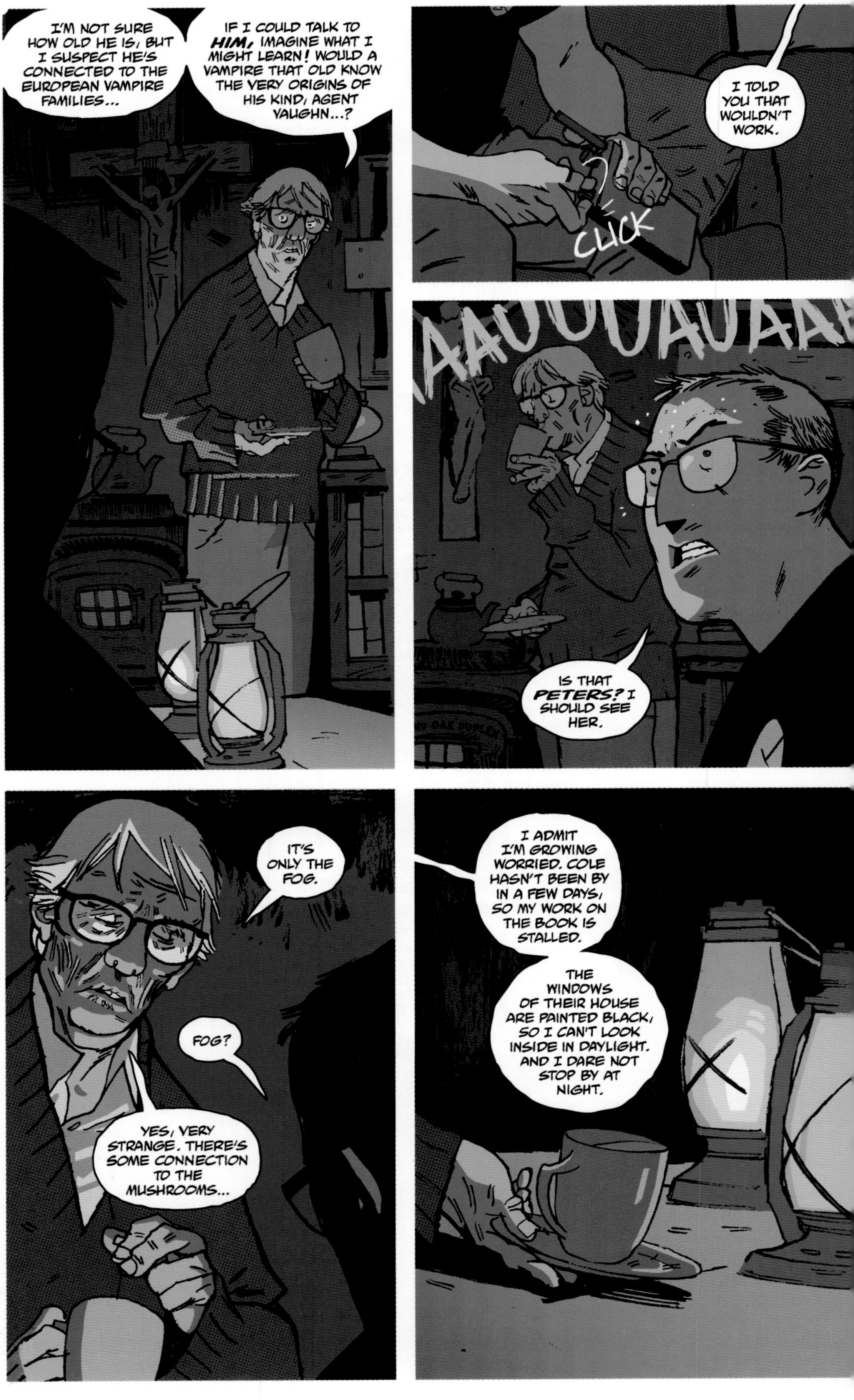
I'M NOT SURE HOW OLD HE IS, BUT I SUSPECT HE'S CONNECTED TO THE EUROPEAN VAMPIRE FAMILIES...
IF I COULD TALK TO HIM, IMAGINE WHAT I MIGHT LEARN! WOULD A VAMPIRE THAT OLD KNOW THE VERY ORIGINS OF HIS KIND, AGENT VAUGHN...?
I TOLD YOU THAT WOULDN'T WORK.
CLICK
AAUUUUAUAAE
IS THAT PETERS? I SHOULD SEE HER.
IT'S ONLY THE FOG.
FOG?
YES, VERY STRANGE. THERE'S SOME CONNECTION TO THE MUSHROOMS...
I ADMIT I'M GROWING WORRIED. COLE HASN'T BEEN BY IN A FEW DAYS, SO MY WORK ON THE BOOK IS STALLED.
THE WINDOWS OF THEIR HOUSE ARE PAINTED BLACK, SO I CAN'T LOOK INSIDE IN DAYLIGHT. AND I DARE NOT STOP BY AT NIGHT.

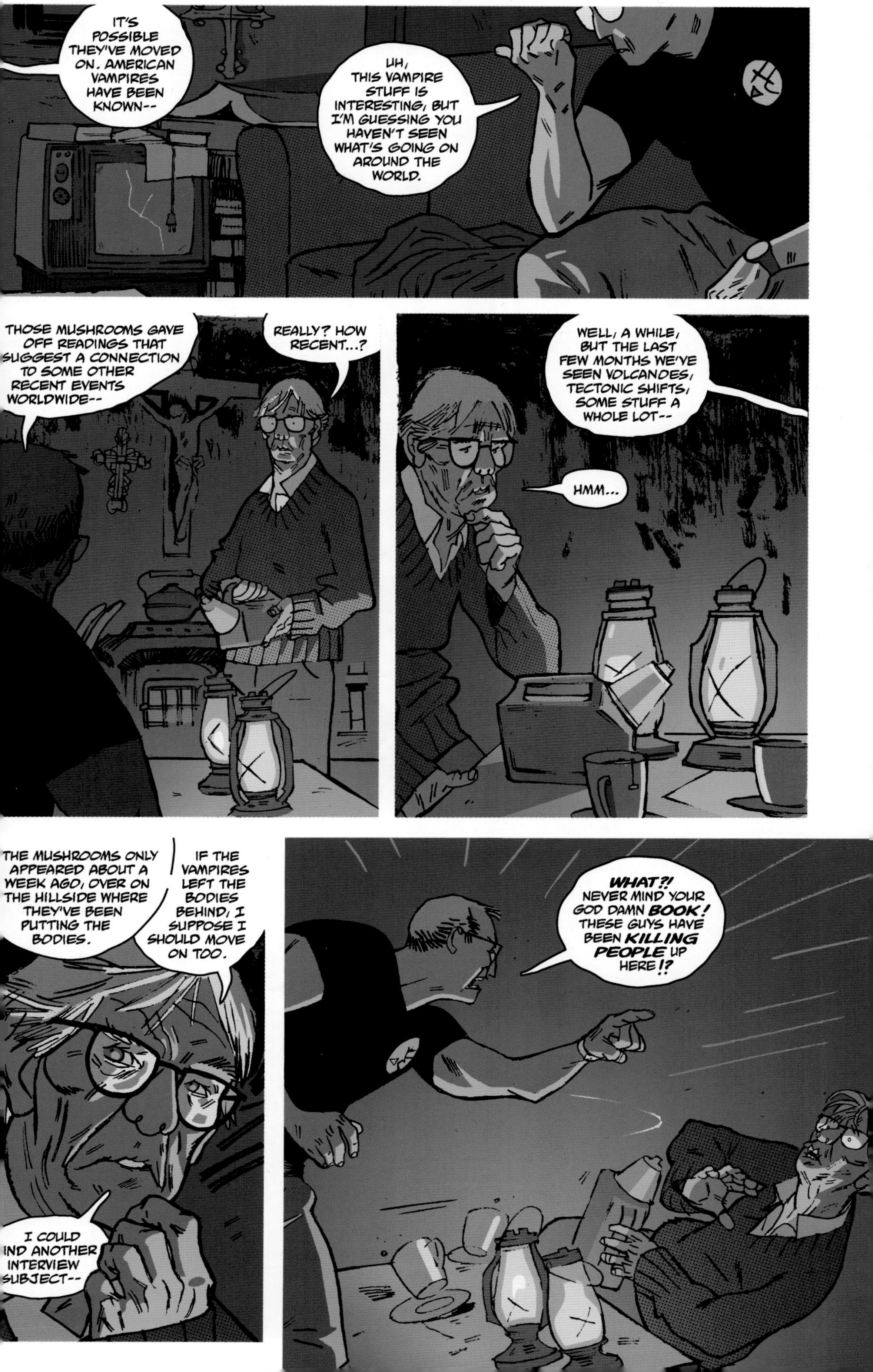
IT'S POSSIBLE THEY'VE MOVED ON. AMERICAN VAMPIRES HAVE BEEN KNOWN--
UH, THIS VAMPIRE STUFF IS INTERESTING, BUT I'M GUESSING YOU HAVEN'T SEEN WHAT'S GOING ON AROUND THE WORLD.
THOSE MUSHROOMS GAVE OFF READINGS THAT SUGGEST A CONNECTION TO SOME OTHER RECENT EVENTS WORLDWIDE--
REALLY? HOW RECENT...?
WELL, A WHILE, BUT THE LAST FEW MONTHS WE'VE SEEN VOLCANOES, TECTONIC SHIFTS, SOME STUFF A WHOLE LOT--
HMM...
THE MUSHROOMS ONLY APPEARED ABOUT A WEEK AGO, OVER ON THE HILLSIDE WHERE THEY'VE BEEN PUTTING THE BODIES.
IF THE VAMPIRES LEFT THE BODIES BEHIND, I SUPPOSE I SHOULD MOVE ON TOO.
I COULD IND ANOTHER INTERVIEW SUBJECT--
WHAT?! NEVER MIND YOUR GOD DAMN BOOK! THESE GUYS HAVE BEEN KILLING PEOPLE UP HERE!?

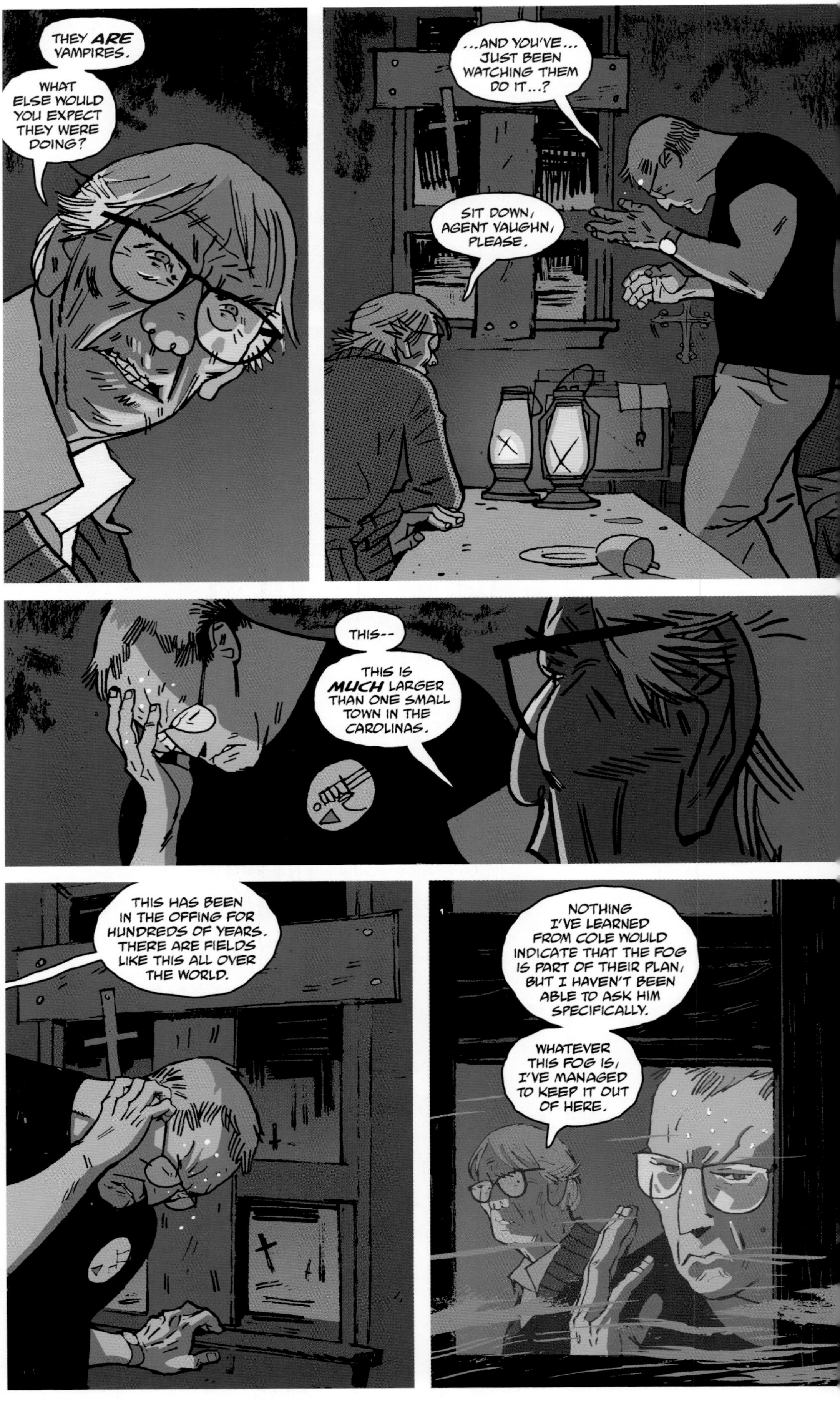
THEY ARE VAMPIRES.
WHAT ELSE WOULD YOU EXPECT THEY WERE DOING?
...AND YOU'VE... JUST BEEN WATCHING THEM DO IT...?
SIT DOWN, AGENT VAUGHN, PLEASE.
THIS--
THIS IS MUCH LARGER THAN ONE SMALL TOWN IN THE CAROLINAS.
THIS HAS BEEN IN THE OFFING FOR HUNDREDS OF YEARS. THERE ARE FIELDS LIKE THIS ALL OVER THE WORLD.
NOTHING I'VE LEARNED FROM COLE WOULD INDICATE THAT THE FOG IS PART OF THEIR PLAN, BUT I HAVEN'T BEEN ABLE TO ASK HIM SPECIFICALLY.
WHATEVER THIS FOG IS, I'VE MANAGED TO KEEP IT OUT OF HERE.

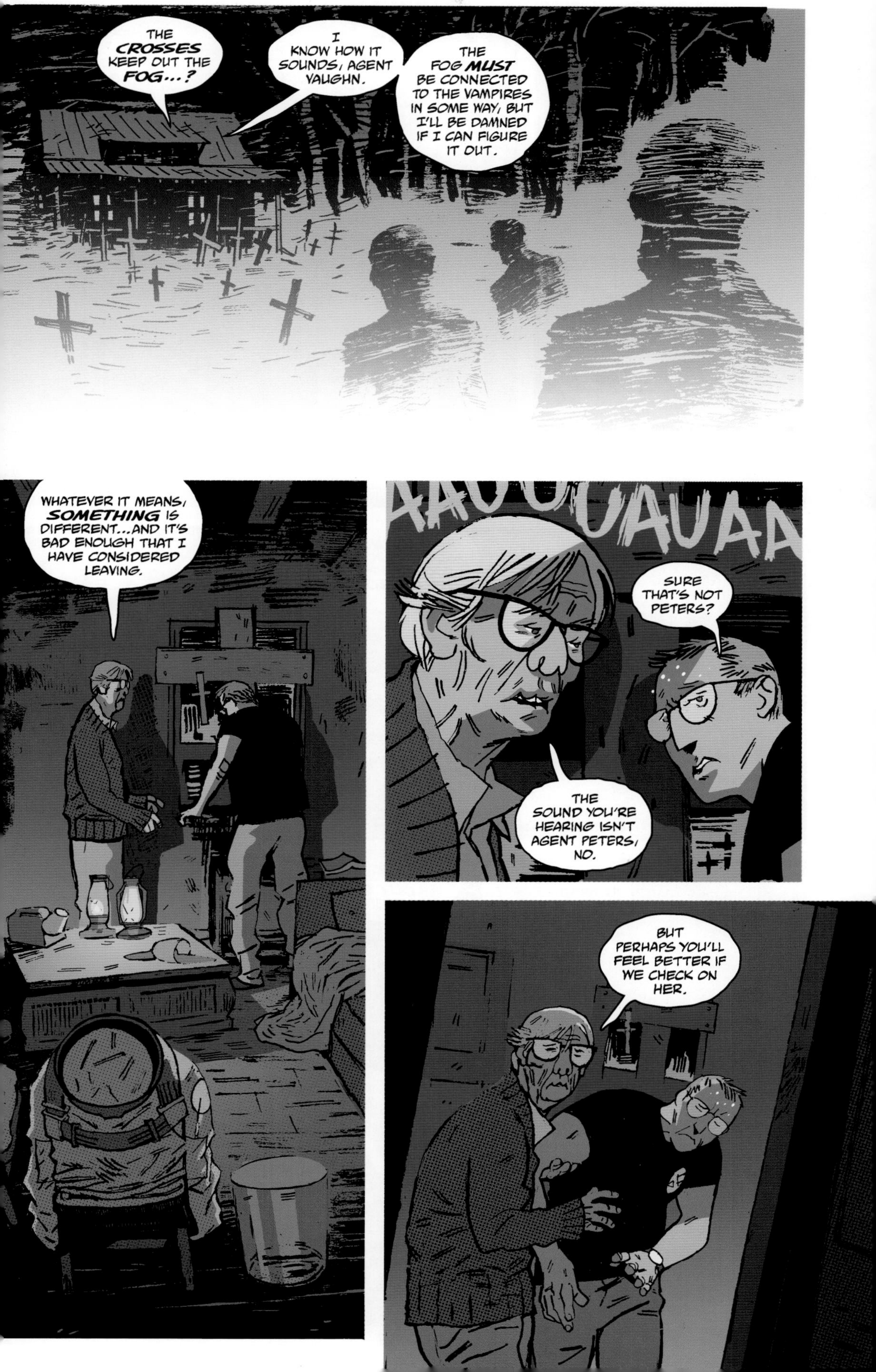
THE CROSSES KEEP OUT THE FOG...?
I KNOW HOW IT SOUNDS, AGENT VAUGHN.
THE FOG MUST BE CONNECTED TO THE VAMPIRES IN SOME WAY, BUT I'LL BE DAMNED IF I CAN FIGURE IT OUT.
WHATEVER IT MEANS, SOMETHING IS DIFFERENT...AND IT'S BAD ENOUGH THAT I HAVE CONSIDERED LEAVING.
AAOOOUAUAA
SURE THAT'S NOT PETERS?
THE SOUND YOU'RE HEARING ISN'T AGENT PETERS, NO.
BUT PERHAPS YOU'LL FEEL BETTER IF WE CHECK ON HER.

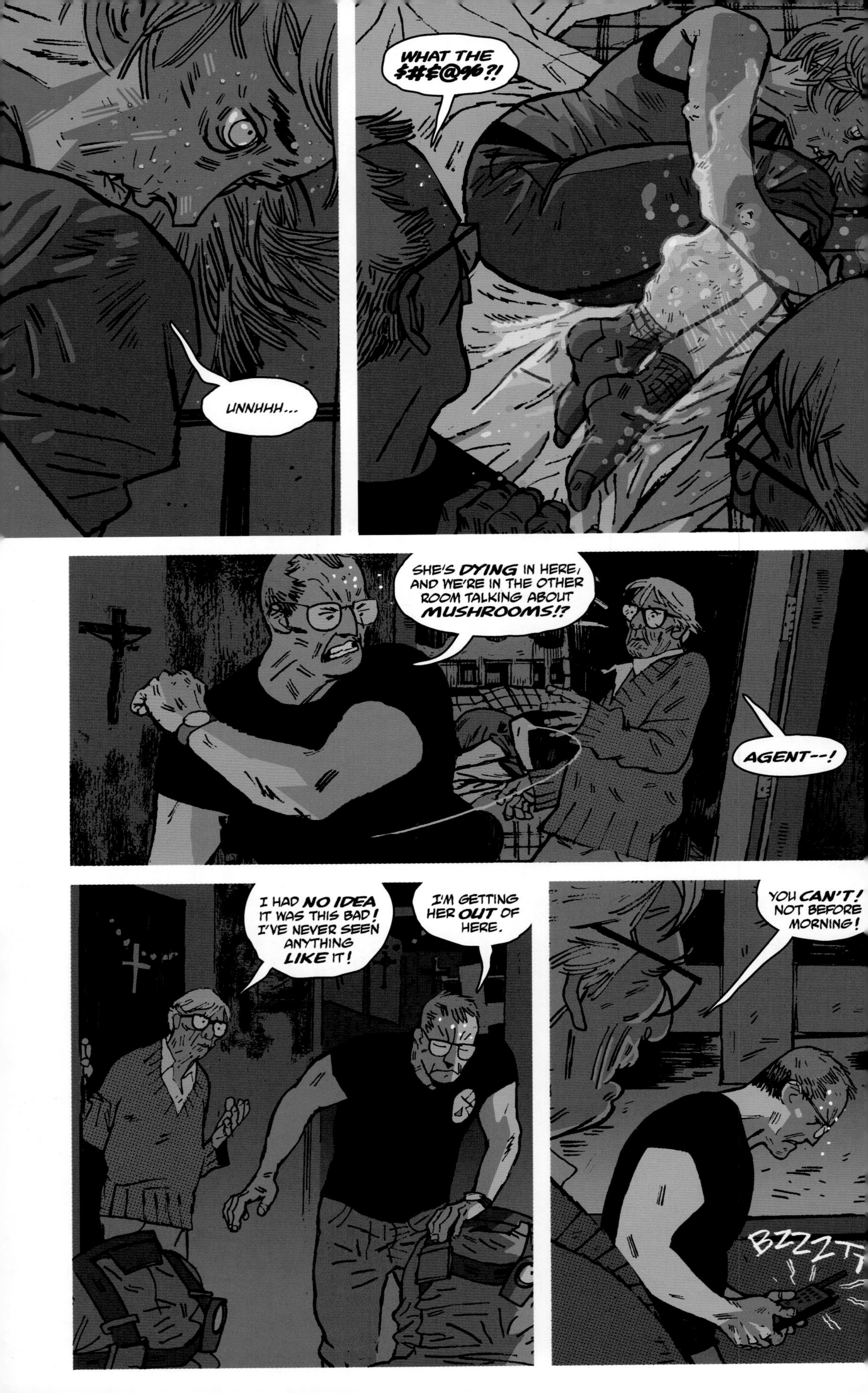
UNNHHH...
WHAT THE $#&@%?!
SHE'S DYING IN HERE, AND WE'RE IN THE OTHER ROOM TALKING ABOUT MUSHROOMS!?
AGENT--!
I HAD NO IDEA IT WAS THIS BAD! I'VE NEVER SEEN ANYTHING LIKE IT!
I'M GETTING HER OUT OF HERE.
YOU CAN'T! NOT BEFORE MORNING!
BZZZT

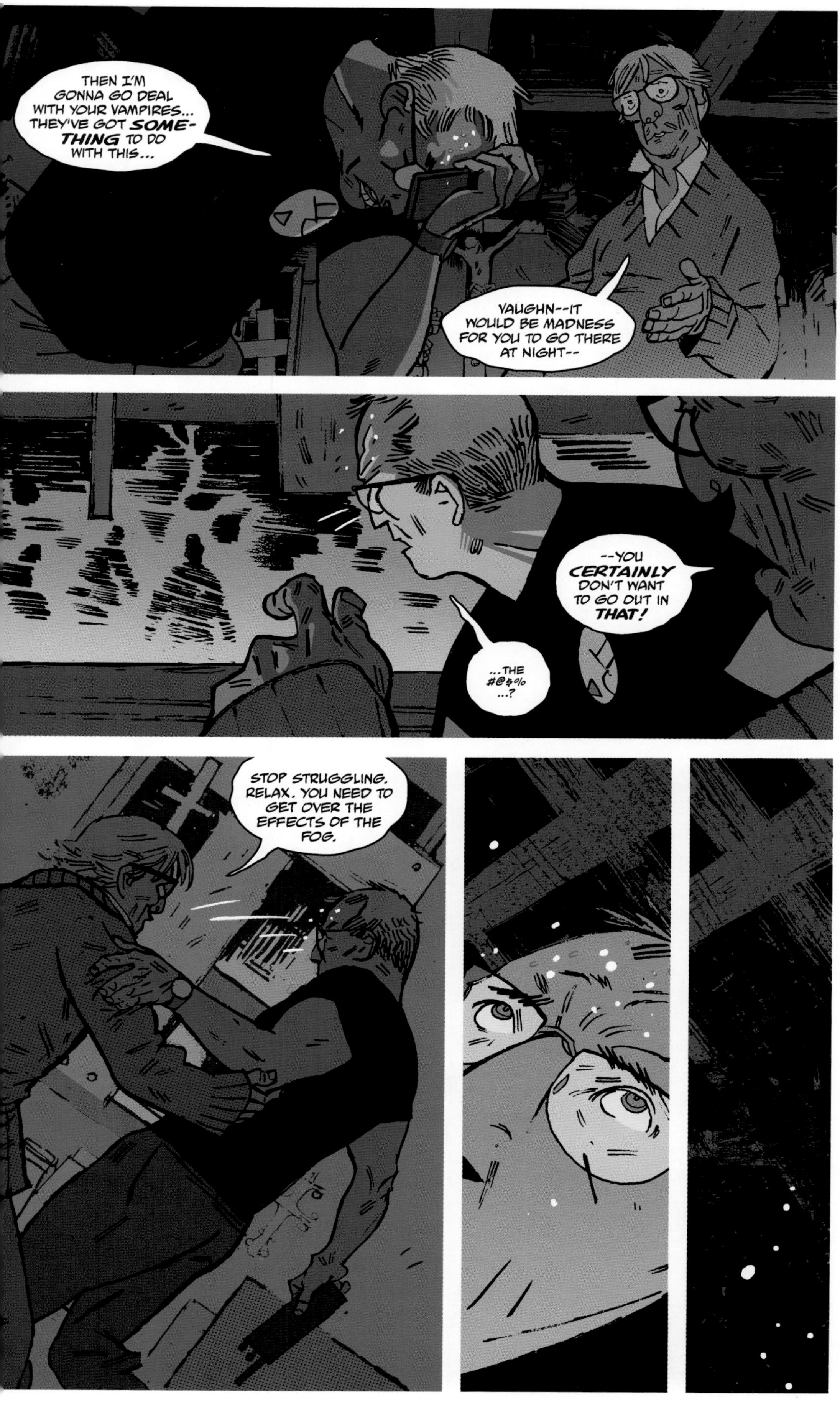
THEN I'M GONNA GO DEAL WITH YOUR VAMPIRES... THEY'VE GOT SOME-THING TO DO WITH THIS...
VAUGHN--IT WOULD BE MADNESS FOR YOU TO GO THERE AT NIGHT--
--YOU CERTAINLY DON'T WANT TO GO OUT IN THAT!
...THE #@$% ...?
STOP STRUGGLING. RELAX. YOU NEED TO GET OVER THE EFFECTS OF THE FOG.

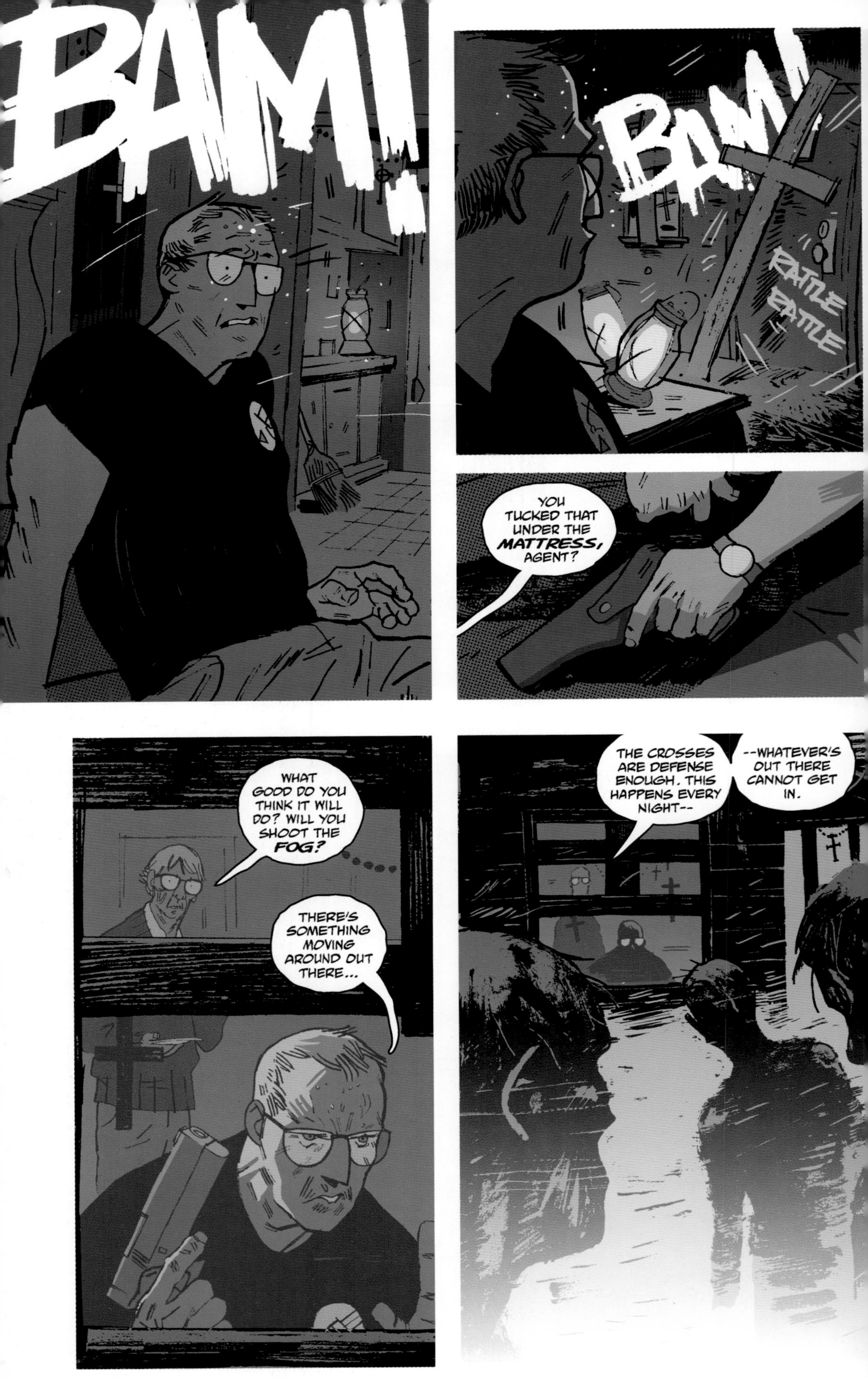
BAM!
BAM!
RATTLE
RATTLE
YOU TUCKED THAT UNDER THE MATTRESS, AGENT?
WHAT GOOD DO YOU THINK IT WILL DO? WILL YOU SHOOT THE FOG?
THERE'S SOMETHING MOVING AROUND OUT THERE...
THE CROSSES ARE DEFENSE ENOUGH. THIS HAPPENS EVERY NIGHT--
--WHATEVER'S OUT THERE CANNOT GET IN.

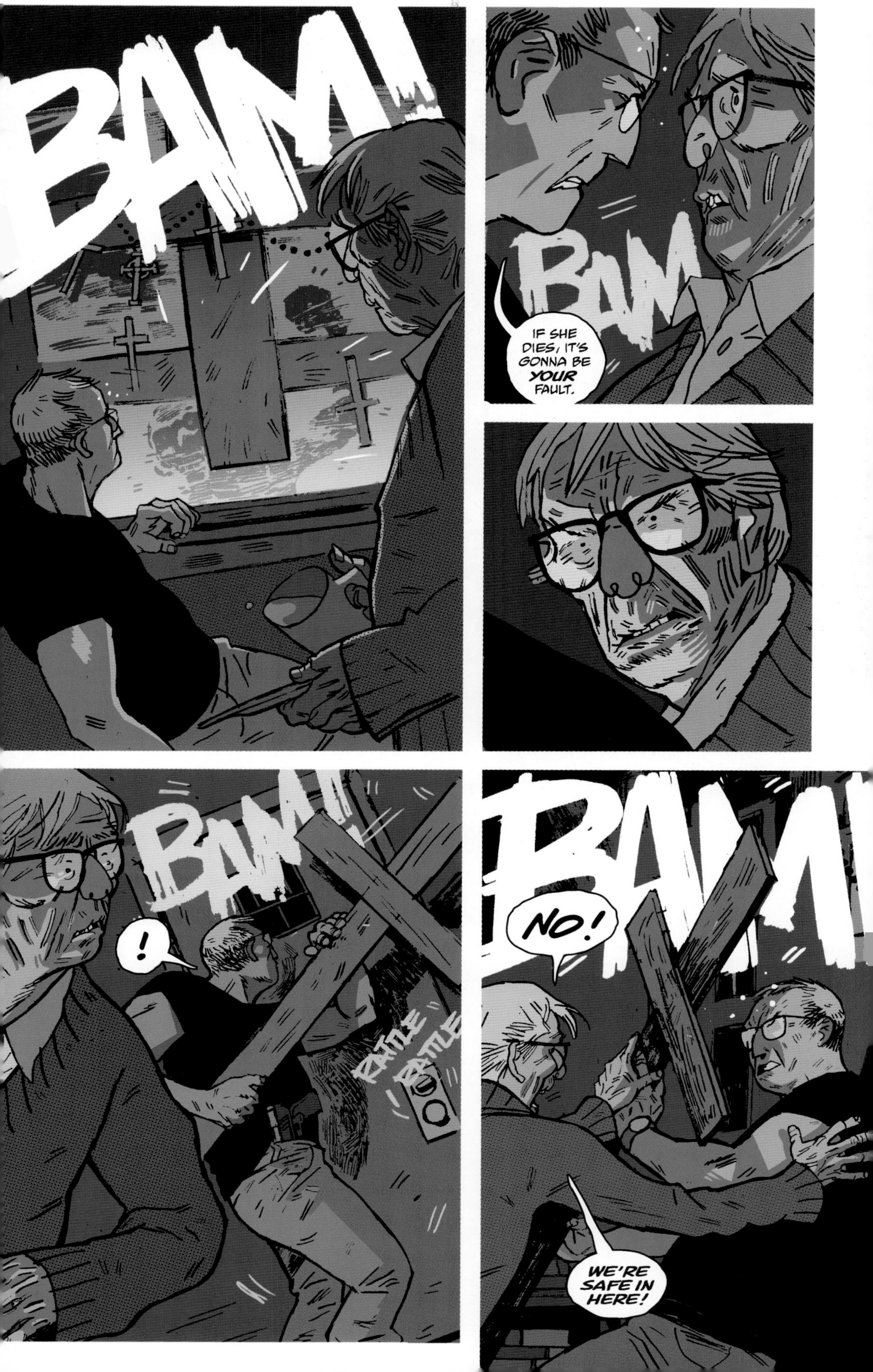
BAM!
BAM
IF SHE DIES, IT'S GONNA BE *YOUR* FAULT.
BAM!
!
RATTLE RATTLE
BAM!
NO!
WE'RE SAFE IN HERE!

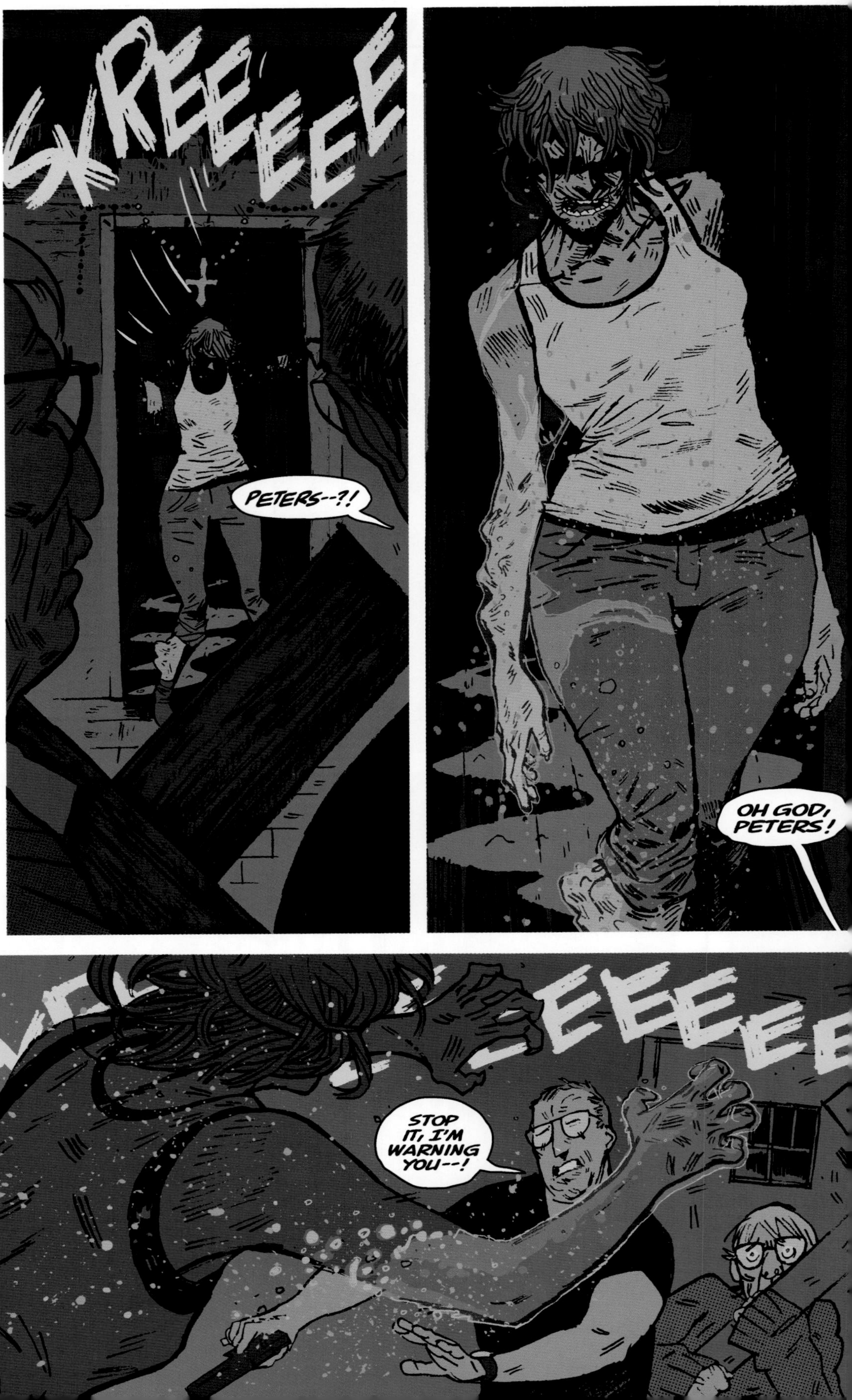
SKREEEEEE
PETERS--?!
OH GOD, PETERS!
STOP IT, I'M WARNING YOU--!

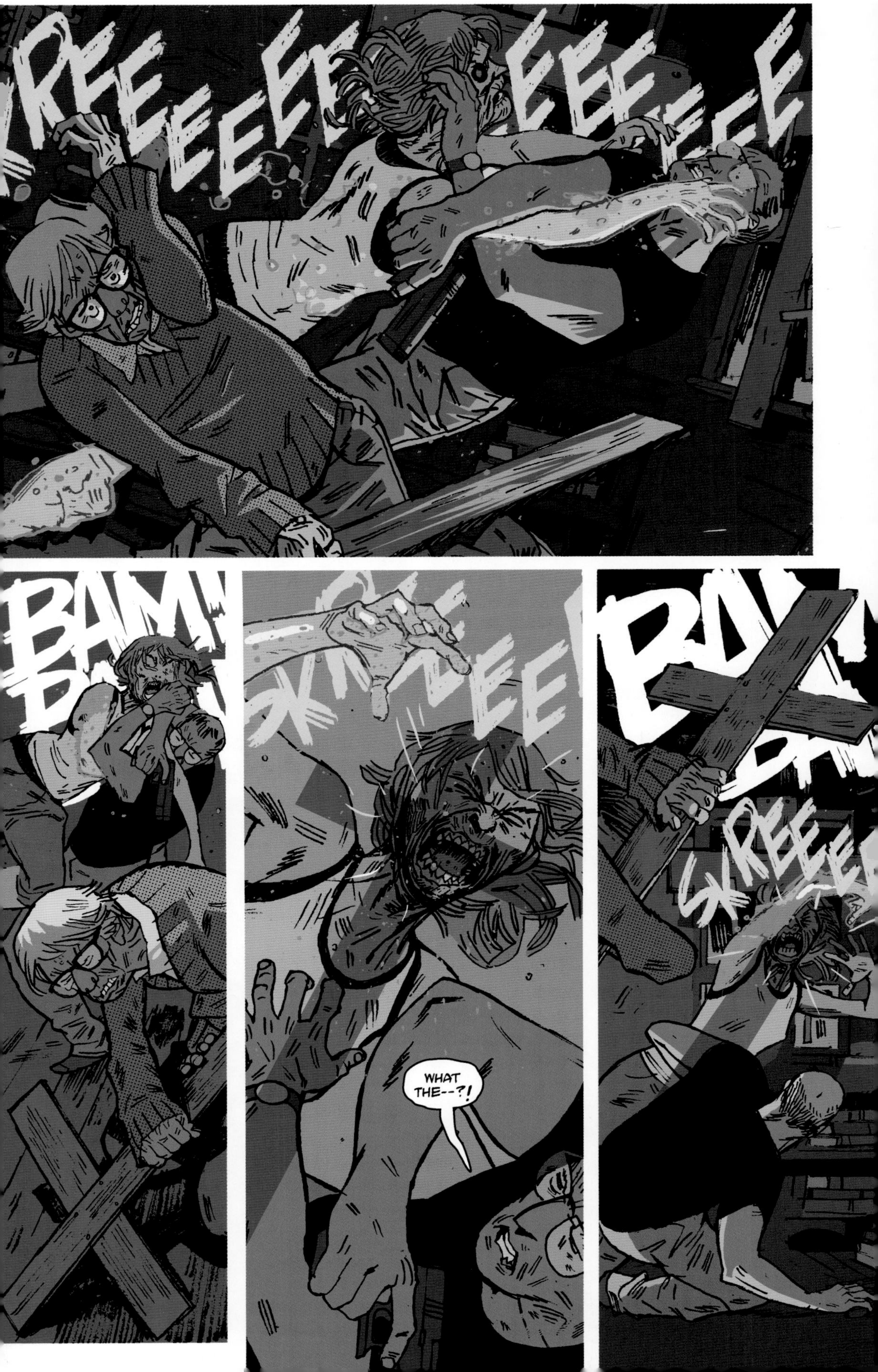
WHAT THE--?!

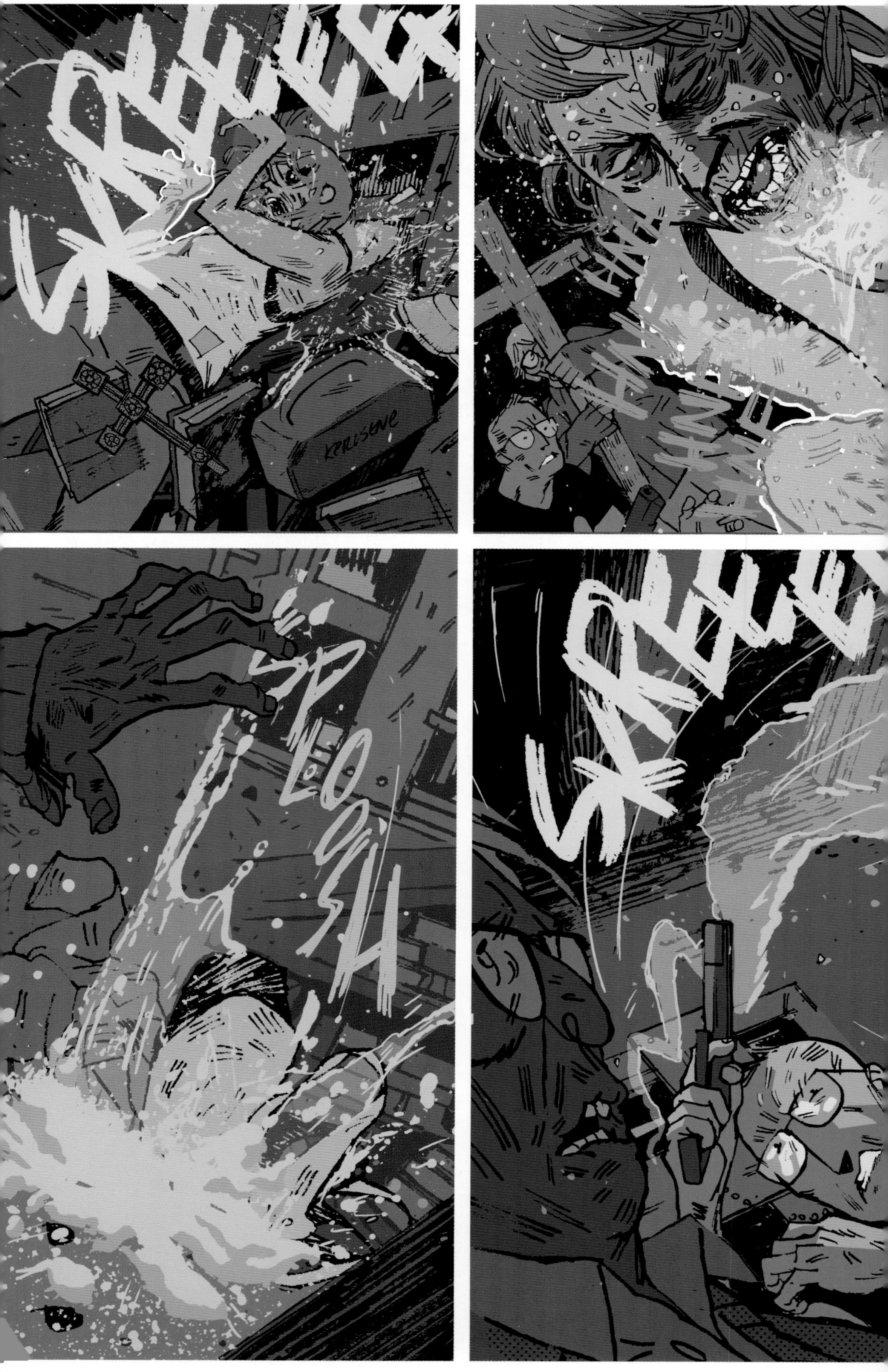
KEROSENE
SPLOOSH

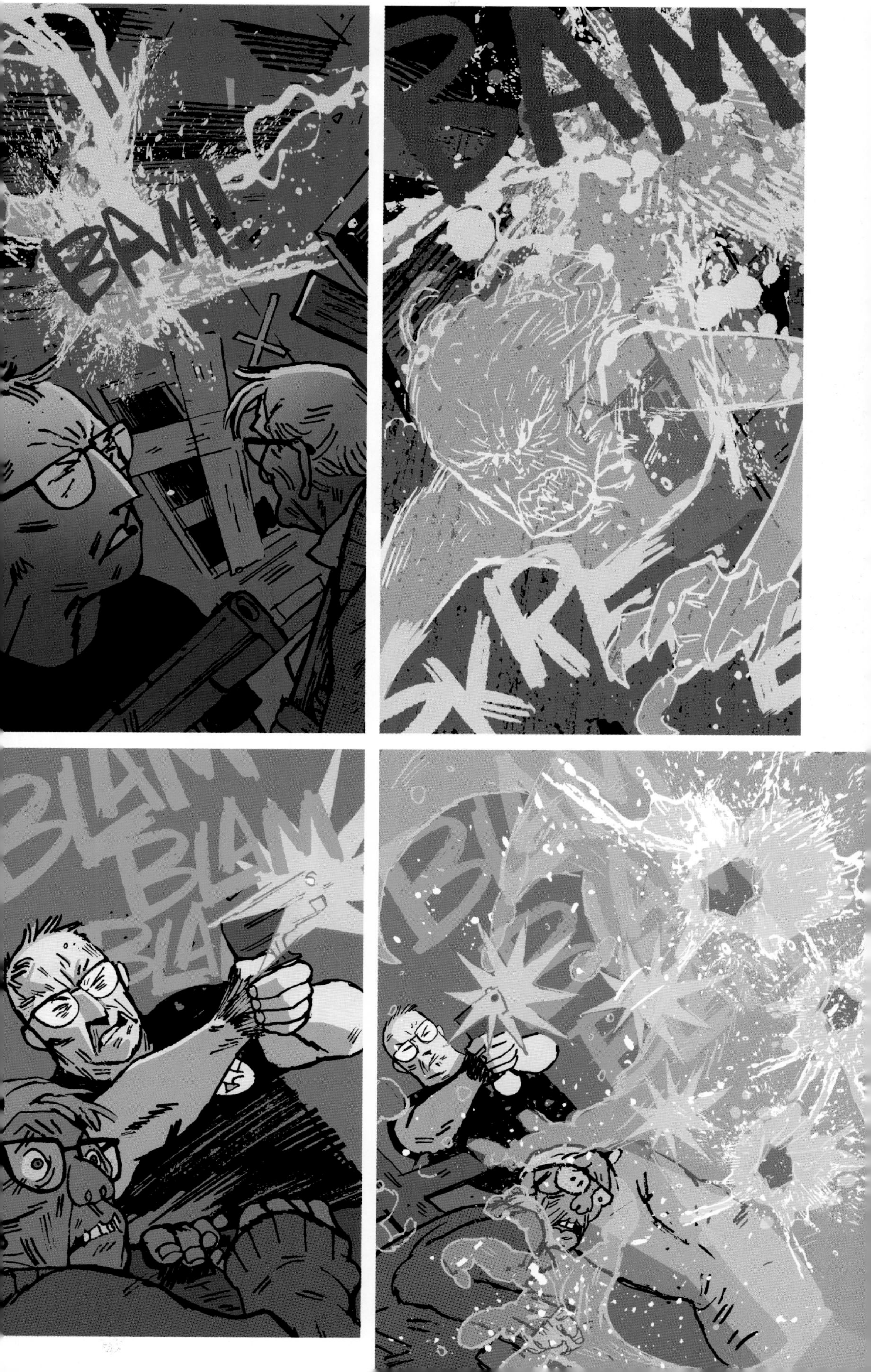
BAM!
BAM!
BLAM
BLAM

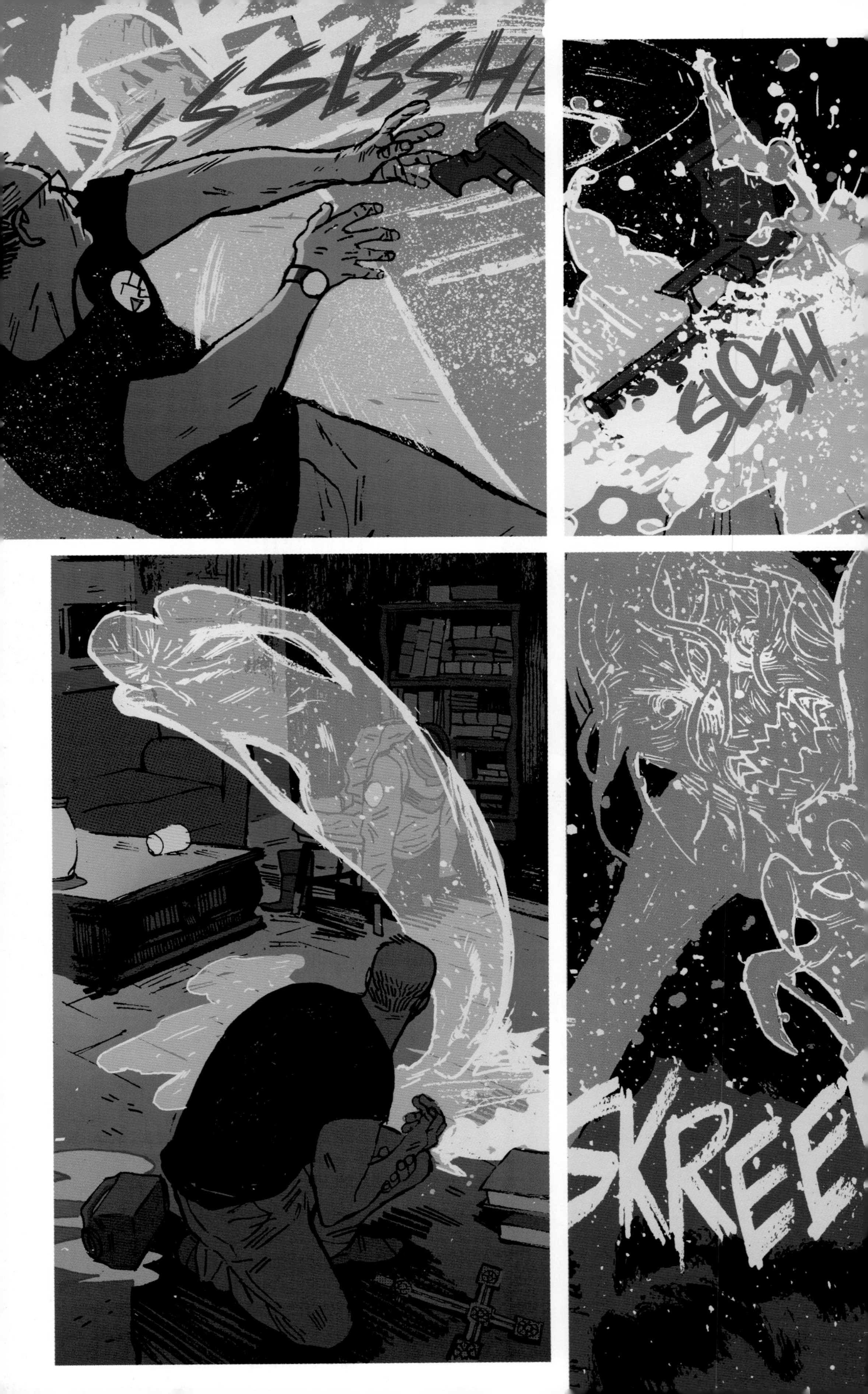
SSSLSSH
SLOSH
SKREE

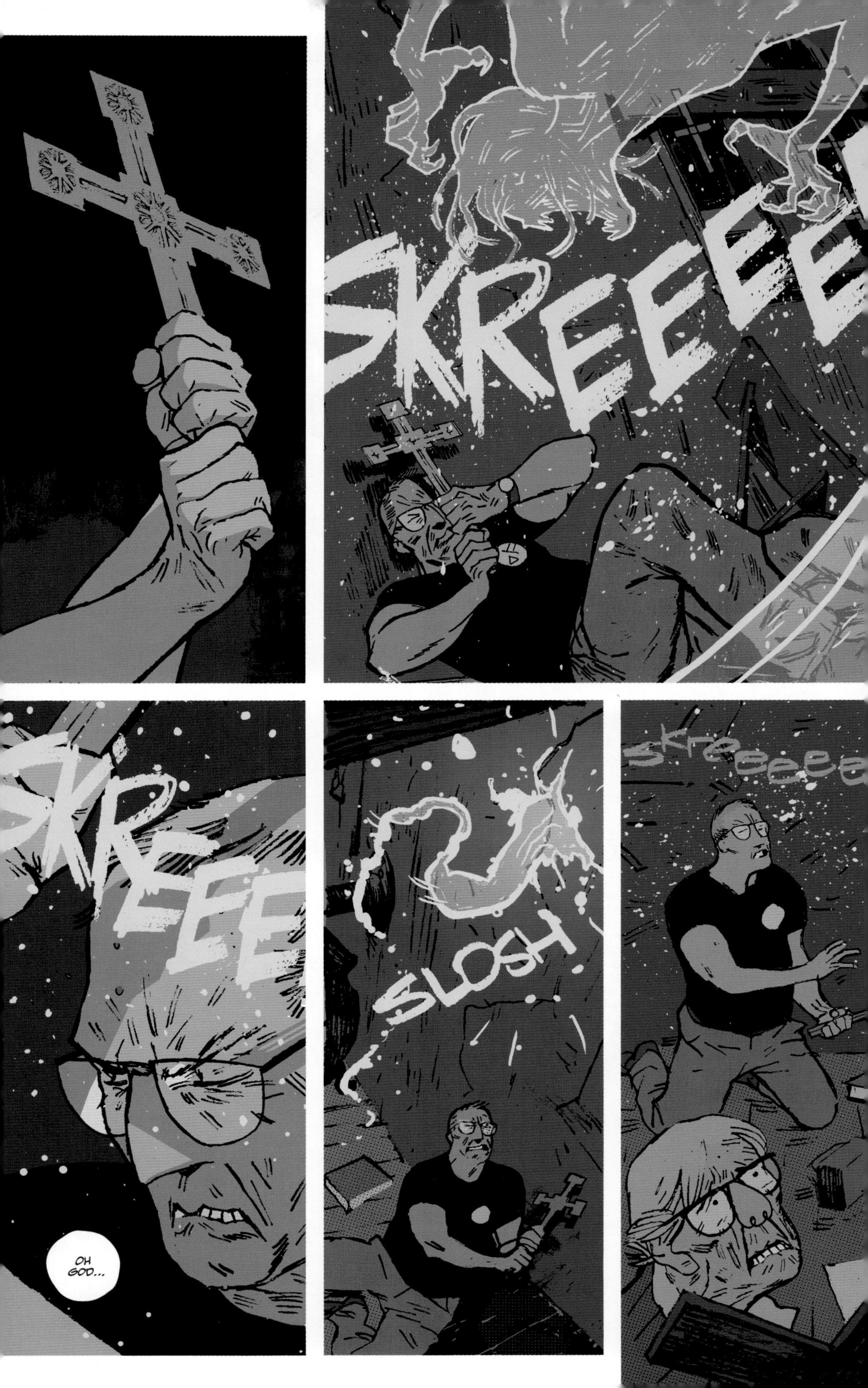
SKREEEE
SKREEE
OH GOD...
SLOSH
sKreeeeee

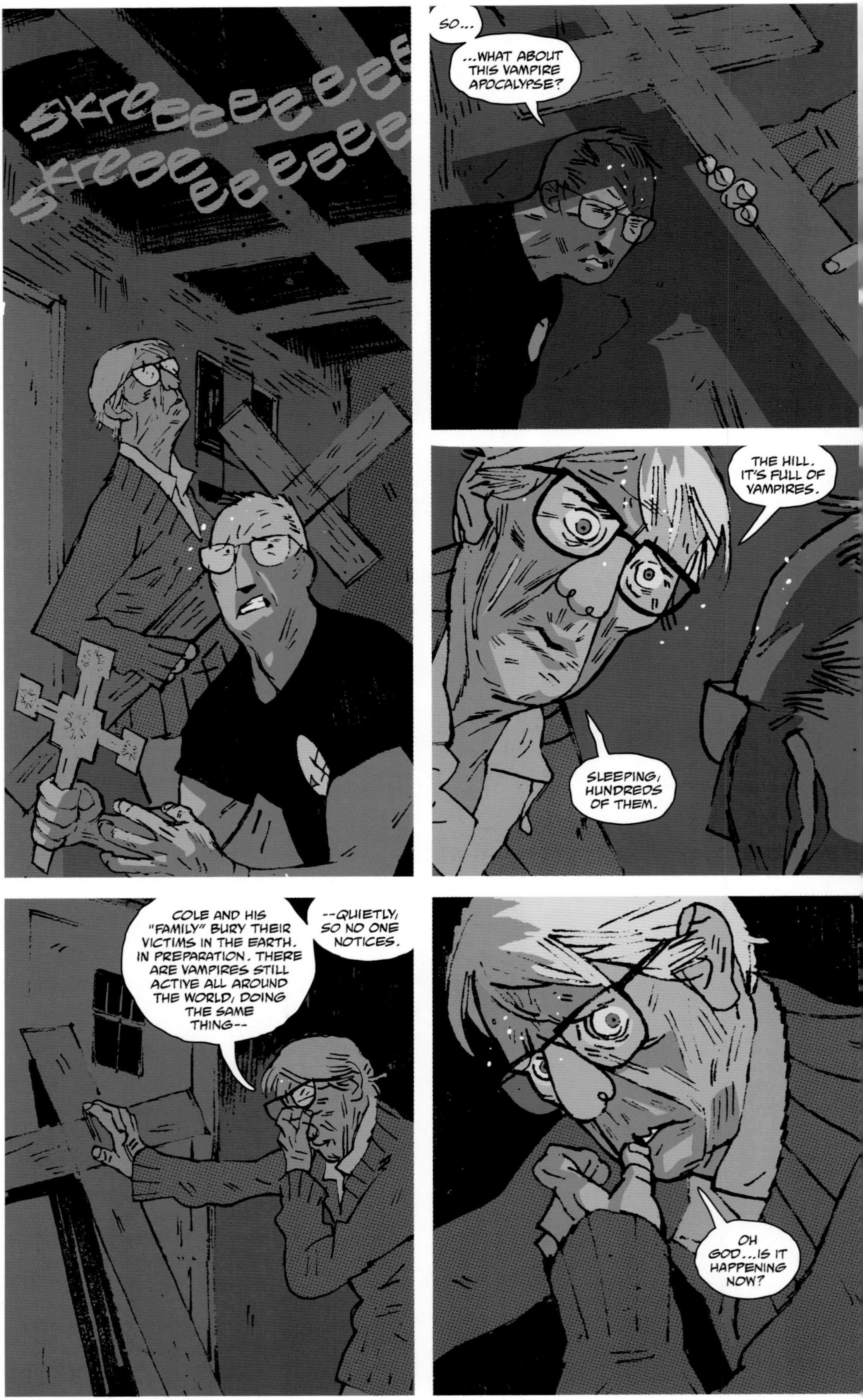
SKREEEEEEEEE
SKREEEEEEEEE
SO...
...WHAT ABOUT THIS VAMPIRE APOCALYPSE?
THE HILL. IT'S FULL OF VAMPIRES.
SLEEPING, HUNDREDS OF THEM.
COLE AND HIS "FAMILY" BURY THEIR VICTIMS IN THE EARTH. IN PREPARATION. THERE ARE VAMPIRES STILL ACTIVE ALL AROUND THE WORLD, DOING THE SAME THING--
--QUIETLY, SO NO ONE NOTICES.
OH GOD...IS IT HAPPENING NOW?

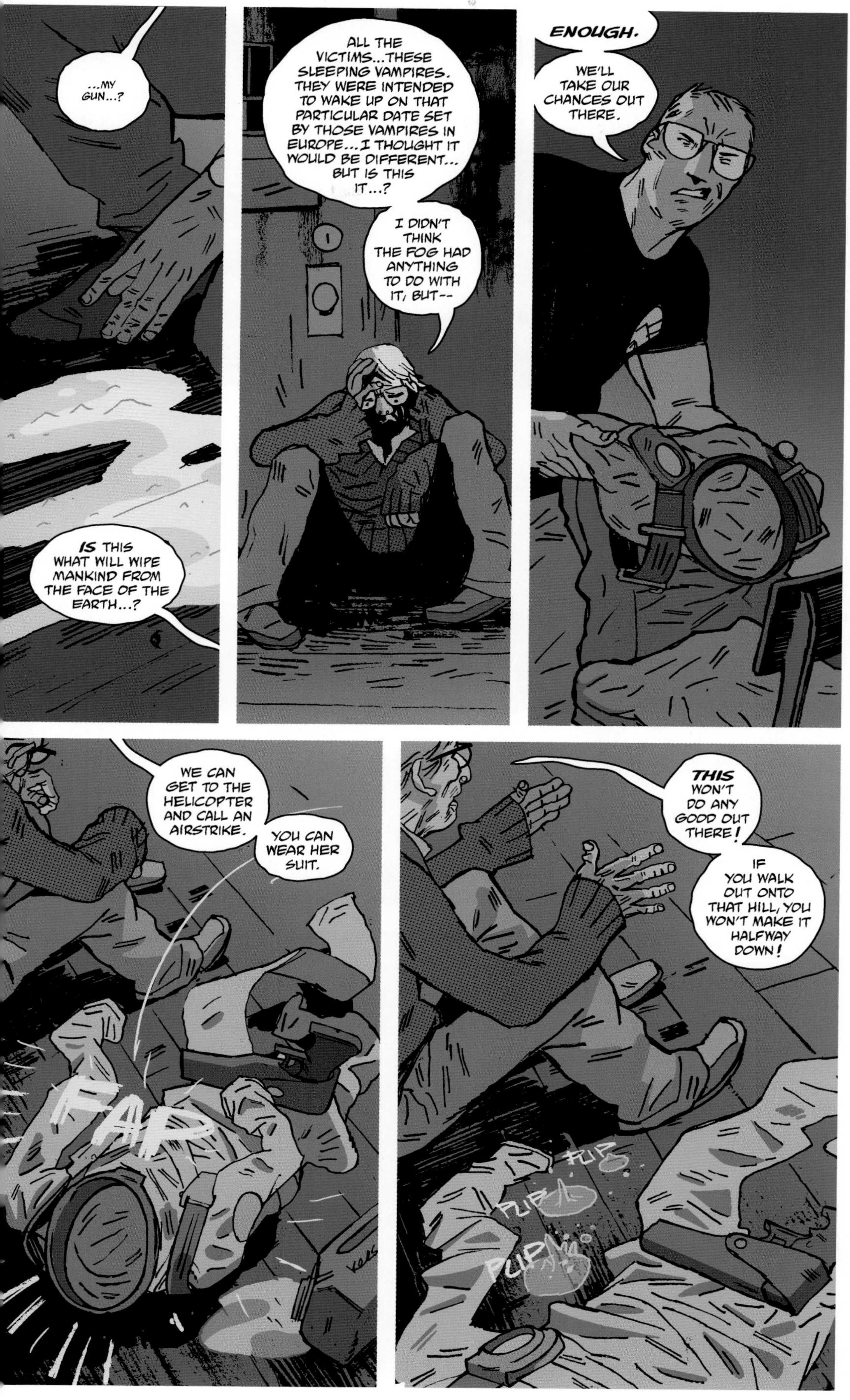
...MY GUN...?
IS THIS WHAT WILL WIPE MANKIND FROM THE FACE OF THE EARTH...?
ALL THE VICTIMS...THESE SLEEPING VAMPIRES. THEY WERE INTENDED TO WAKE UP ON THAT PARTICULAR DATE SET BY THOSE VAMPIRES IN EUROPE...I THOUGHT IT WOULD BE DIFFERENT... BUT IS THIS IT...?
I DIDN'T THINK THE FOG HAD ANYTHING TO DO WITH IT, BUT--
ENOUGH.
WE'LL TAKE OUR CHANCES OUT THERE.
WE CAN GET TO THE HELICOPTER AND CALL AN AIRSTRIKE.
YOU CAN WEAR HER SUIT.
FAP
THIS WON'T DO ANY GOOD OUT THERE!
IF YOU WALK OUT ONTO THAT HILL, YOU WON'T MAKE IT HALFWAY DOWN!
PLIP
PLIP
PLIP

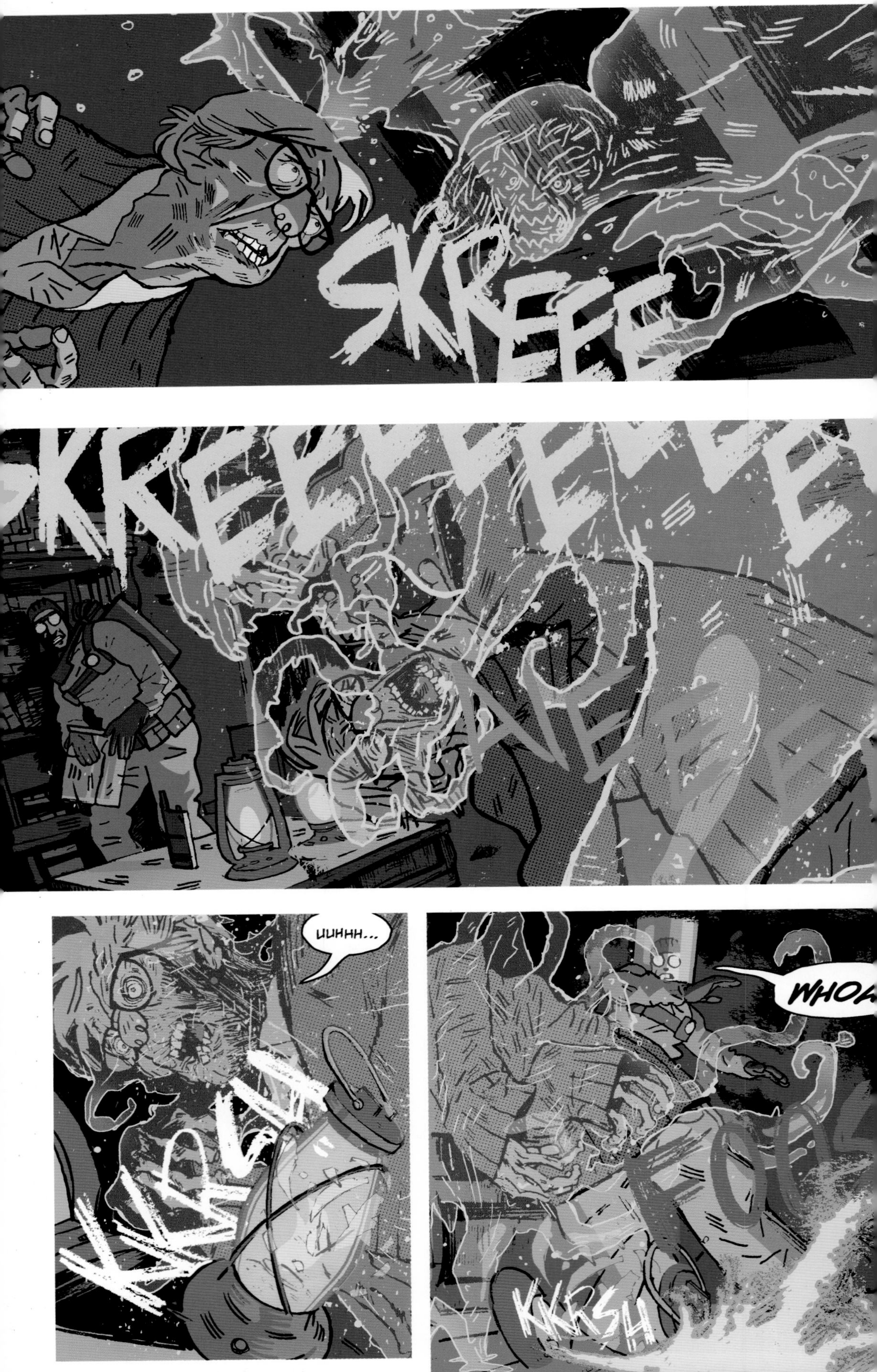
SKREEE
UUHHH...
WHOA
KKKSH

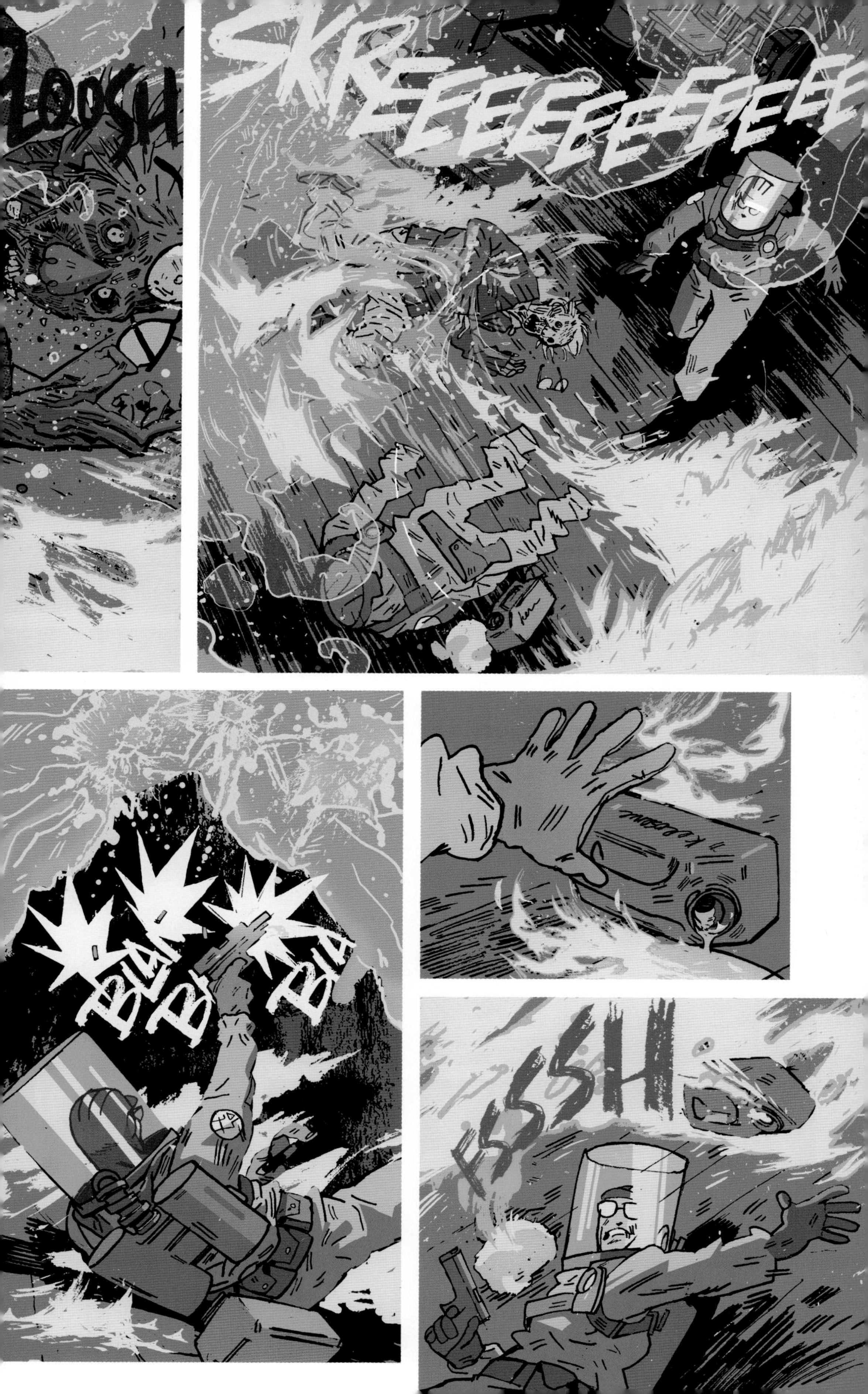
ZOOSH
SKREEEEEEEEEEEE
BLA
BLA
BLA
FSSSH

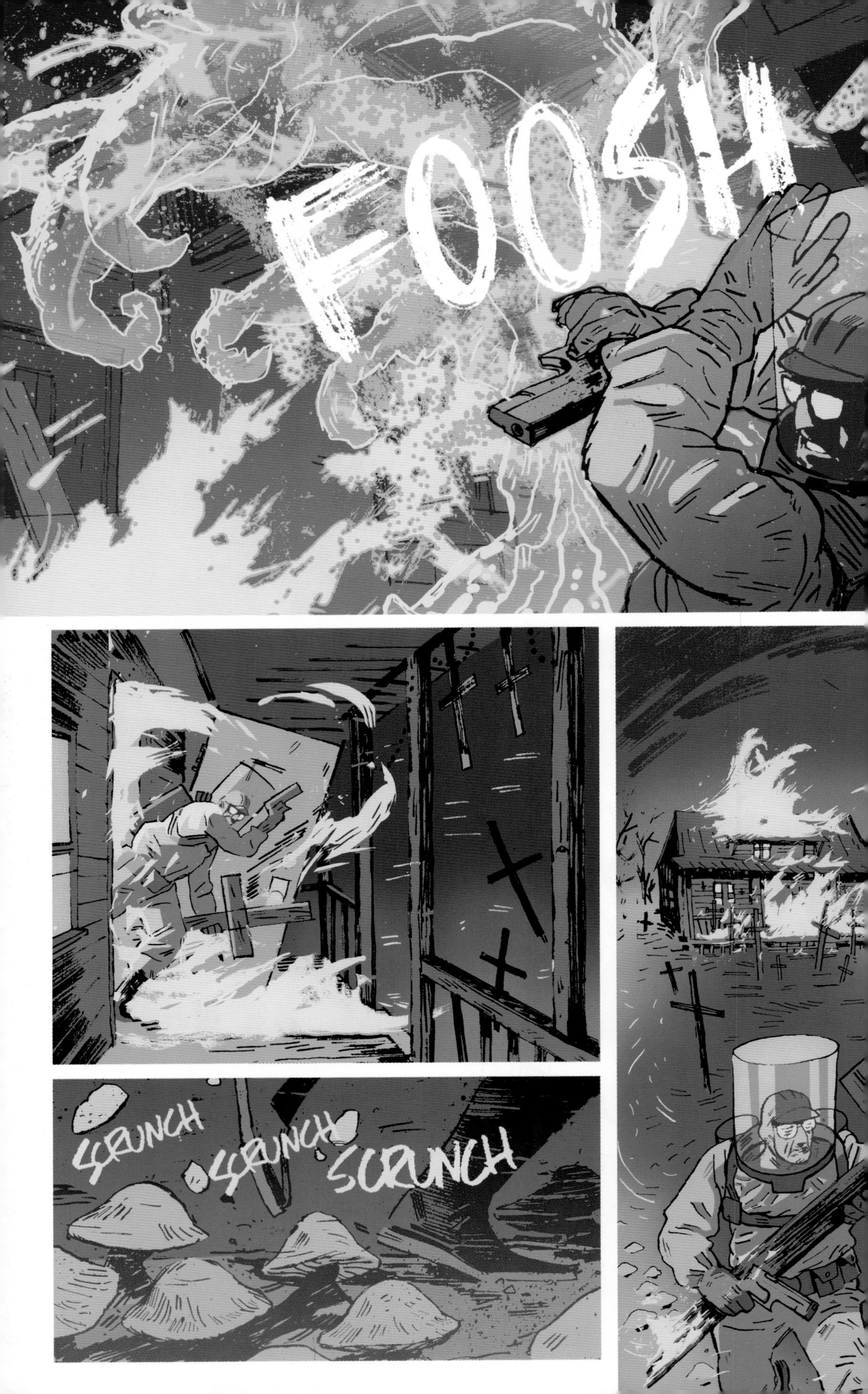
FOOSH
SCRUNCH
SCRUNCH
SCRUNCH

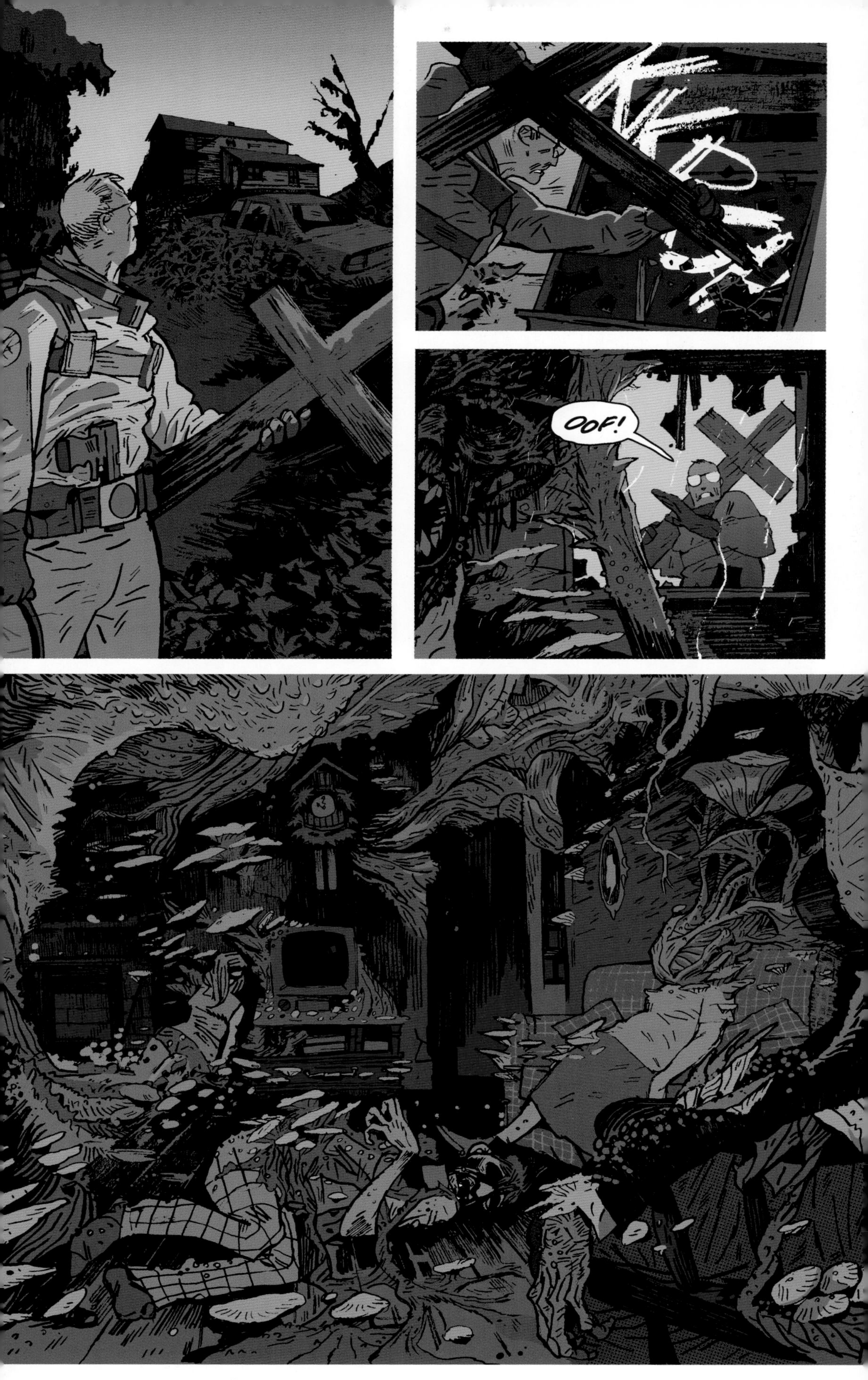
OOF!

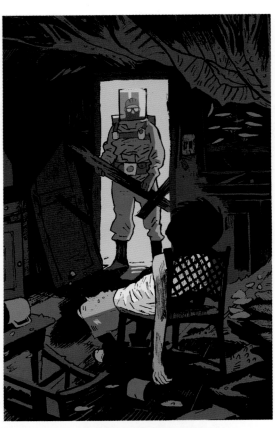

WHAT THE HELL DID YOU GUYS DO...?

THE END

THE TRANSFORMATION OF J. H. O'DONNELL

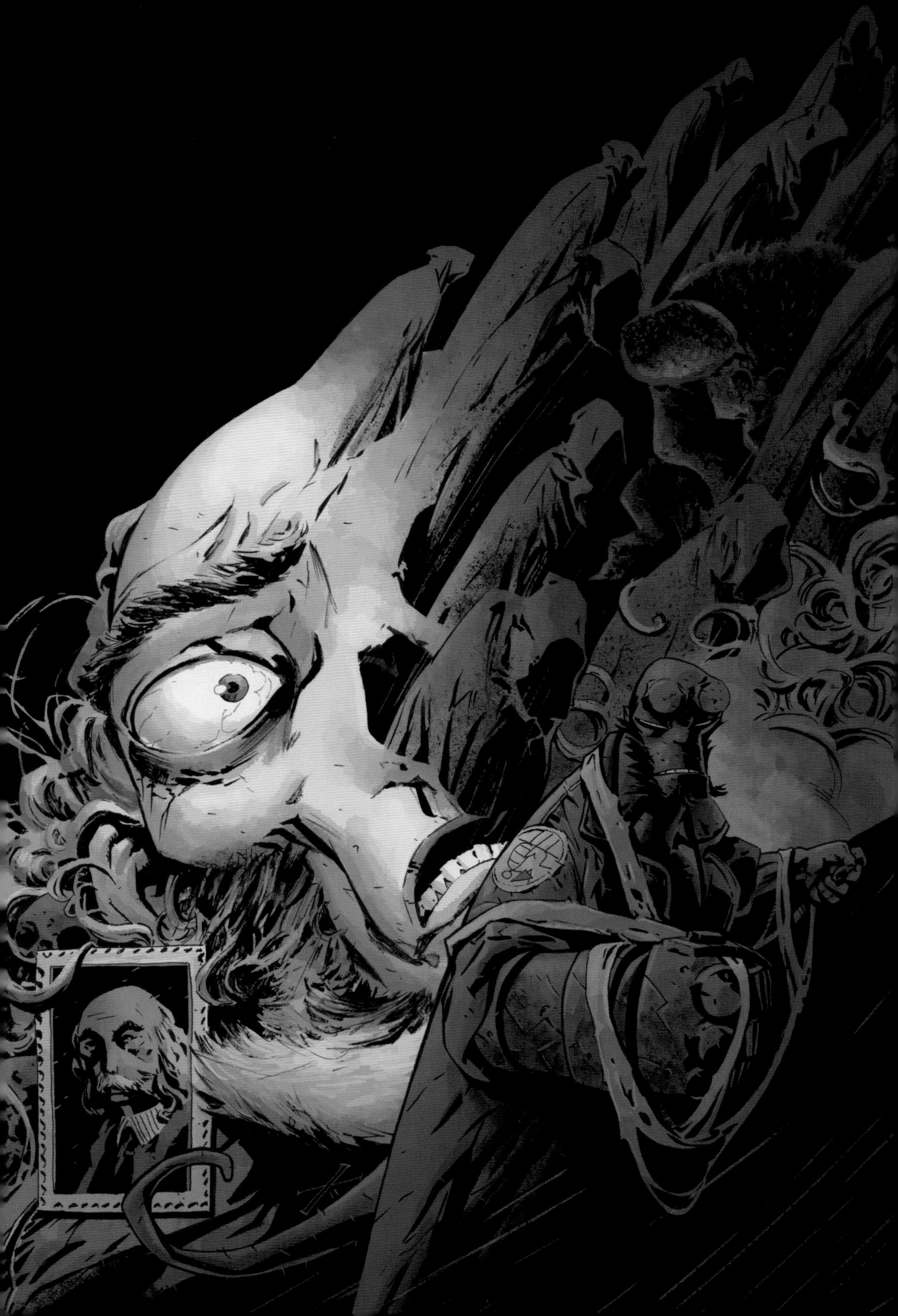

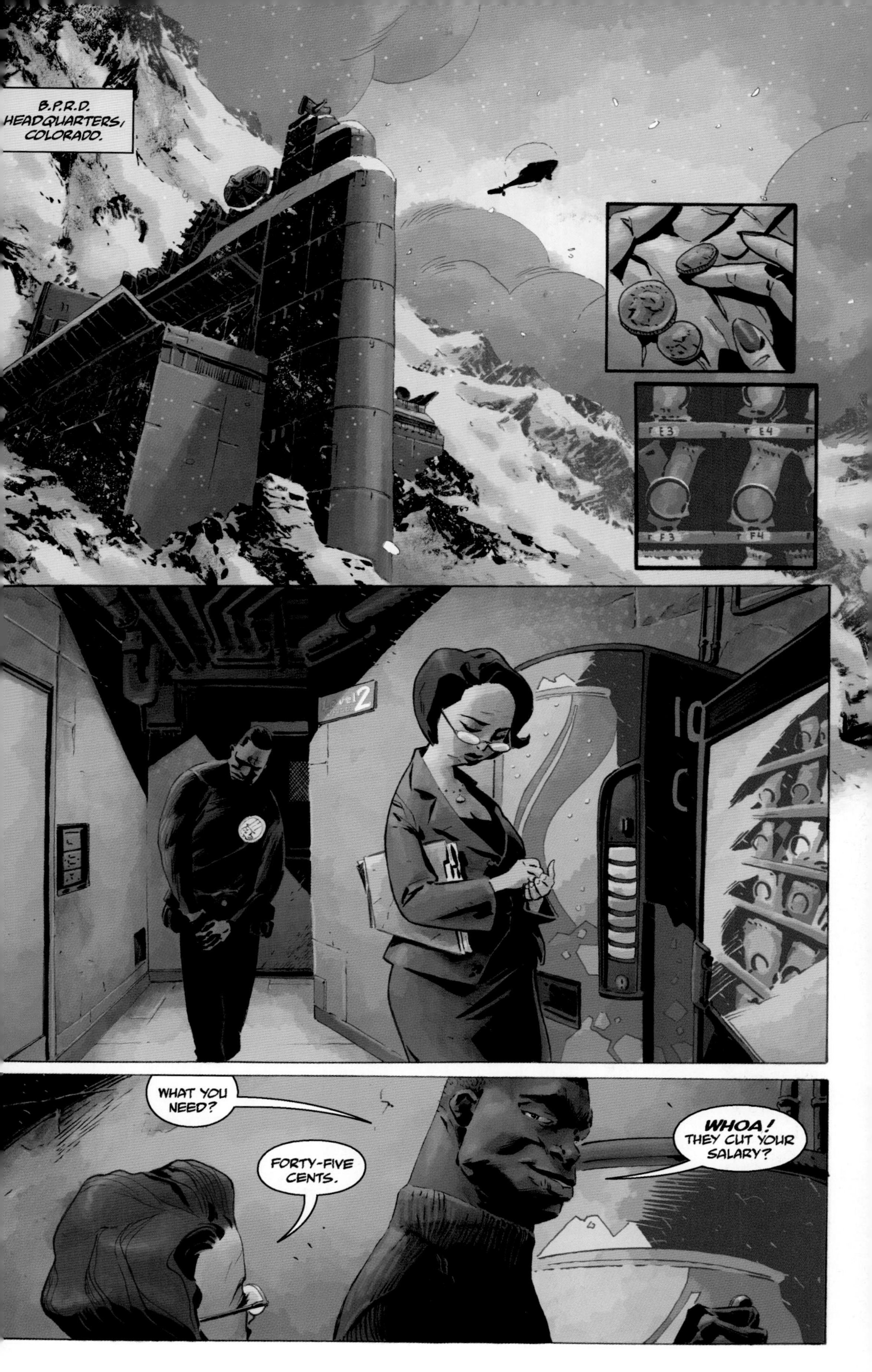
B.P.R.D. HEADQUARTERS, COLORADO.
E3
E4
F3
F4
Level 2
WHAT YOU NEED?
FORTY-FIVE CENTS.
WHOA! THEY CUT YOUR SALARY?

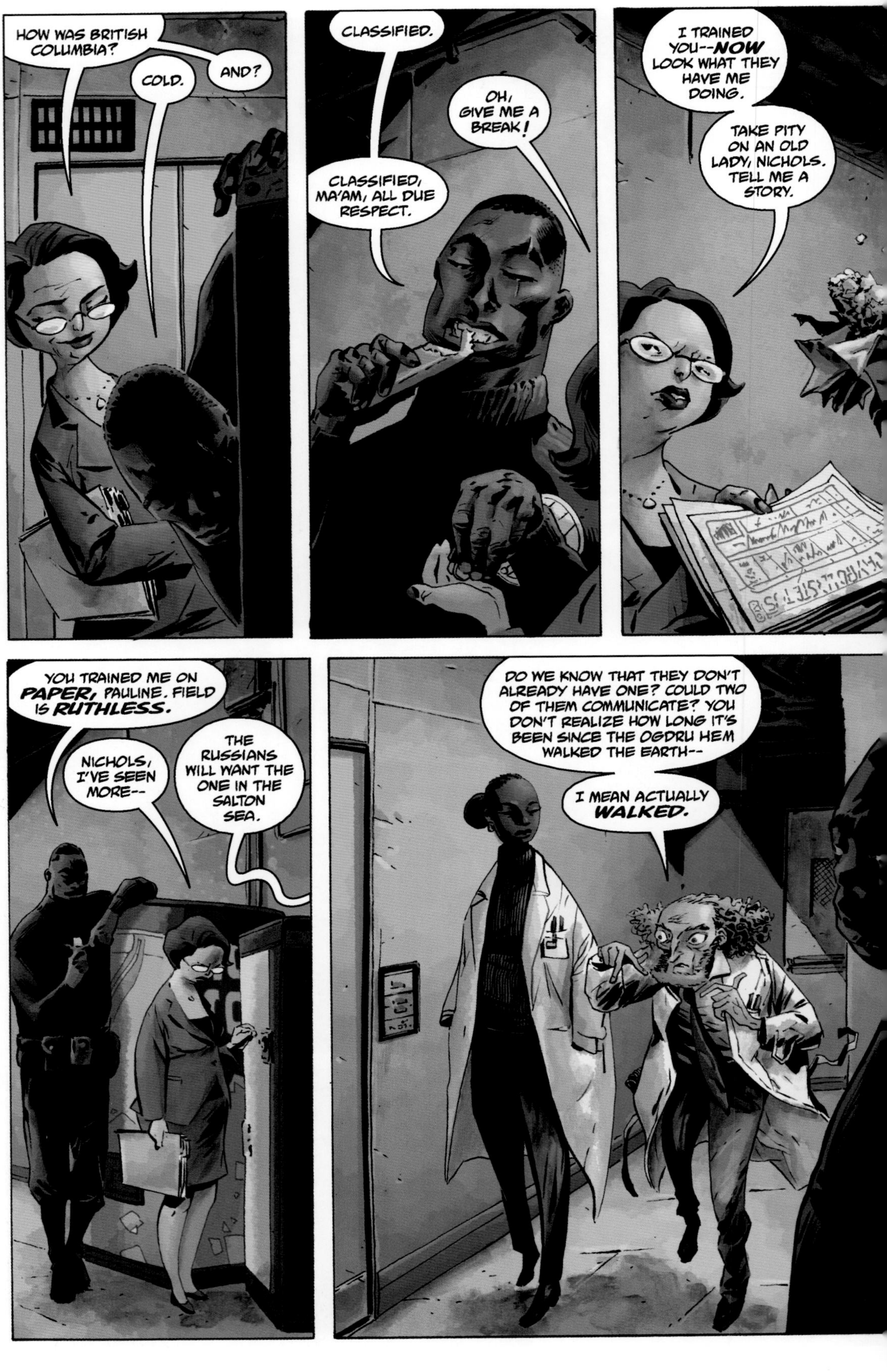
HOW WAS BRITISH COLUMBIA?
COLD.
AND?
CLASSIFIED.
OH, GIVE ME A BREAK!
CLASSIFIED, MA'AM, ALL DUE RESPECT.
I TRAINED YOU--NOW LOOK WHAT THEY HAVE ME DOING.
TAKE PITY ON AN OLD LADY, NICHOLS. TELL ME A STORY.
YOU TRAINED ME ON PAPER, PAULINE. FIELD IS RUTHLESS.
NICHOLS, I'VE SEEN MORE--
THE RUSSIANS WILL WANT THE ONE IN THE SALTON SEA.
DO WE KNOW THAT THEY DON'T ALREADY HAVE ONE? COULD TWO OF THEM COMMUNICATE? YOU DON'T REALIZE HOW LONG IT'S BEEN SINCE THE OGDRU HEM WALKED THE EARTH--
I MEAN ACTUALLY WALKED.

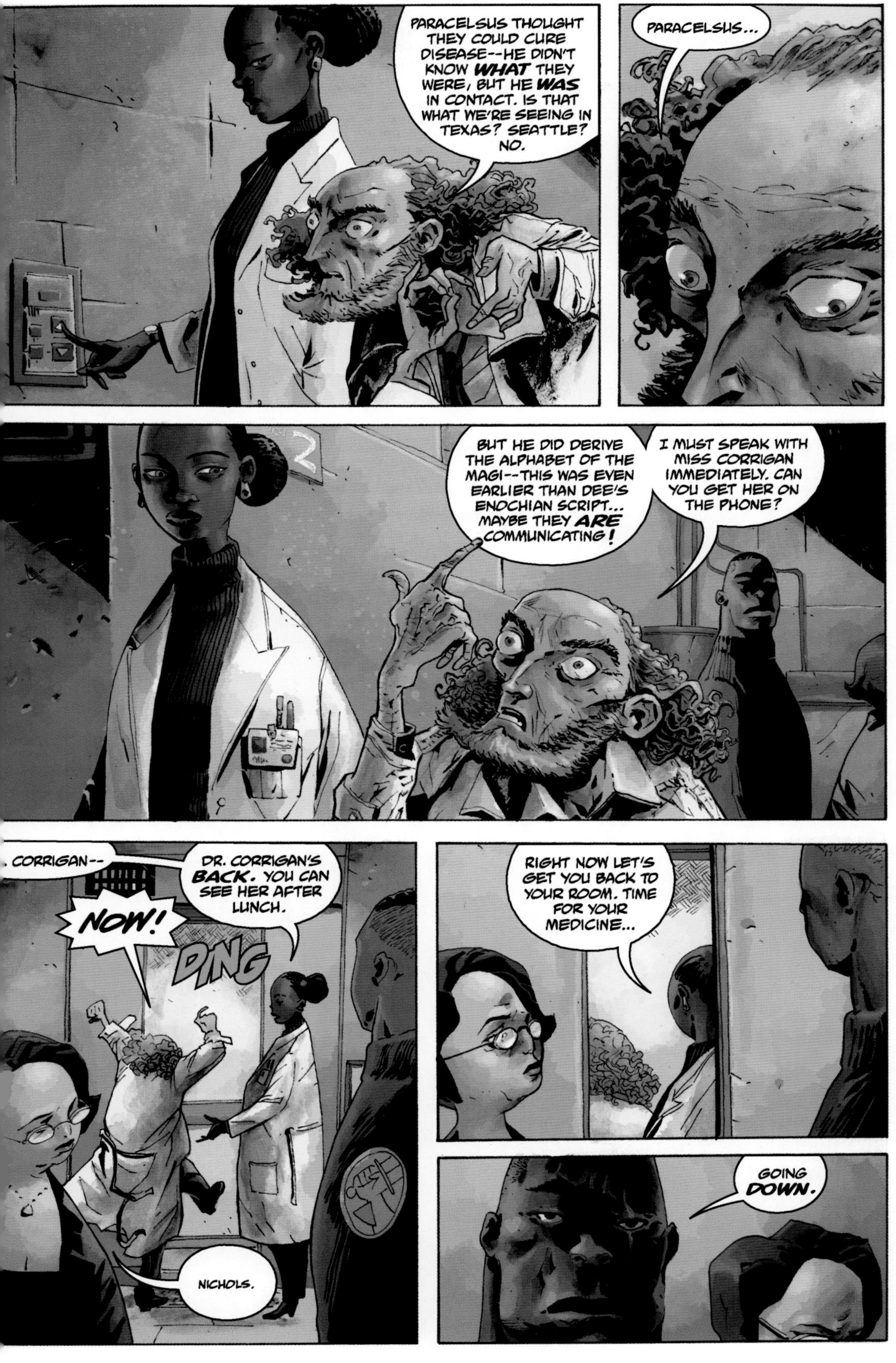
PARACELSUS THOUGHT THEY COULD CURE DISEASE--HE DIDN'T KNOW WHAT THEY WERE, BUT HE WAS IN CONTACT. IS THAT WHAT WE'RE SEEING IN TEXAS? SEATTLE? NO.
PARACELSUS...
BUT HE DID DERIVE THE ALPHABET OF THE MAGI--THIS WAS EVEN EARLIER THAN DEE'S ENOCHIAN SCRIPT... MAYBE THEY ARE COMMUNICATING!
I MUST SPEAK WITH MISS CORRIGAN IMMEDIATELY. CAN YOU GET HER ON THE PHONE?
. CORRIGAN--
DR. CORRIGAN'S BACK. YOU CAN SEE HER AFTER LUNCH.
NOW!
DING
NICHOLS.
RIGHT NOW LET'S GET YOU BACK TO YOUR ROOM. TIME FOR YOUR MEDICINE...
GOING DOWN.

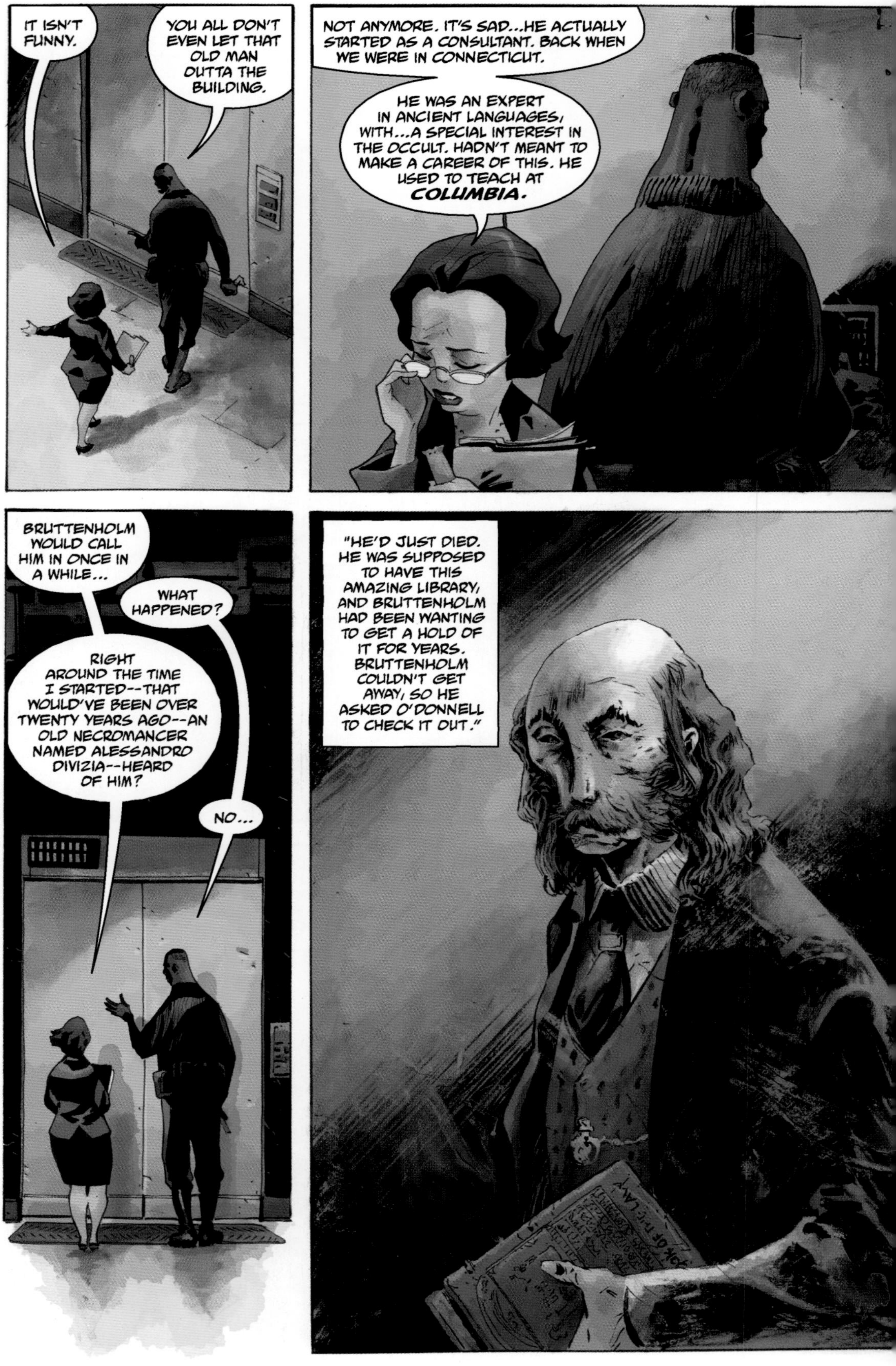
IT ISN'T FUNNY.
YOU ALL DON'T EVEN LET THAT OLD MAN OUTTA THE BUILDING.
NOT ANYMORE. IT'S SAD...HE ACTUALLY STARTED AS A CONSULTANT. BACK WHEN WE WERE IN CONNECTICUT.
HE WAS AN EXPERT IN ANCIENT LANGUAGES, WITH...A SPECIAL INTEREST IN THE OCCULT. HADN'T MEANT TO MAKE A CAREER OF THIS. HE USED TO TEACH AT COLUMBIA.
BRUTTENHOLM WOULD CALL HIM IN ONCE IN A WHILE...
WHAT HAPPENED?
RIGHT AROUND THE TIME I STARTED--THAT WOULD'VE BEEN OVER TWENTY YEARS AGO--AN OLD NECROMANCER NAMED ALESSANDRO DIVIZIA--HEARD OF HIM?
NO...
"HE'D JUST DIED. HE WAS SUPPOSED TO HAVE THIS AMAZING LIBRARY, AND BRUTTENHOLM HAD BEEN WANTING TO GET A HOLD OF IT FOR YEARS. BRUTTENHOLM COULDN'T GET AWAY, SO HE ASKED O'DONNELL TO CHECK IT OUT."

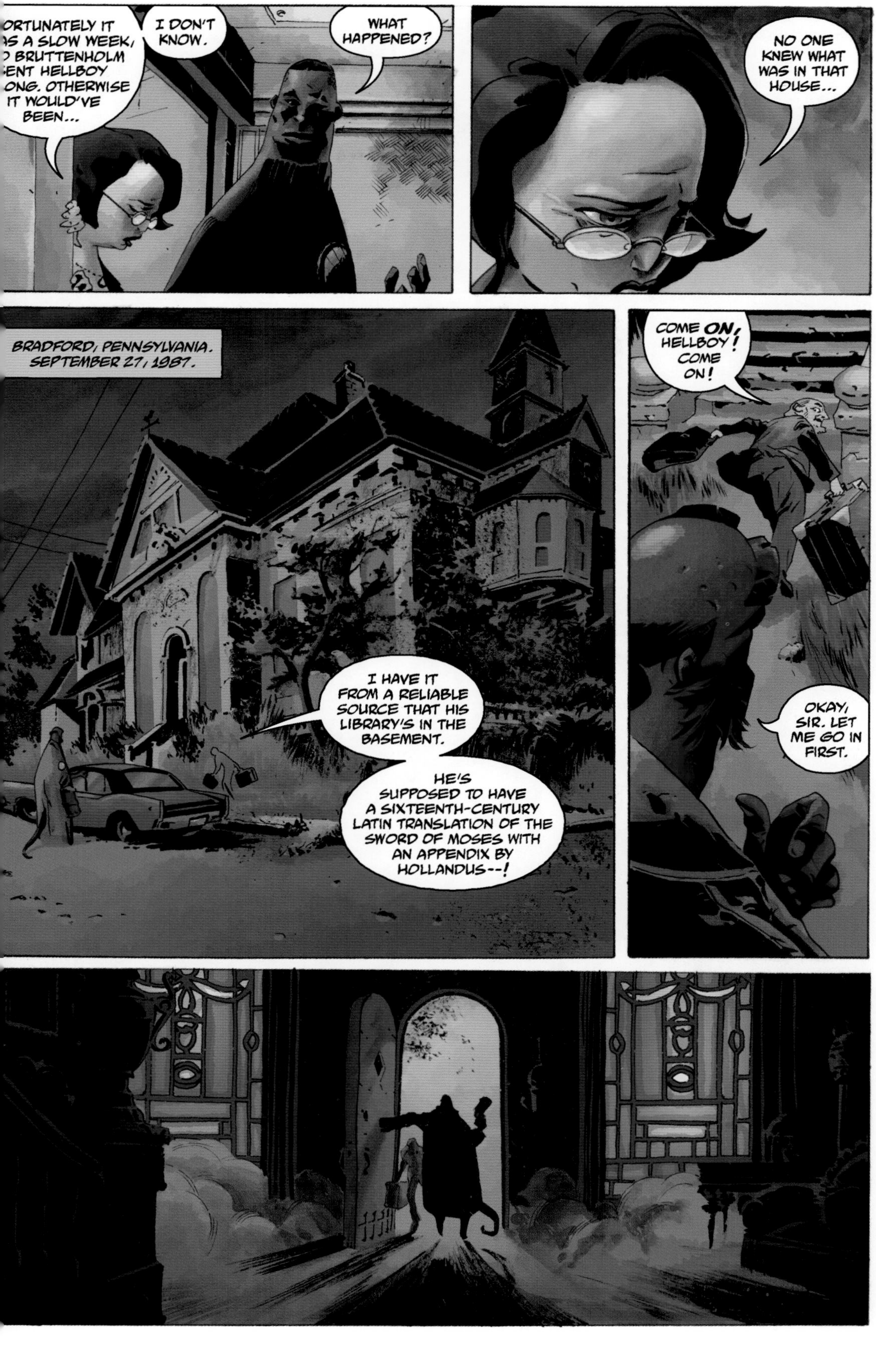
ORTUNATELY IT AS A SLOW WEEK, O BRUTTENHOLM ENT HELLBOY ONG. OTHERWISE IT WOULD'VE BEEN...
I DON'T KNOW.
WHAT HAPPENED?
NO ONE KNEW WHAT WAS IN THAT HOUSE...
BRADFORD, PENNSYLVANIA. SEPTEMBER 27, 1987.
I HAVE IT FROM A RELIABLE SOURCE THAT HIS LIBRARY'S IN THE BASEMENT.
HE'S SUPPOSED TO HAVE A SIXTEENTH-CENTURY LATIN TRANSLATION OF THE SWORD OF MOSES WITH AN APPENDIX BY HOLLANDUS--!
COME ON, HELLBOY! COME ON!
OKAY, SIR. LET ME GO IN FIRST.

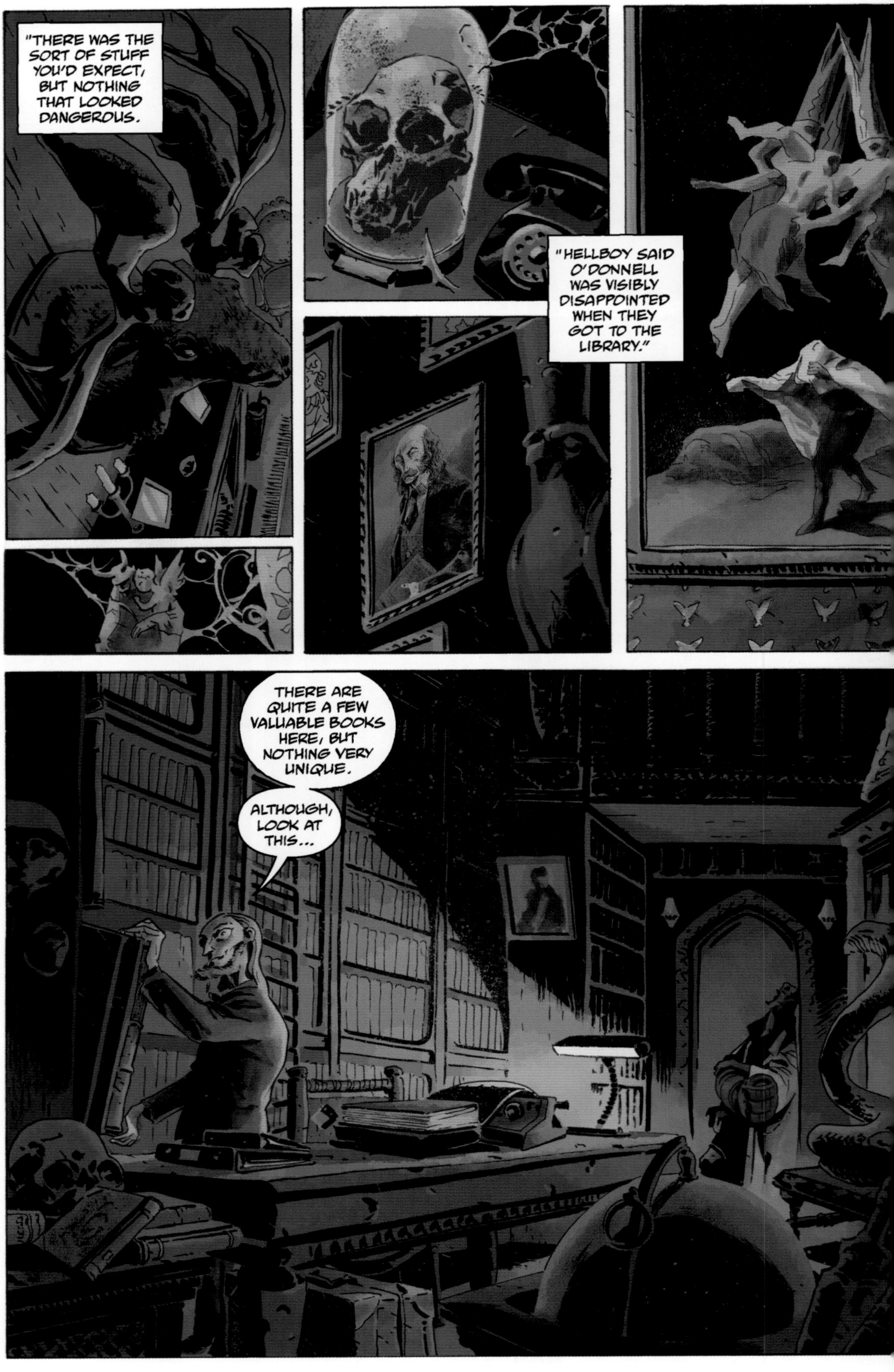
"THERE WAS THE SORT OF STUFF YOU'D EXPECT, BUT NOTHING THAT LOOKED DANGEROUS.
"HELLBOY SAID O'DONNELL WAS VISIBLY DISAPPOINTED WHEN THEY GOT TO THE LIBRARY."
THERE ARE QUITE A FEW VALUABLE BOOKS HERE, BUT NOTHING VERY UNIQUE.
ALTHOUGH, LOOK AT THIS...

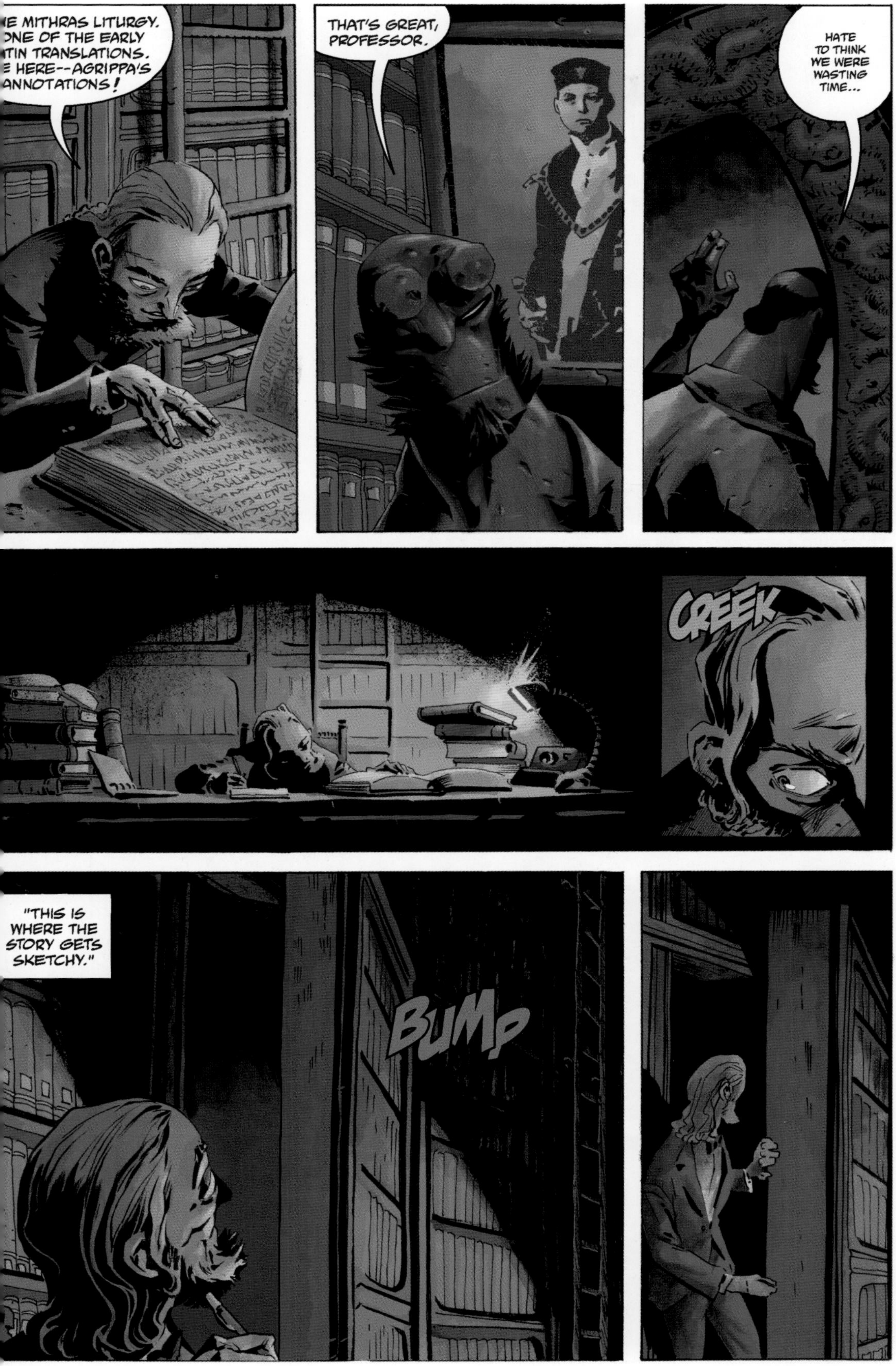
E MITHRAS LITURGY. ONE OF THE EARLY TIN TRANSLATIONS. E HERE--AGRIPPA'S ANNOTATIONS!
THAT'S GREAT, PROFESSOR.
HATE TO THINK WE WERE WASTING TIME...
CREEK
"THIS IS WHERE THE STORY GETS SKETCHY."
BUMP

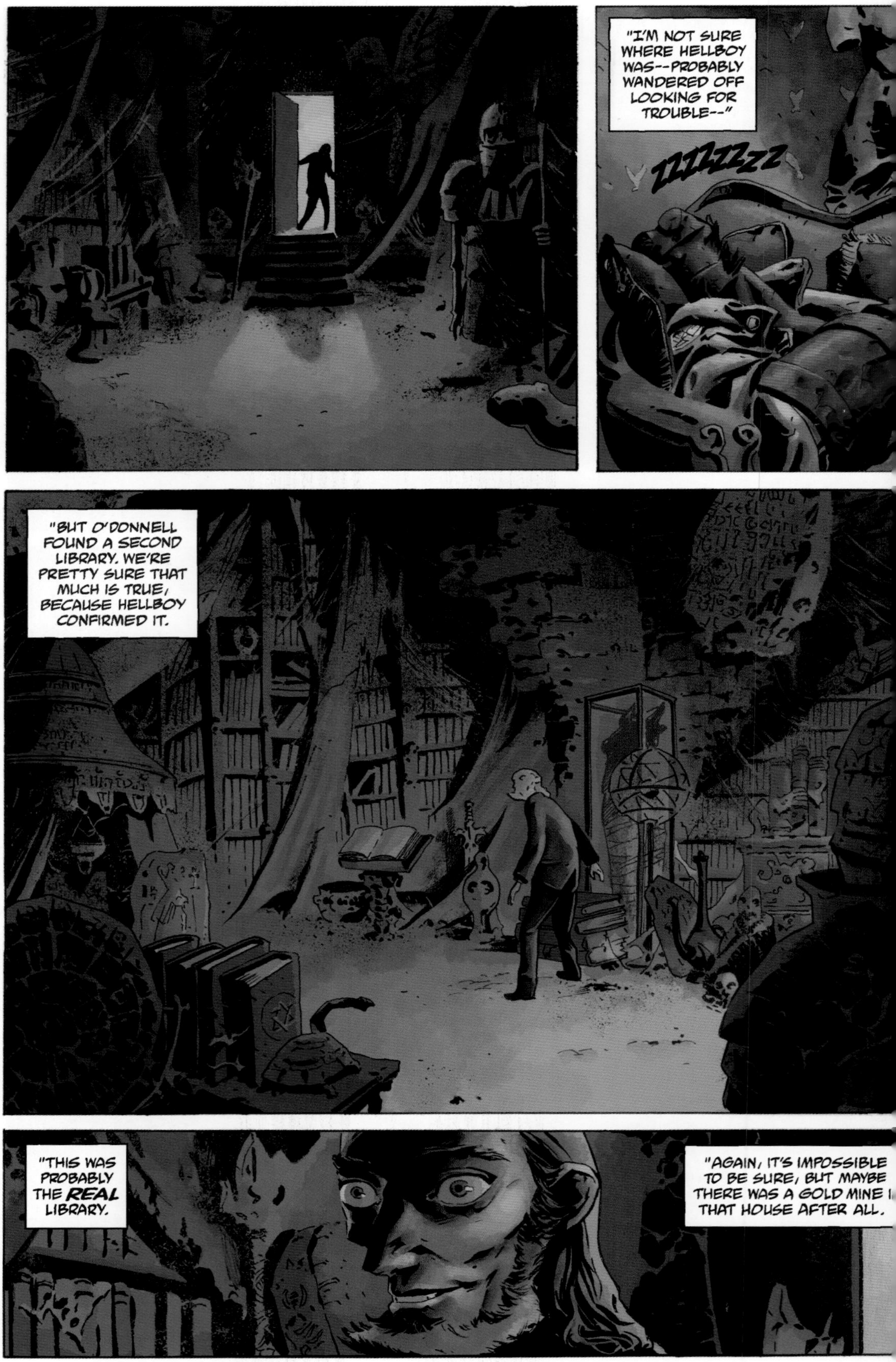
"I'M NOT SURE WHERE HELLBOY WAS--PROBABLY WANDERED OFF LOOKING FOR TROUBLE--"
ZZZZZZZZ
"BUT O'DONNELL FOUND A SECOND LIBRARY. WE'RE PRETTY SURE THAT MUCH IS TRUE, BECAUSE HELLBOY CONFIRMED IT.
"THIS WAS PROBABLY THE REAL LIBRARY.
"AGAIN, IT'S IMPOSSIBLE TO BE SURE, BUT MAYBE THERE WAS A GOLD MINE I THAT HOUSE AFTER ALL.

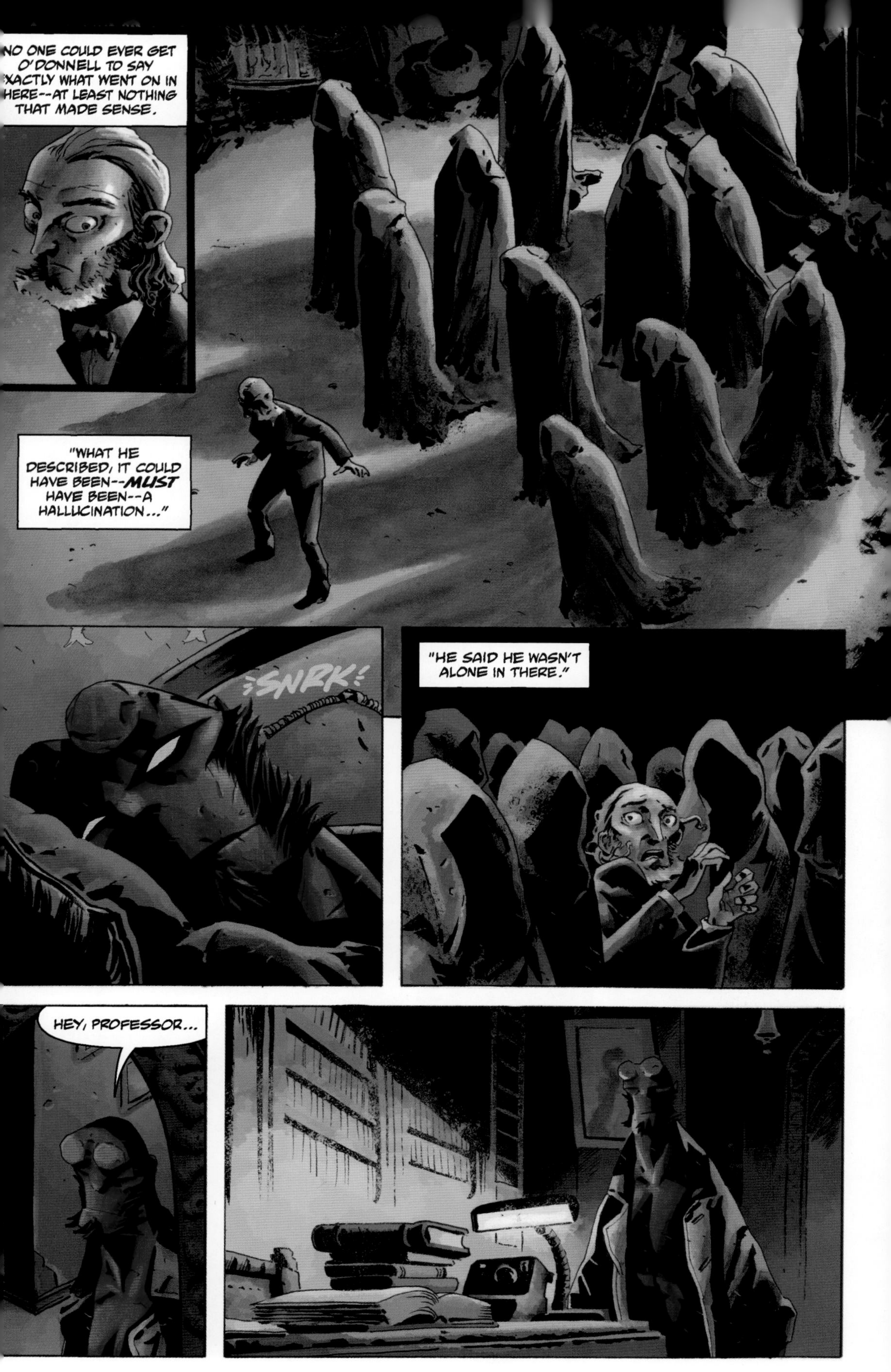
NO ONE COULD EVER GET O'DONNELL TO SAY EXACTLY WHAT WENT ON IN HERE--AT LEAST NOTHING THAT MADE SENSE.
"WHAT HE DESCRIBED, IT COULD HAVE BEEN--MUST HAVE BEEN--A HALLUCINATION..."
SNRK!
"HE SAID HE WASN'T ALONE IN THERE."
HEY, PROFESSOR...

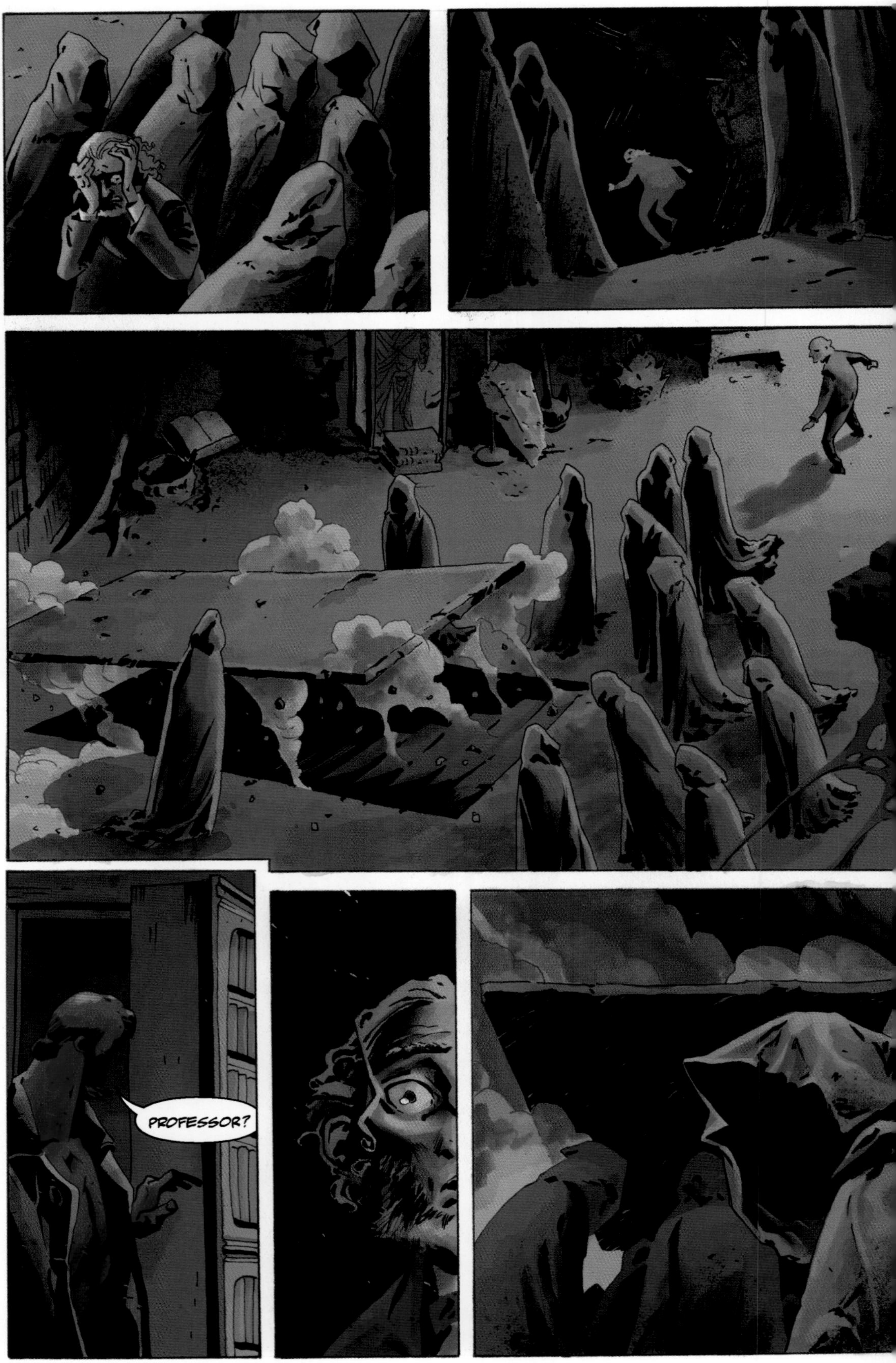
PROFESSOR?

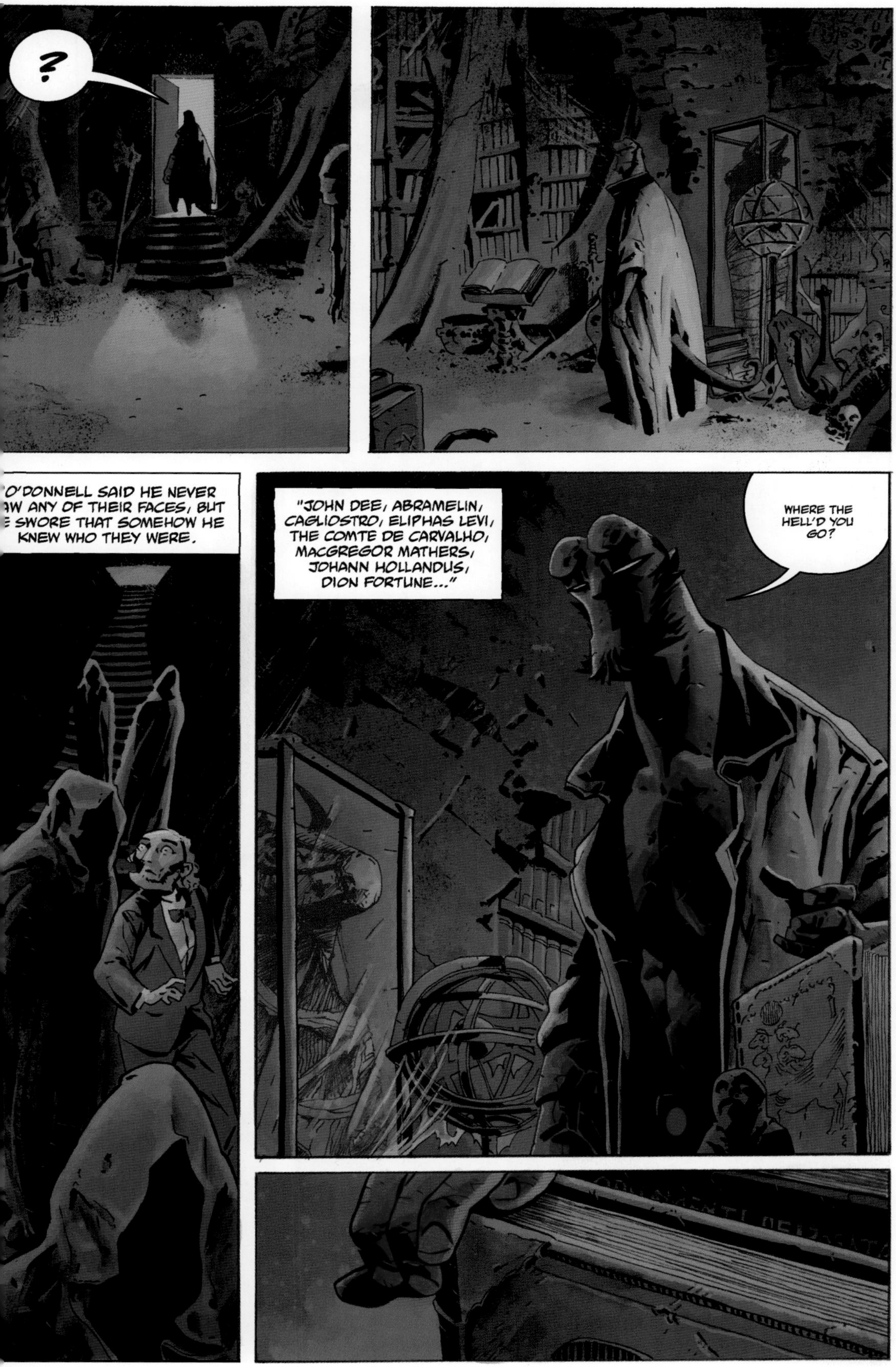

?
'O'DONNELL SAID HE NEVER
AW ANY OF THEIR FACES, BUT
E SWORE THAT SOMEHOW HE
KNEW WHO THEY WERE.
"JOHN DEE, ABRAMELIN, CAGLIOSTRO, ELIPHAS LEVI, THE COMTE DE CARVALHO, MACGREGOR MATHERS, JOHANN HOLLANDUS, DION FORTUNE..."
WHERE THE HELL'D YOU GO?

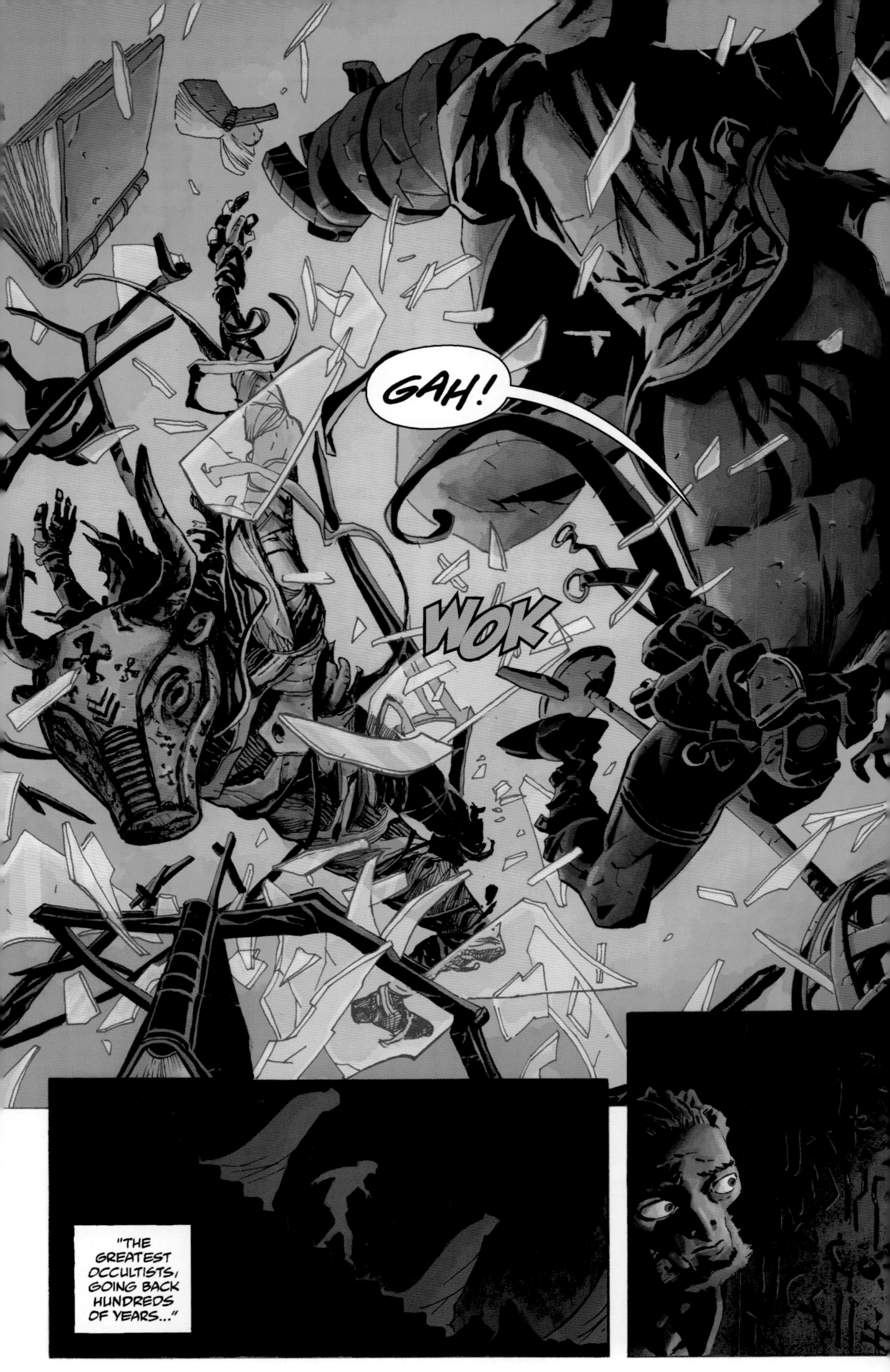
GAH!
WOK
"THE GREATEST OCCULTISTS, GOING BACK HUNDREDS OF YEARS..."

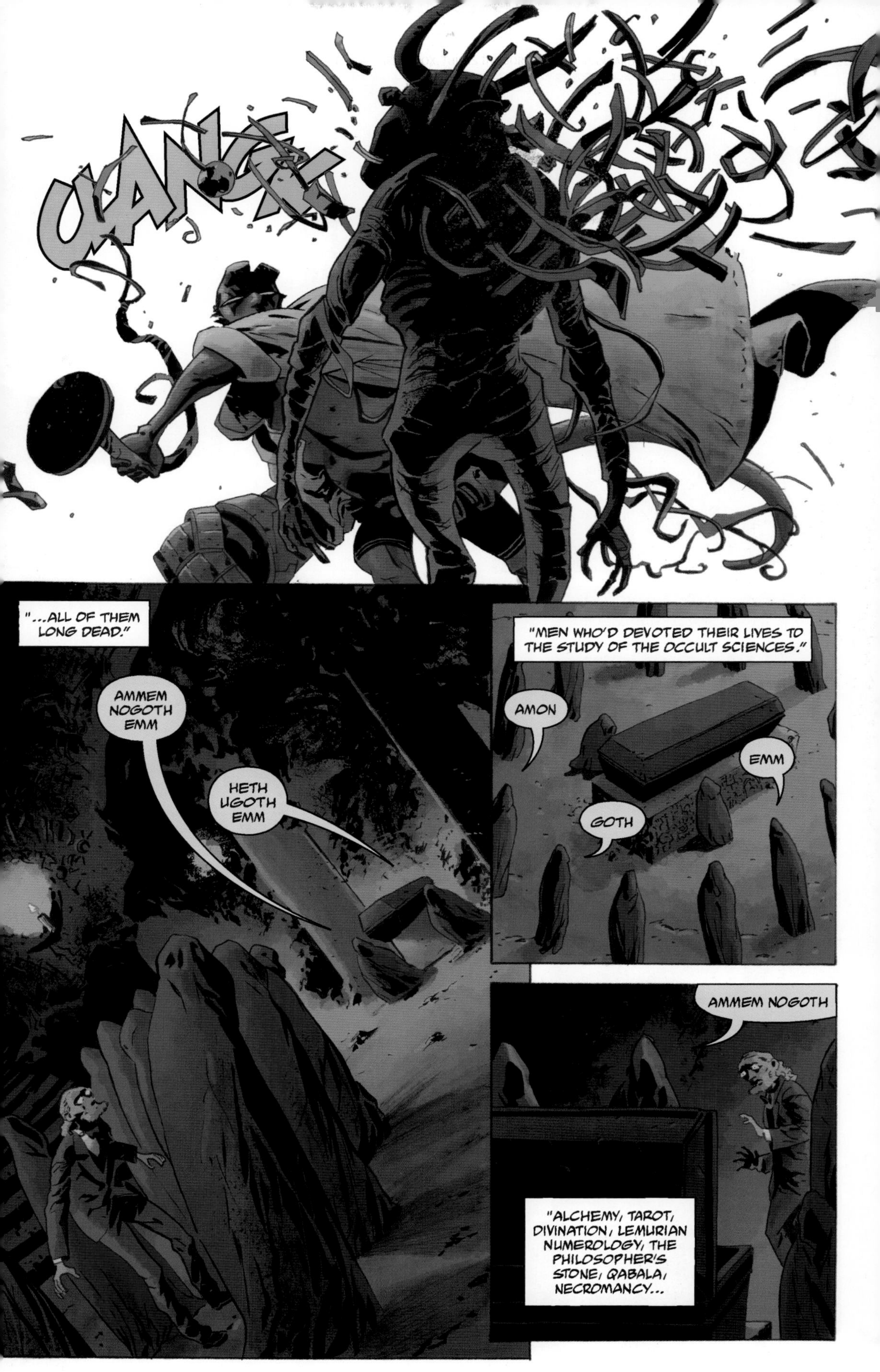
CLANG!
"...ALL OF THEM LONG DEAD."
AMMEM NOGOTH EMM
HETH UGOTH EMM
"MEN WHO'D DEVOTED THEIR LIVES TO THE STUDY OF THE OCCULT SCIENCES."
AMON
EMM
GOTH
AMMEM NOGOTH
"ALCHEMY, TAROT, DIVINATION, LEMURIAN NUMEROLOGY, THE PHILOSOPHER'S STONE, QABALA, NECROMANCY...

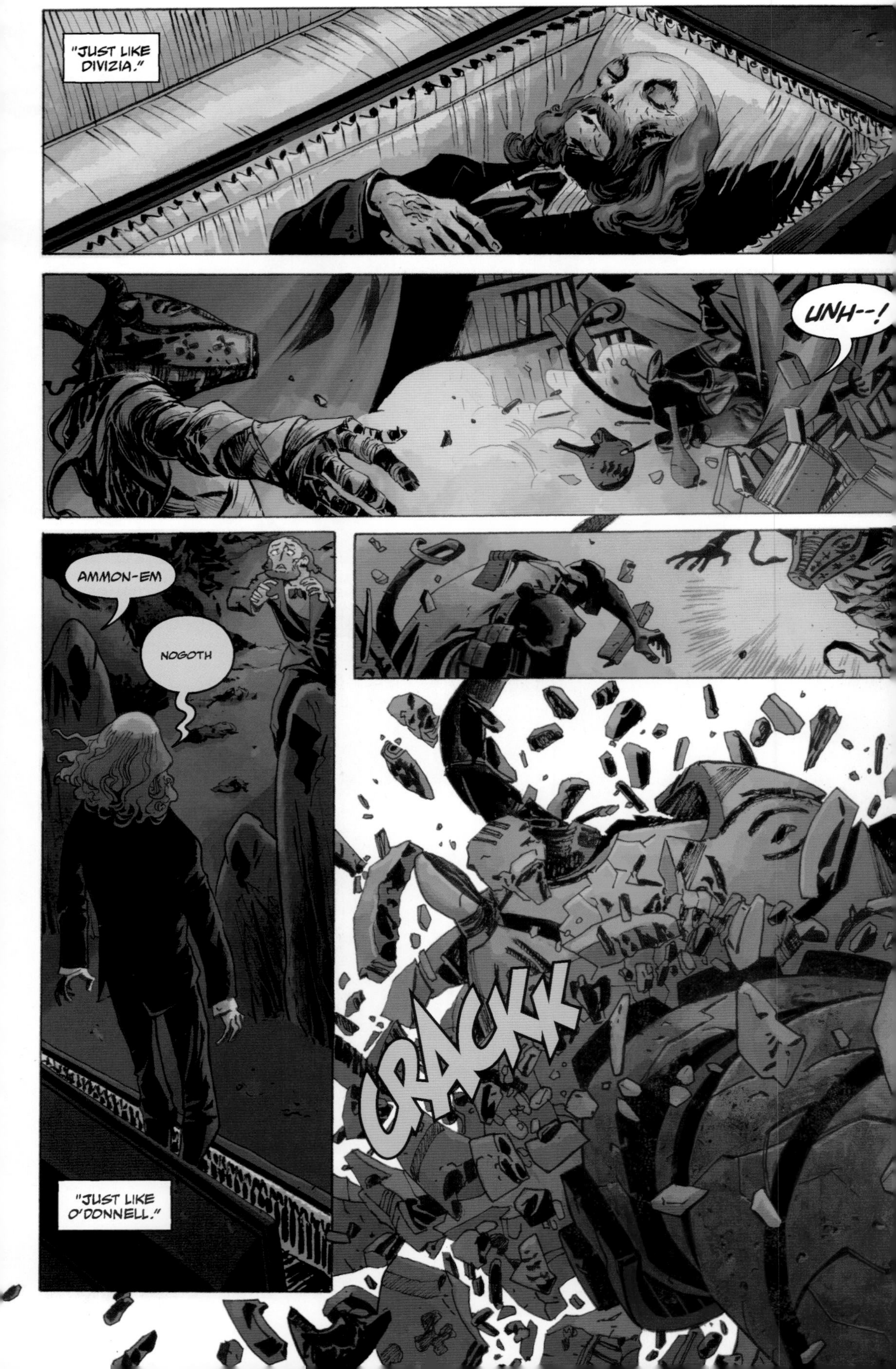
"JUST LIKE DIVIZIA."
UNH--!
AMMON-EM
NOGOTH
"JUST LIKE O'DONNELL."
CRACKK

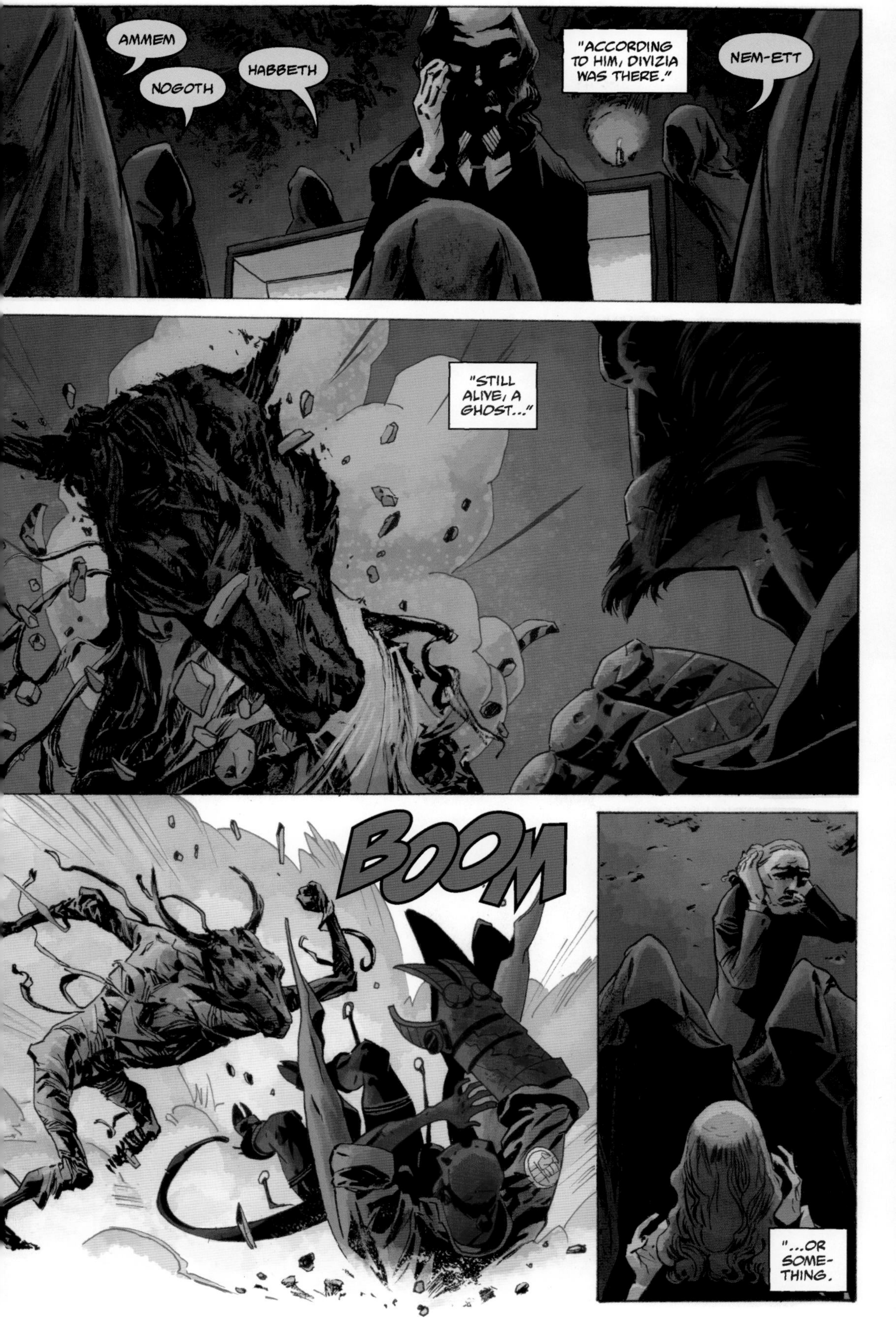
AMMEM
NOGOTH
HABBETH
"ACCORDING TO HIM, DIVIZIA WAS THERE."
NEM-ETT
"STILL ALIVE, A GHOST..."
BOOM
"...OR SOME-THING.

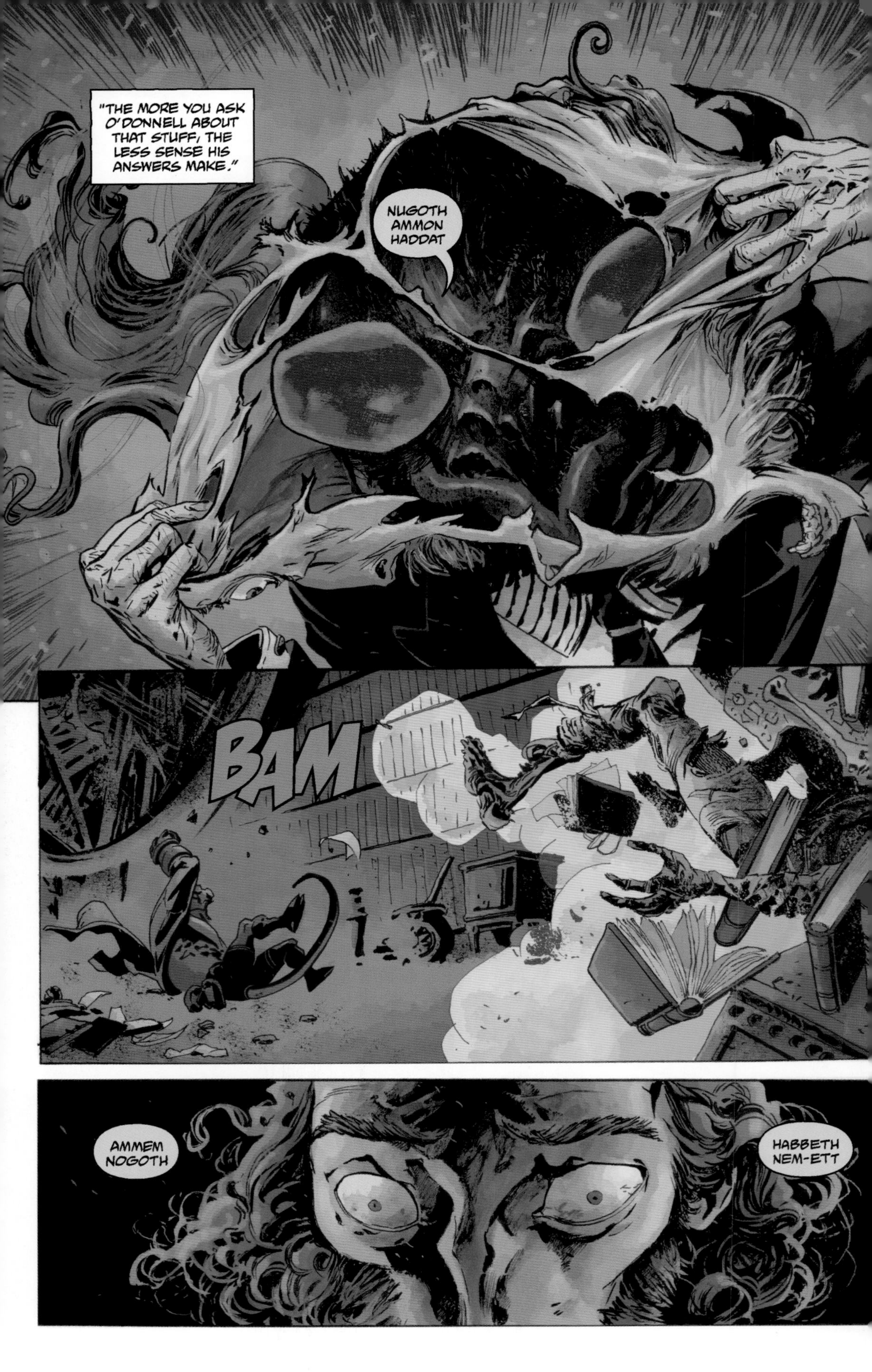
"THE MORE YOU ASK O'DONNELL ABOUT THAT STUFF, THE LESS SENSE HIS ANSWERS MAKE."
NUGOTH AMMON HADDAT
BAM
AMMEM NOGOTH
HABBETH NEM-ETT

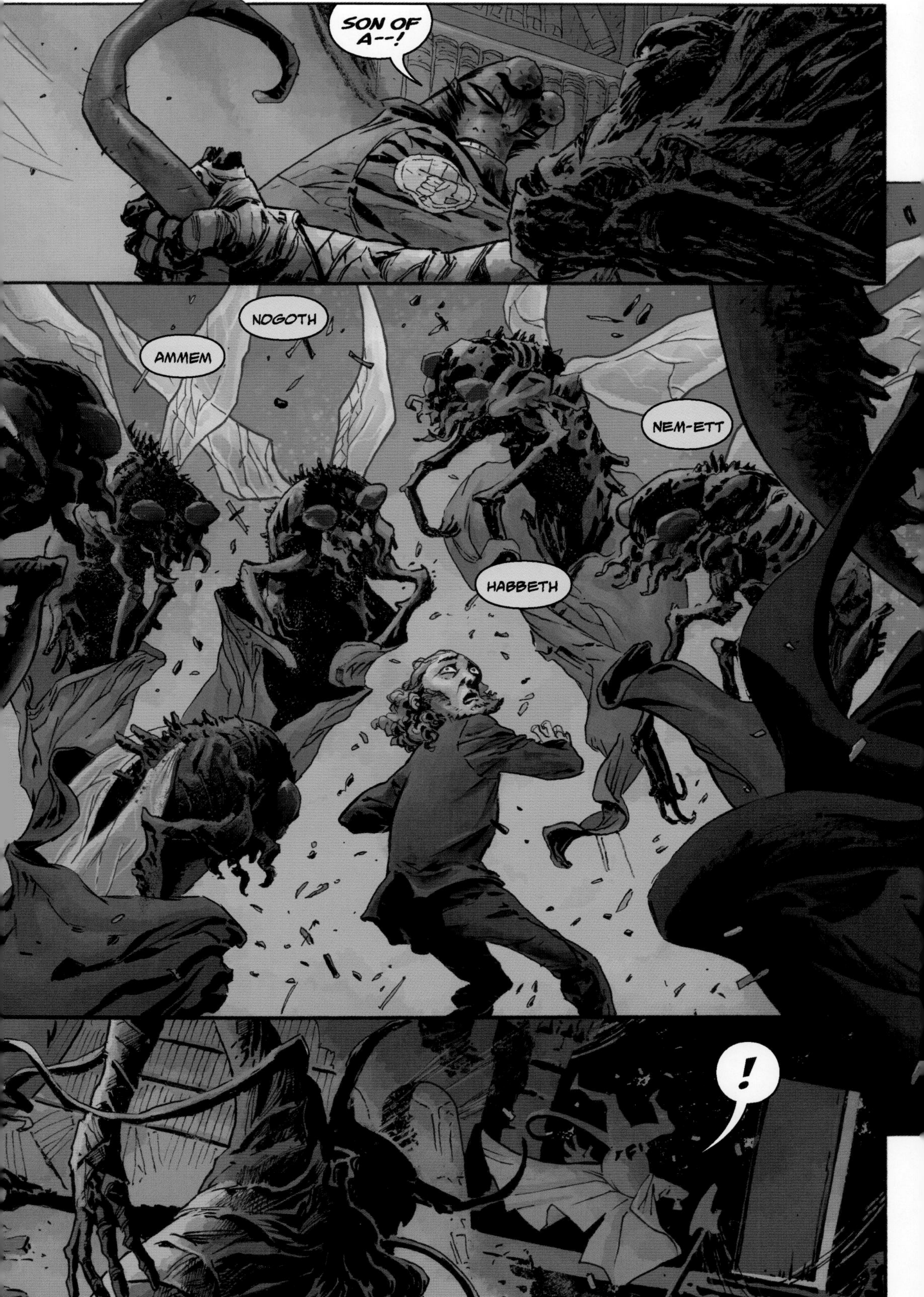
SON OF A--!
NOGOTH
AMMEM
NEM-ETT
HABBETH
!

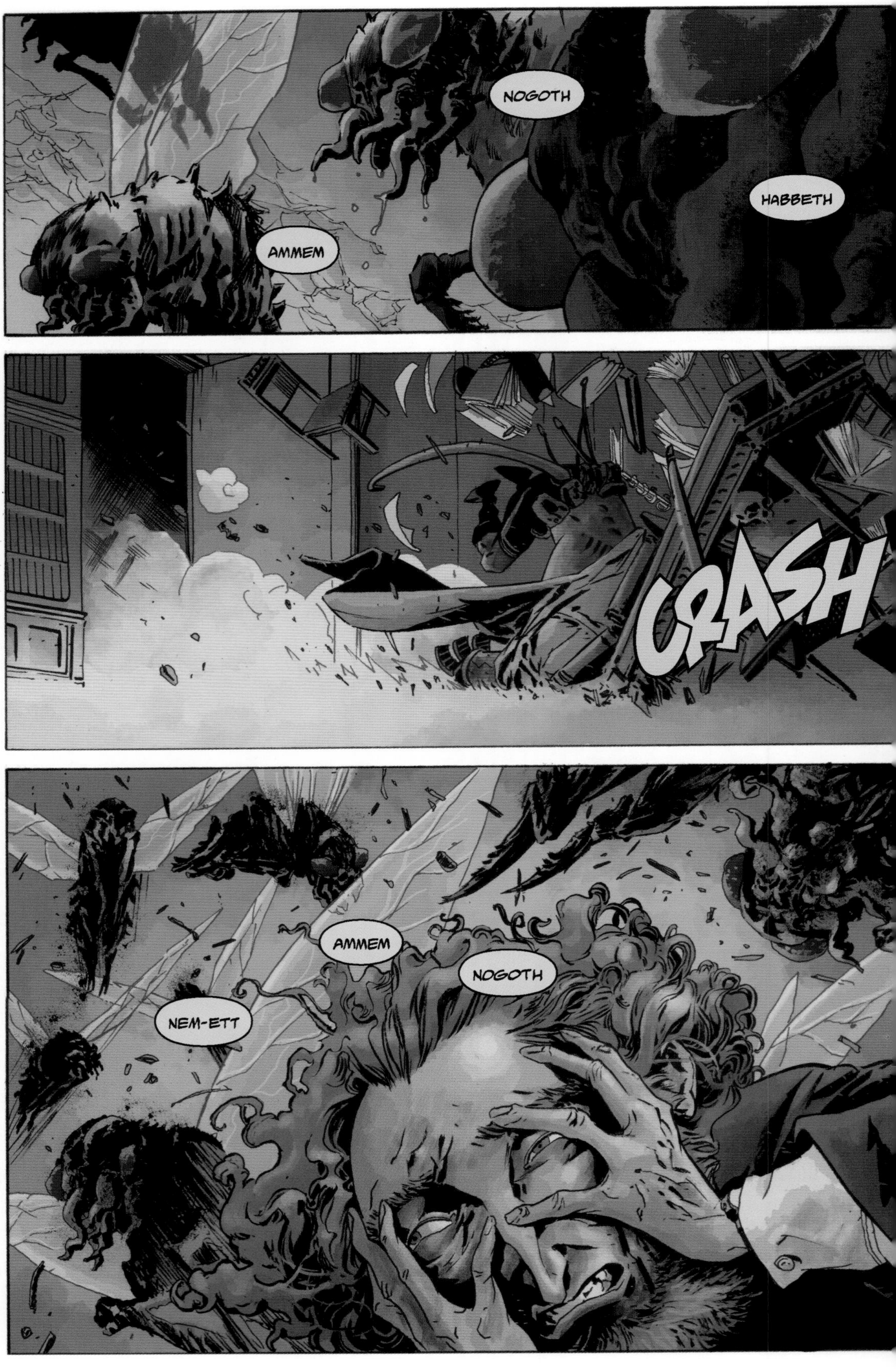
NOGOTH
HABBETH
AMMEM
CRASH
AMMEM
NOGOTH
NEM-ETT

SLAM

NEM-ETT

HABBETH

AMMEM

AIIIE!

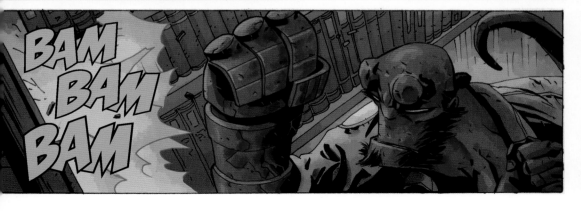

BAM
BAM
BAM

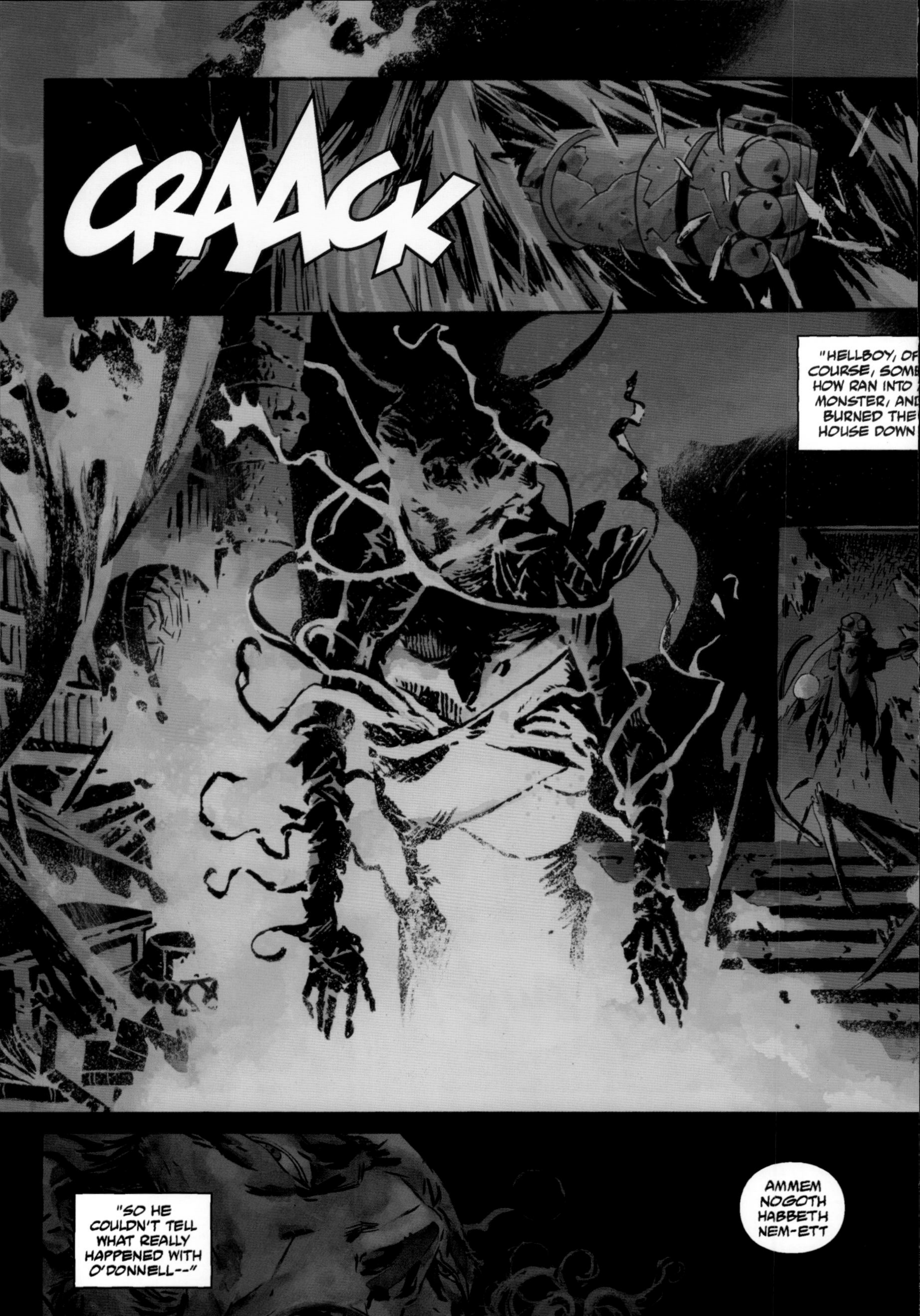
CRAACK
"HELLBOY, OF COURSE, SOME HOW RAN INTO A MONSTER, AND BURNED THE HOUSE DOWN
"SO HE COULDN'T TELL WHAT REALLY HAPPENED WITH O'DONNELL--"
AMMEM NOGOTH HABBETH NEM-ETT

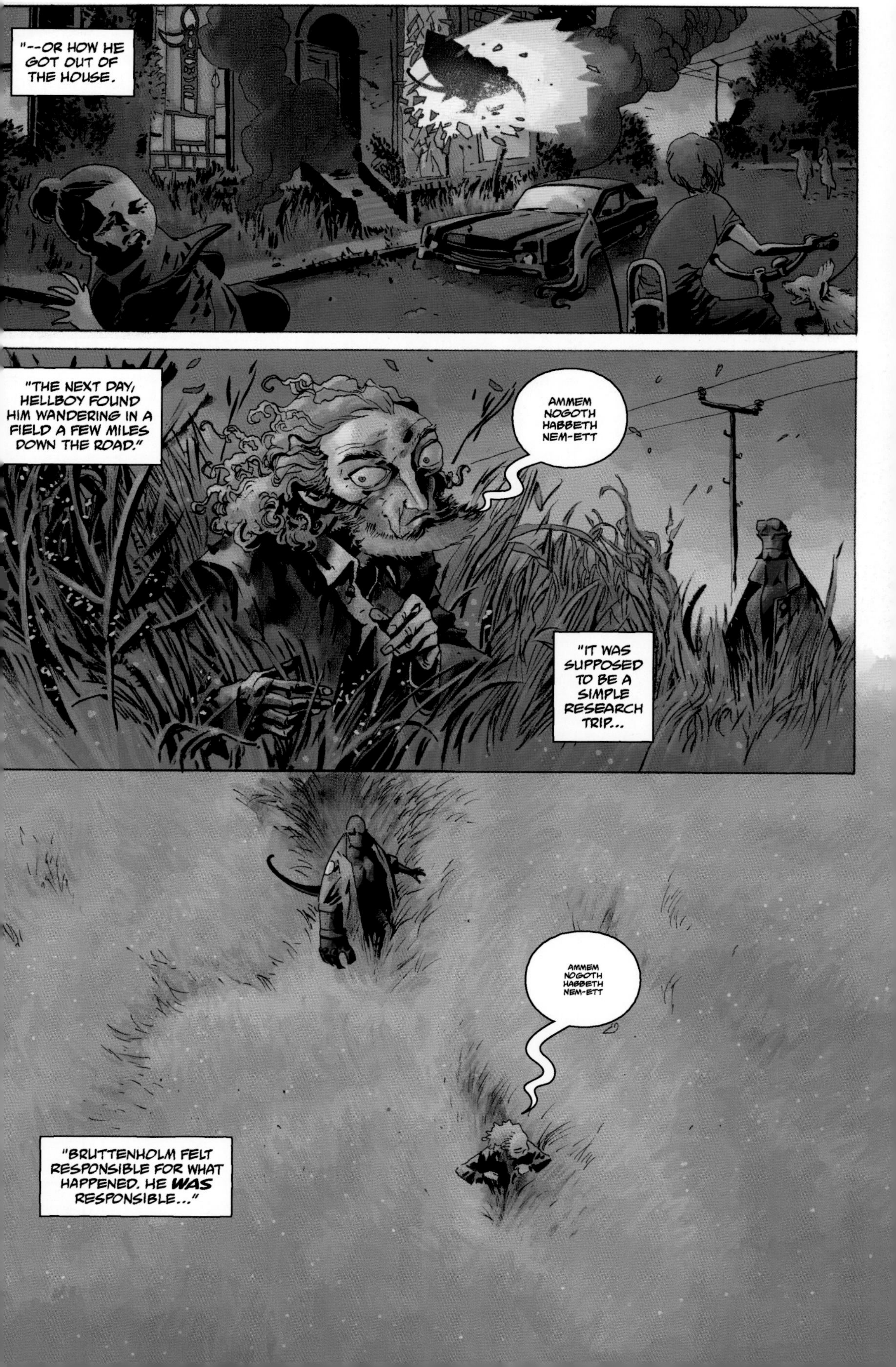
"--OR HOW HE GOT OUT OF THE HOUSE.
"THE NEXT DAY, HELLBOY FOUND HIM WANDERING IN A FIELD A FEW MILES DOWN THE ROAD."
AMMEM NOGOTH HABBETH NEM-ETT
"IT WAS SUPPOSED TO BE A SIMPLE RESEARCH TRIP...
AMMEM NOGOTH HABBETH NEM-ETT
"BRUTTENHOLM FELT RESPONSIBLE FOR WHAT HAPPENED. HE WAS RESPONSIBLE..."

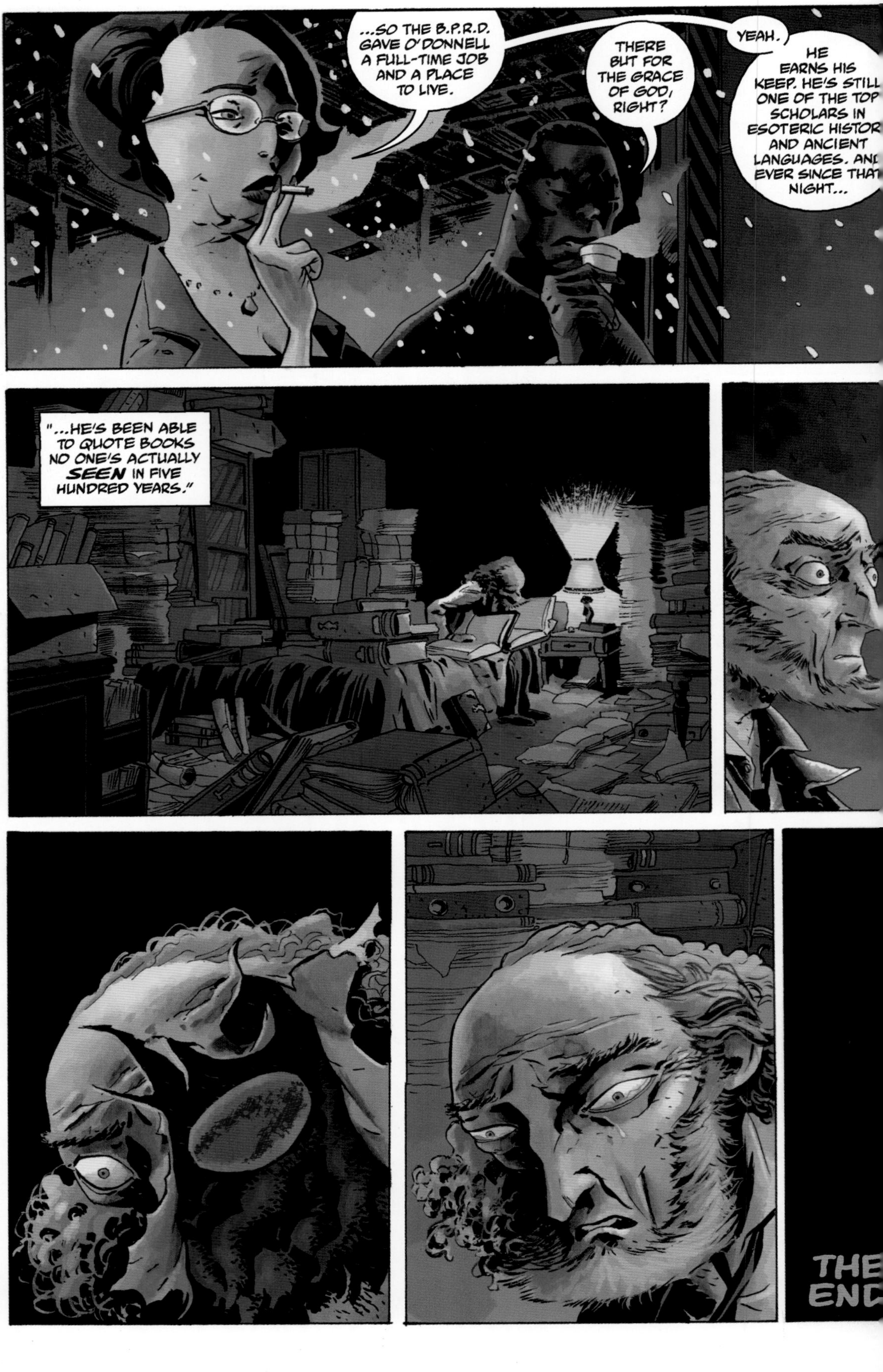
...SO THE B.P.R.D. GAVE O'DONNELL A FULL-TIME JOB AND A PLACE TO LIVE.
THERE BUT FOR THE GRACE OF GOD, RIGHT?
YEAH.
HE EARNS HIS KEEP. HE'S STILL ONE OF THE TOP SCHOLARS IN ESOTERIC HISTOR AND ANCIENT LANGUAGES. AND EVER SINCE THAT NIGHT...
"...HE'S BEEN ABLE TO QUOTE BOOKS NO ONE'S ACTUALLY SEEN IN FIVE HUNDRED YEARS."
THE END

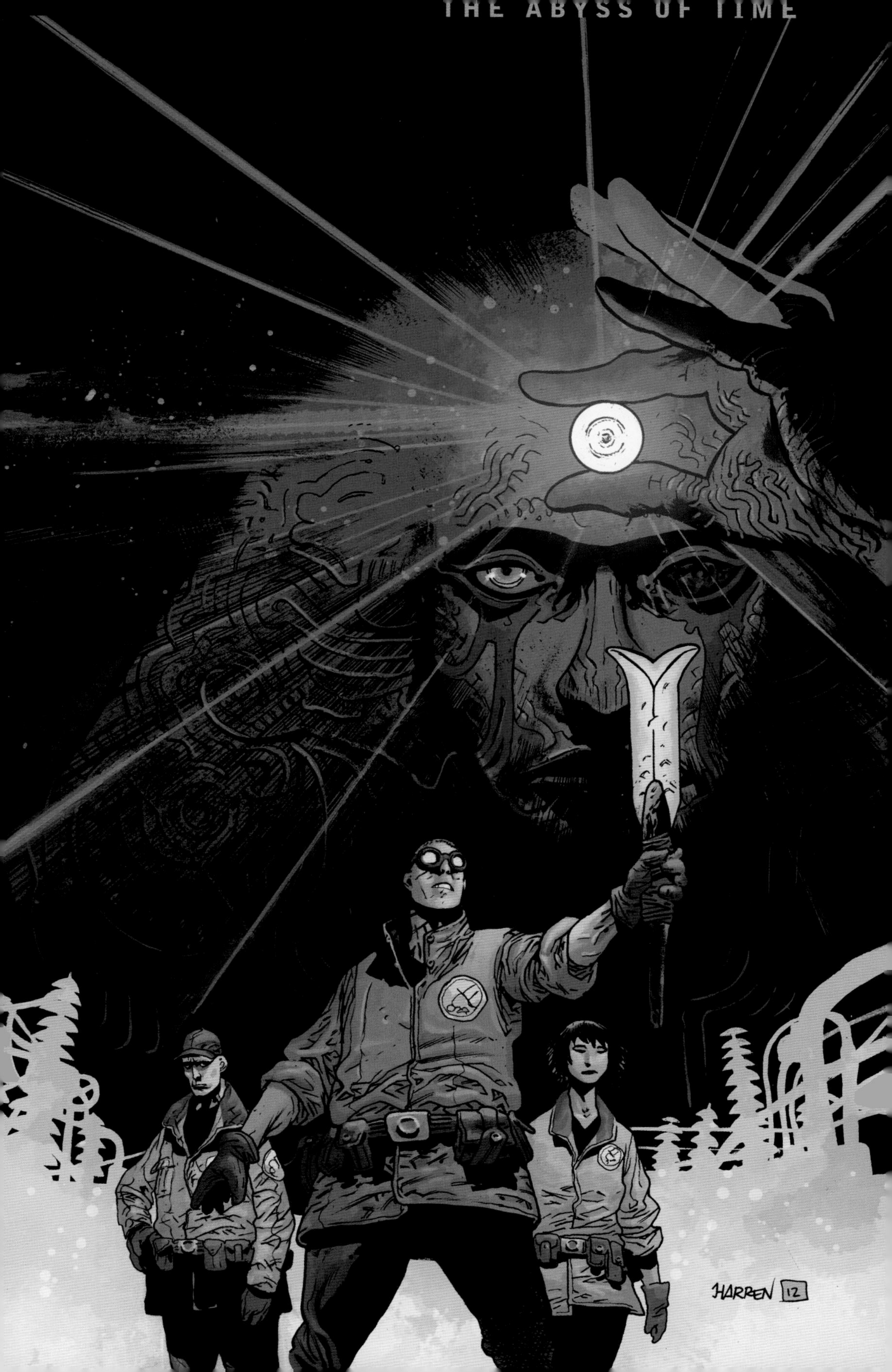
THE ABYSS OF TIME
HARREN 12

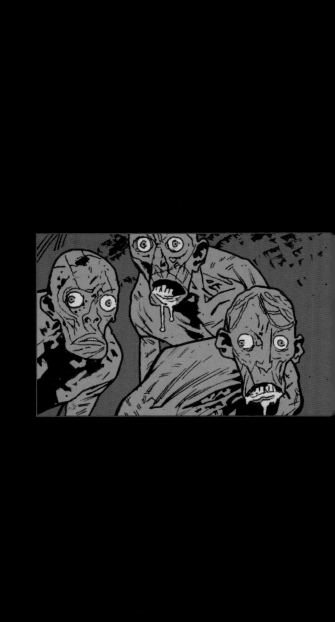

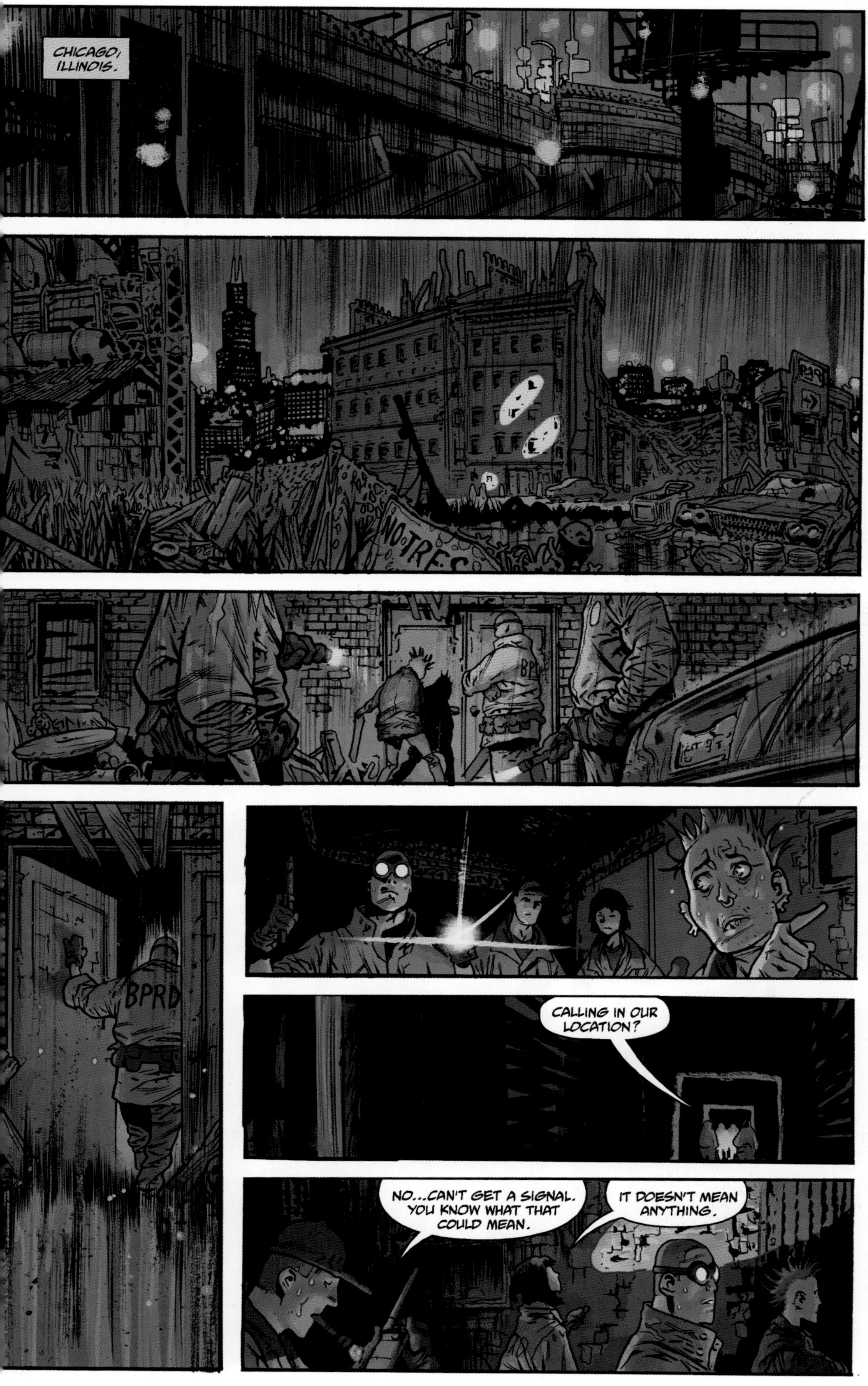
CHICAGO, ILLINOIS.
NO TRES
CALLING IN OUR LOCATION?
NO...CAN'T GET A SIGNAL. YOU KNOW WHAT THAT COULD MEAN.
IT DOESN'T MEAN ANYTHING.

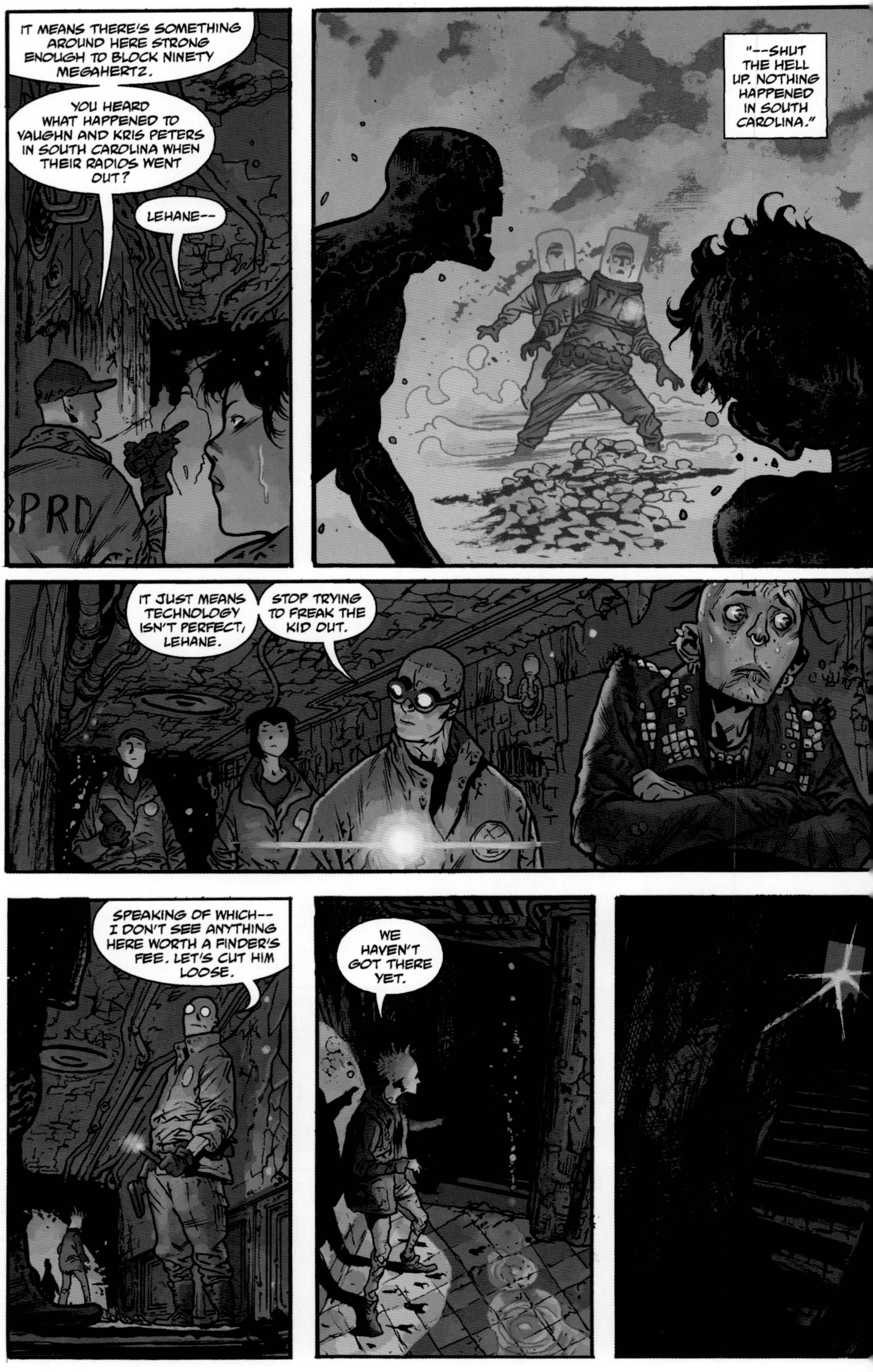
IT MEANS THERE'S SOMETHING AROUND HERE STRONG ENOUGH TO BLOCK NINETY MEGAHERTZ.
YOU HEARD WHAT HAPPENED TO VAUGHN AND KRIS PETERS IN SOUTH CAROLINA WHEN THEIR RADIOS WENT OUT?
LEHANE--
SPRD
"--SHUT THE HELL UP. NOTHING HAPPENED IN SOUTH CAROLINA."
IT JUST MEANS TECHNOLOGY ISN'T PERFECT, LEHANE.
STOP TRYING TO FREAK THE KID OUT.
SPEAKING OF WHICH-- I DON'T SEE ANYTHING HERE WORTH A FINDER'S FEE. LET'S CUT HIM LOOSE.
WE HAVEN'T GOT THERE YET.

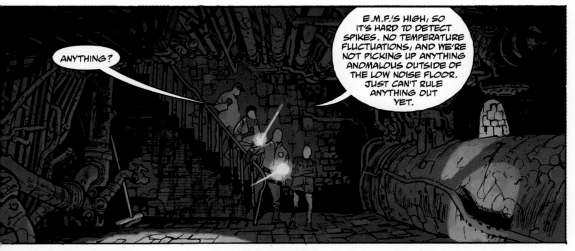

E.M.F.'S HIGH, SO IT'S HARD TO DETECT SPIKES. NO TEMPERATURE FLUCTUATIONS, AND WE'RE NOT PICKING UP ANYTHING ANOMALOUS OUTSIDE OF THE LOW NOISE FLOOR. JUST CAN'T RULE ANYTHING OUT YET.

ANYTHING?

ALL RIGHT. THAT'S IT. AND I AM *NOT* GOING IN THERE.

WHY NOT, SCOTTIE?

I WENT IN ONE TIME. ON A DARE. I FELT SOMETHING WEIRD--

A DARE. STREET KIDS FREAKING EACH OTHER OUT.

TTCH. I FELT A CHILL. OR SOMETHING.

DOESN'T MATTER.

EVERYONE KNOWS THERE'S SOMETHING BAD DOWN HERE. THAT'S WHY NO ONE CRASHES IN THIS PLACE.

OTHERWISE IT'D BE SUCH PRIME REAL ESTATE...

YOU'LL SEE.

THANK YOU, SCOTTIE.

CREEEEEEE

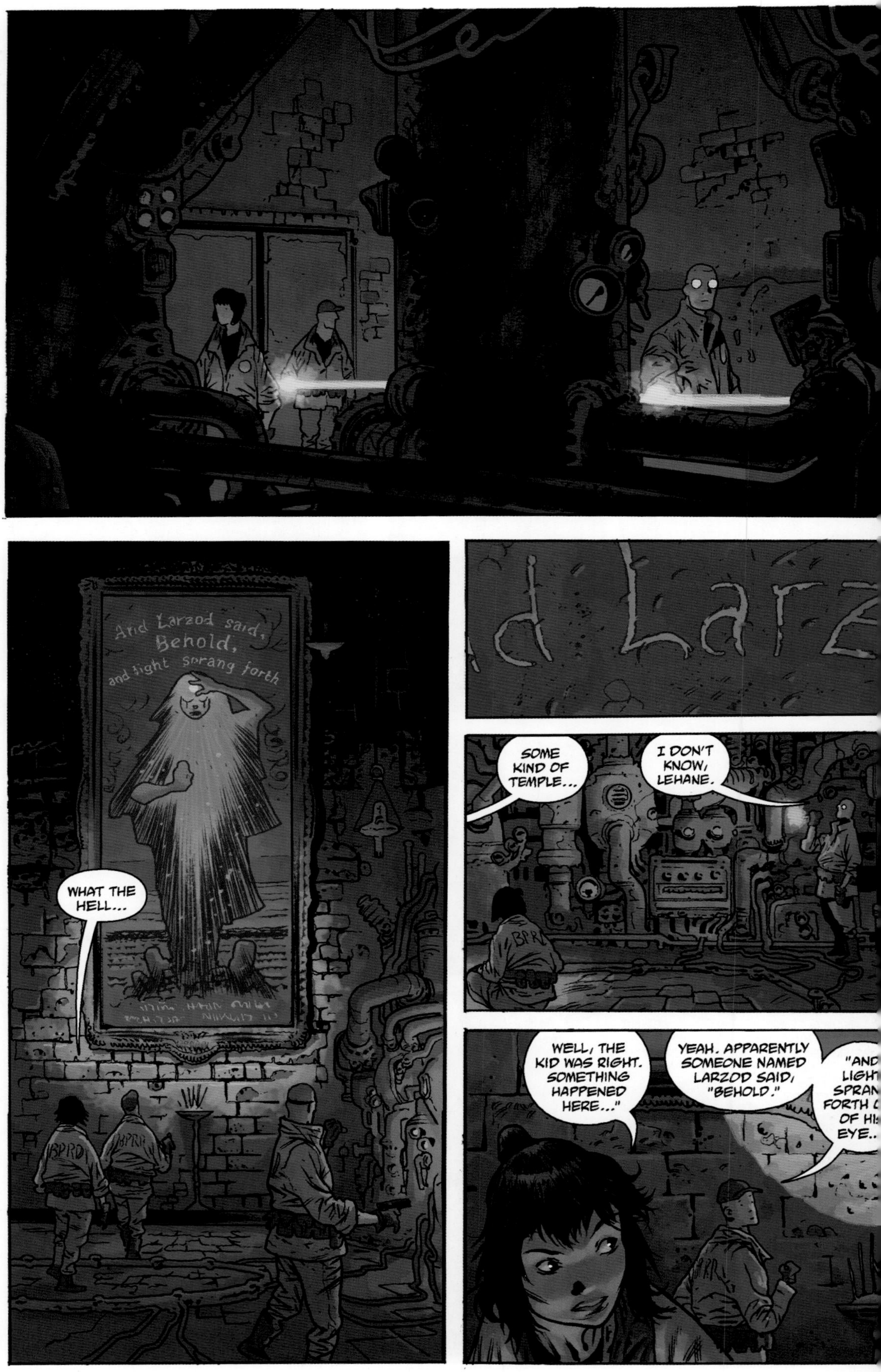
And Larzod said, Behold, and light sprang forth
WHAT THE HELL...
d Larz
SOME KIND OF TEMPLE...
I DON'T KNOW, LEHANE.
WELL, THE KID WAS RIGHT. SOMETHING HAPPENED HERE..."
YEAH. APPARENTLY SOMEONE NAMED LARZOD SAID, "BEHOLD."
"AND LIGH SPRAN FORTH OF HI EYE..

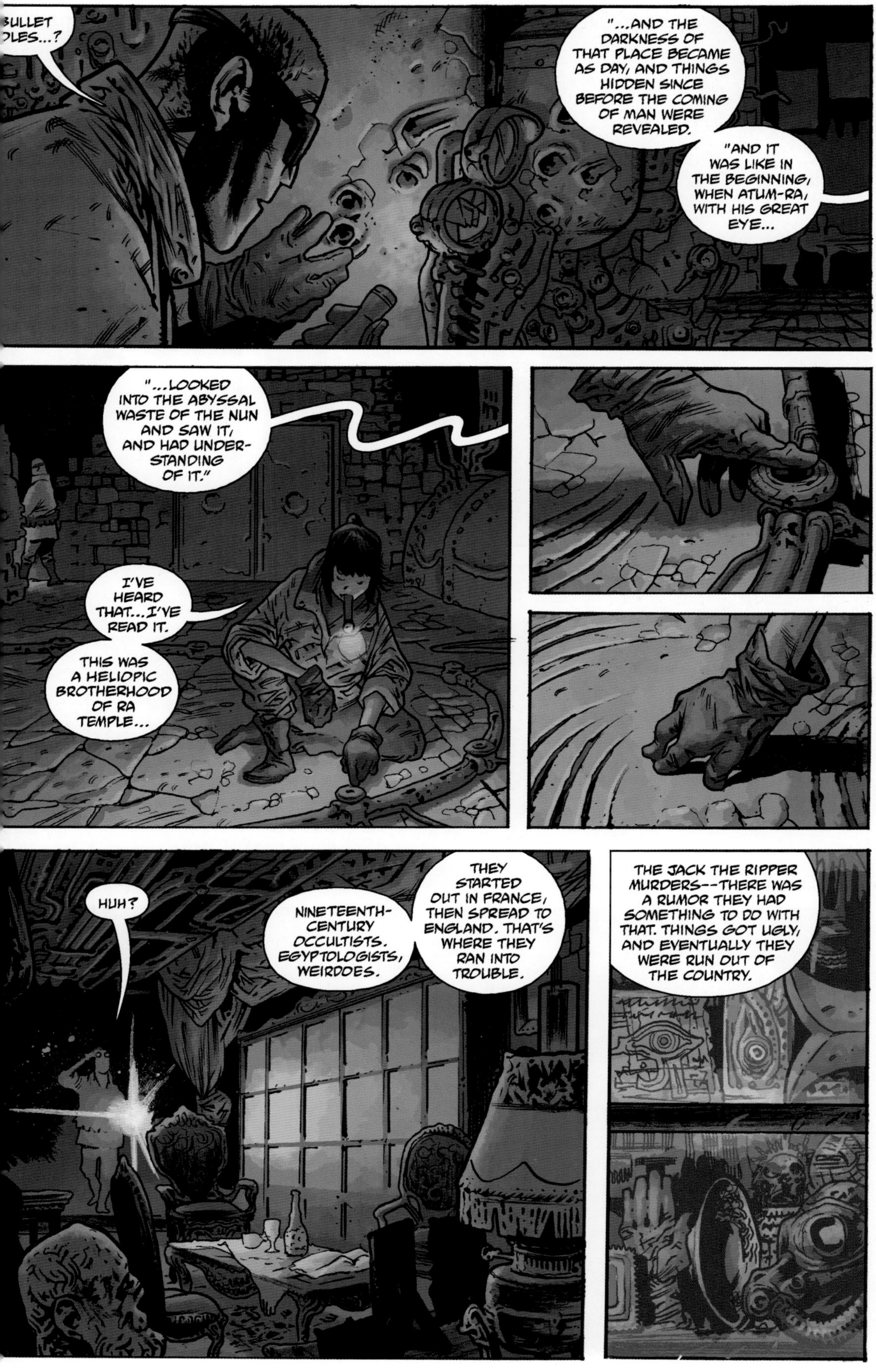
BULLET
OLES...?
"...AND THE DARKNESS OF THAT PLACE BECAME AS DAY, AND THINGS HIDDEN SINCE BEFORE THE COMING OF MAN WERE REVEALED.
"AND IT WAS LIKE IN THE BEGINNING, WHEN ATUM-RA, WITH HIS GREAT EYE...
"...LOOKED INTO THE ABYSSAL WASTE OF THE NUN AND SAW IT, AND HAD UNDER-STANDING OF IT."
I'VE HEARD THAT... I'VE READ IT.
THIS WAS A HELIOPIC BROTHERHOOD OF RA TEMPLE...
HUH?
NINETEENTH-CENTURY OCCULTISTS. EGYPTOLOGISTS, WEIRDOES.
THEY STARTED OUT IN FRANCE, THEN SPREAD TO ENGLAND. THAT'S WHERE THEY RAN INTO TROUBLE.
THE JACK THE RIPPER MURDERS--THERE WAS A RUMOR THEY HAD SOMETHING TO DO WITH THAT. THINGS GOT UGLY, AND EVENTUALLY THEY WERE RUN OUT OF THE COUNTRY.

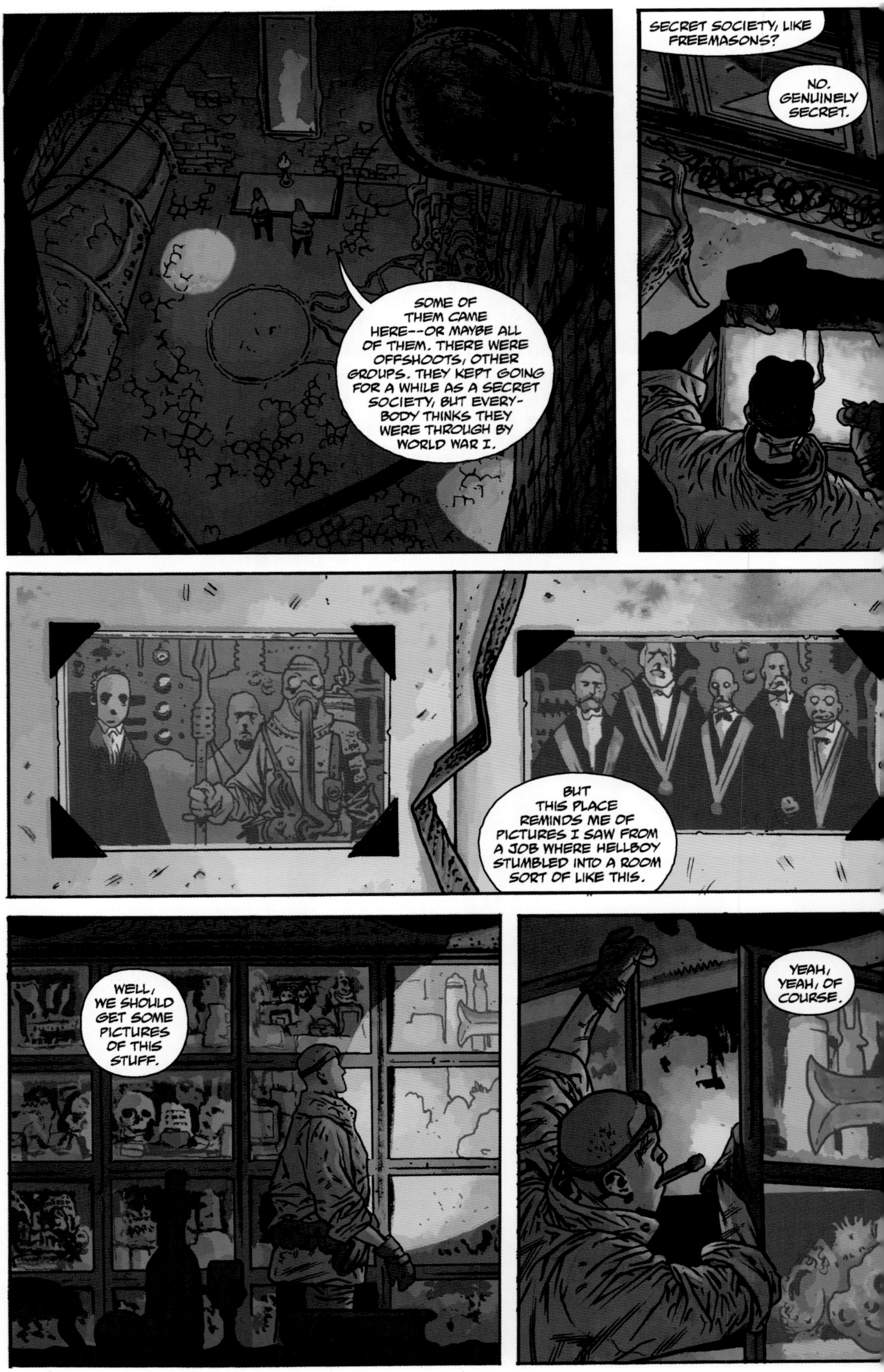
SOME OF THEM CAME HERE--OR MAYBE ALL OF THEM. THERE WERE OFFSHOOTS, OTHER GROUPS. THEY KEPT GOING FOR A WHILE AS A SECRET SOCIETY, BUT EVERY-BODY THINKS THEY WERE THROUGH BY WORLD WAR I.
SECRET SOCIETY, LIKE FREEMASONS?
NO. GENUINELY SECRET.
BUT THIS PLACE REMINDS ME OF PICTURES I SAW FROM A JOB WHERE HELLBOY STUMBLED INTO A ROOM SORT OF LIKE THIS.
WELL, WE SHOULD GET SOME PICTURES OF THIS STUFF.
YEAH, YEAH, OF COURSE.

I'D LOVE TO BOX SOME OF THIS UP, ACTUALLY...

...BUT WITH EVERY-THING ELSE GOING ON RIGHT NOW, THIS ROOM IS PRETTY SMALL POTATOES.

THEY WON'T GET AROUND TO SENDING A CREW OUT TO--

THUMP

?

HOWARDS?

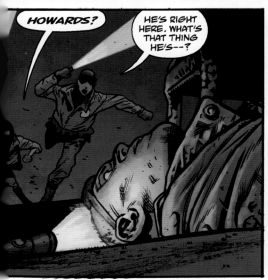

HOWARDS?

HE'S RIGHT HERE. WHAT'S THAT THING HE'S--?

HOWARDS? CAN YOU HEAR ME?

IS HE DEAD?

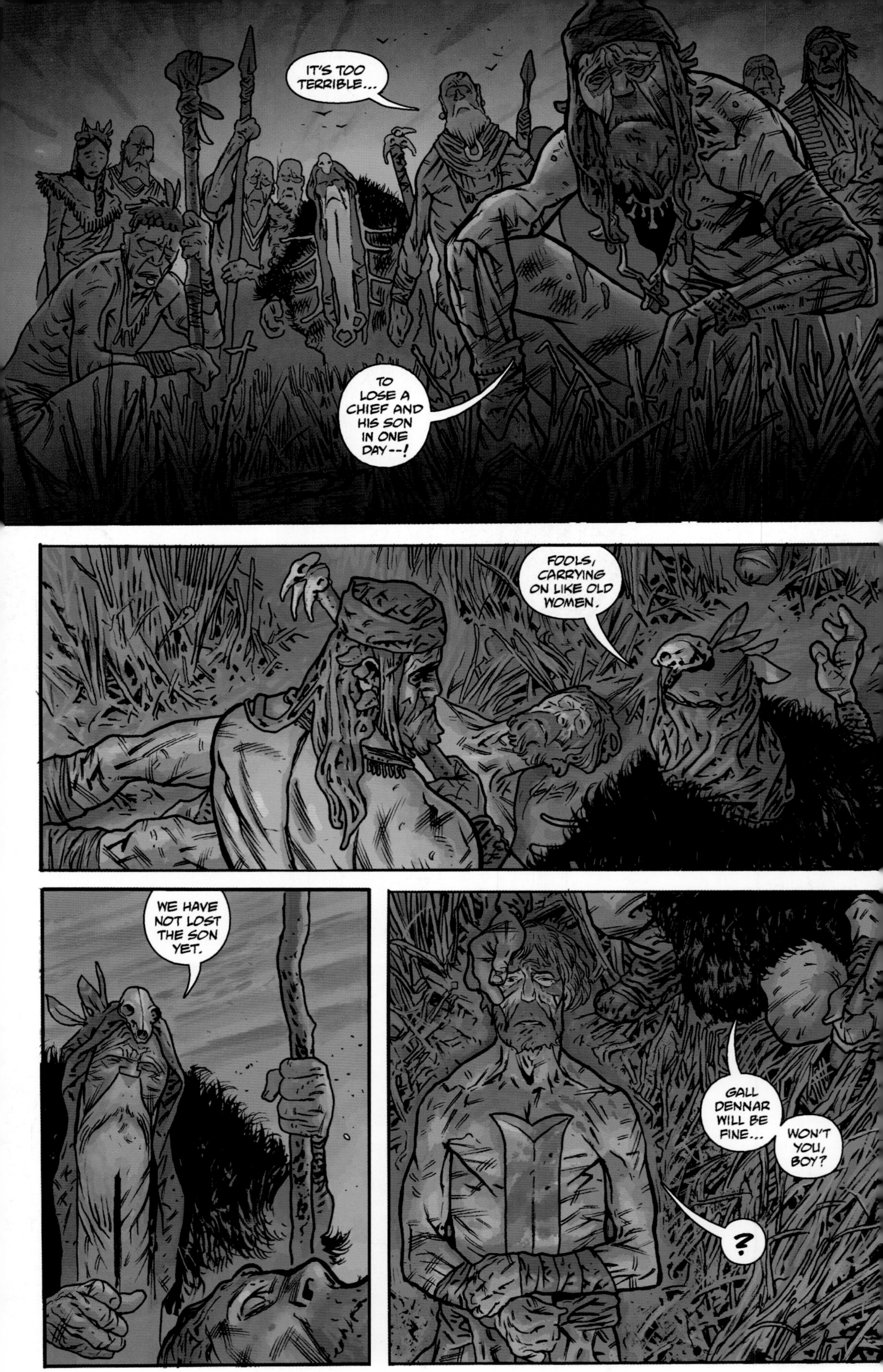
IT'S TOO TERRIBLE...
TO LOSE A CHIEF AND HIS SON IN ONE DAY--!
FOOLS, CARRYING ON LIKE OLD WOMEN.
WE HAVE NOT LOST THE SON YET.
GALL DENNAR WILL BE FINE...
WON'T YOU, BOY?
?

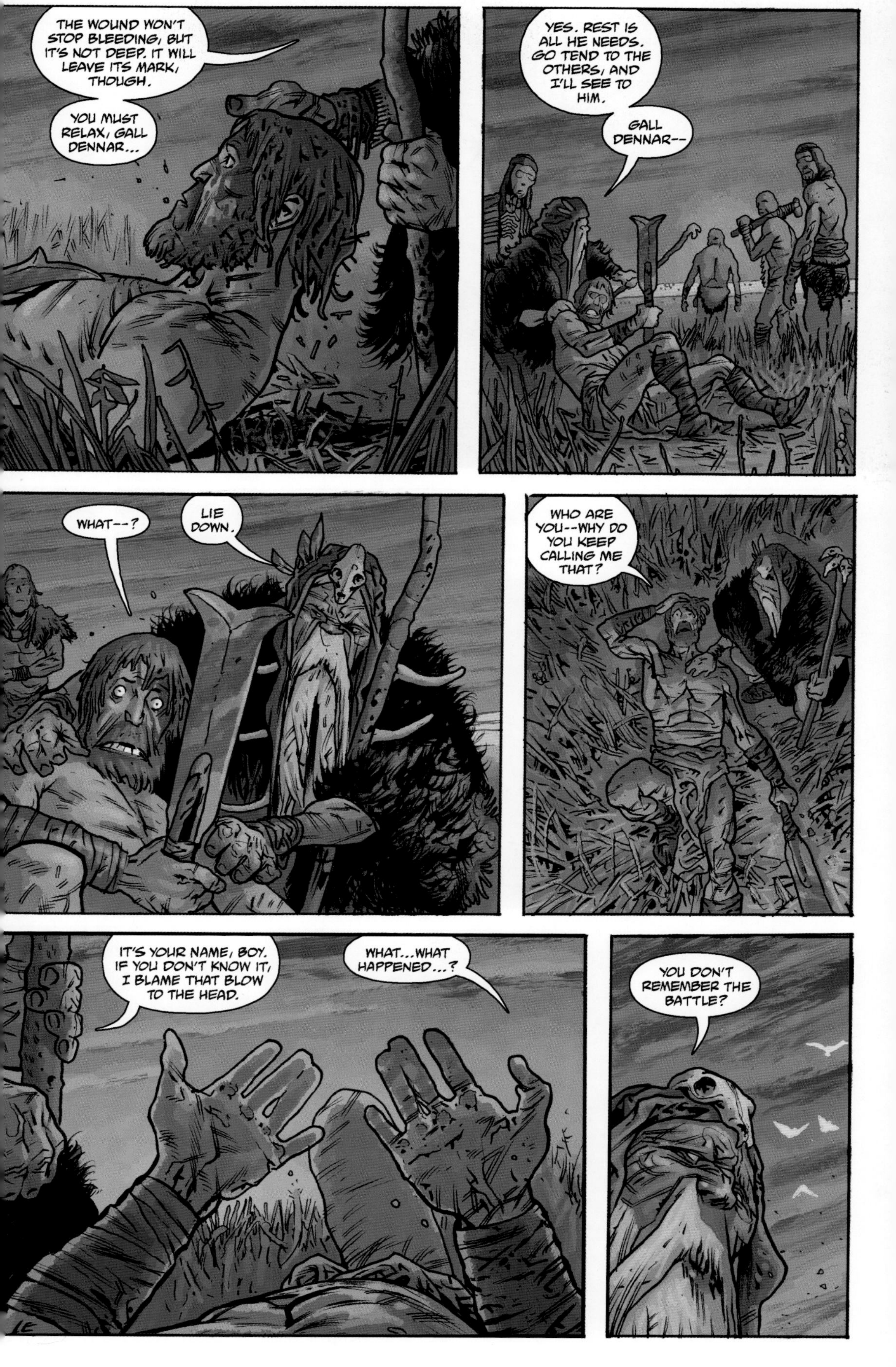
THE WOUND WON'T STOP BLEEDING, BUT IT'S NOT DEEP. IT WILL LEAVE ITS MARK, THOUGH.
YOU MUST RELAX, GALL DENNAR...
YES. REST IS ALL HE NEEDS. GO TEND TO THE OTHERS, AND I'LL SEE TO HIM.
GALL DENNAR--
WHAT--?
LIE DOWN.
WHO ARE YOU--WHY DO YOU KEEP CALLING ME THAT?
IT'S YOUR NAME, BOY. IF YOU DON'T KNOW IT, I BLAME THAT BLOW TO THE HEAD.
WHAT...WHAT HAPPENED...?
YOU DON'T REMEMBER THE BATTLE?

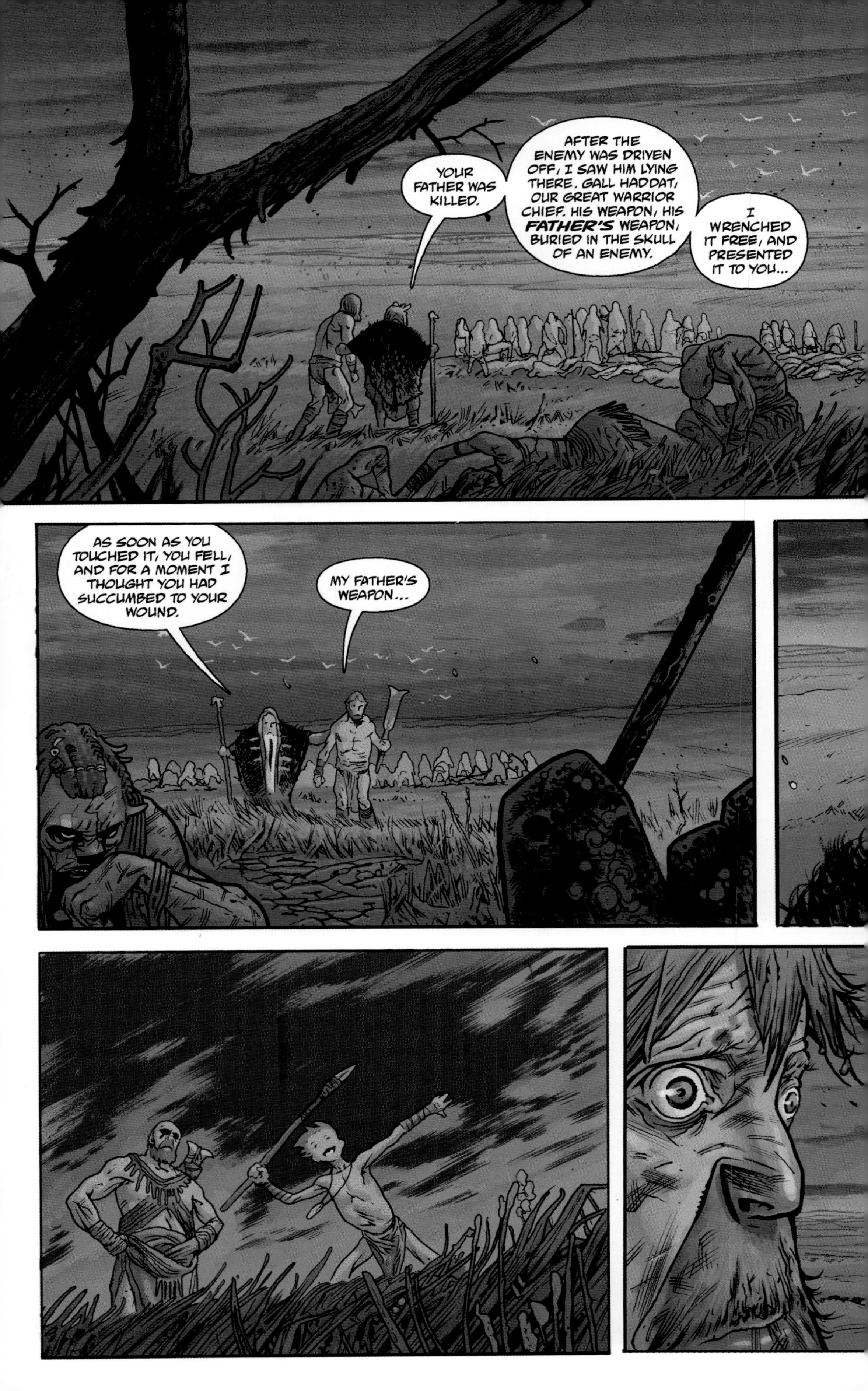
YOUR FATHER WAS KILLED.
AFTER THE ENEMY WAS DRIVEN OFF, I SAW HIM LYING THERE. GALL HADDAT, OUR GREAT WARRIOR CHIEF. HIS WEAPON, HIS **FATHER'S** WEAPON, BURIED IN THE SKULL OF AN ENEMY.
I WRENCHED IT FREE, AND PRESENTED IT TO YOU...
AS SOON AS YOU TOUCHED IT, YOU FELL, AND FOR A MOMENT I THOUGHT YOU HAD SUCCUMBED TO YOUR WOUND.
MY FATHER'S WEAPON...

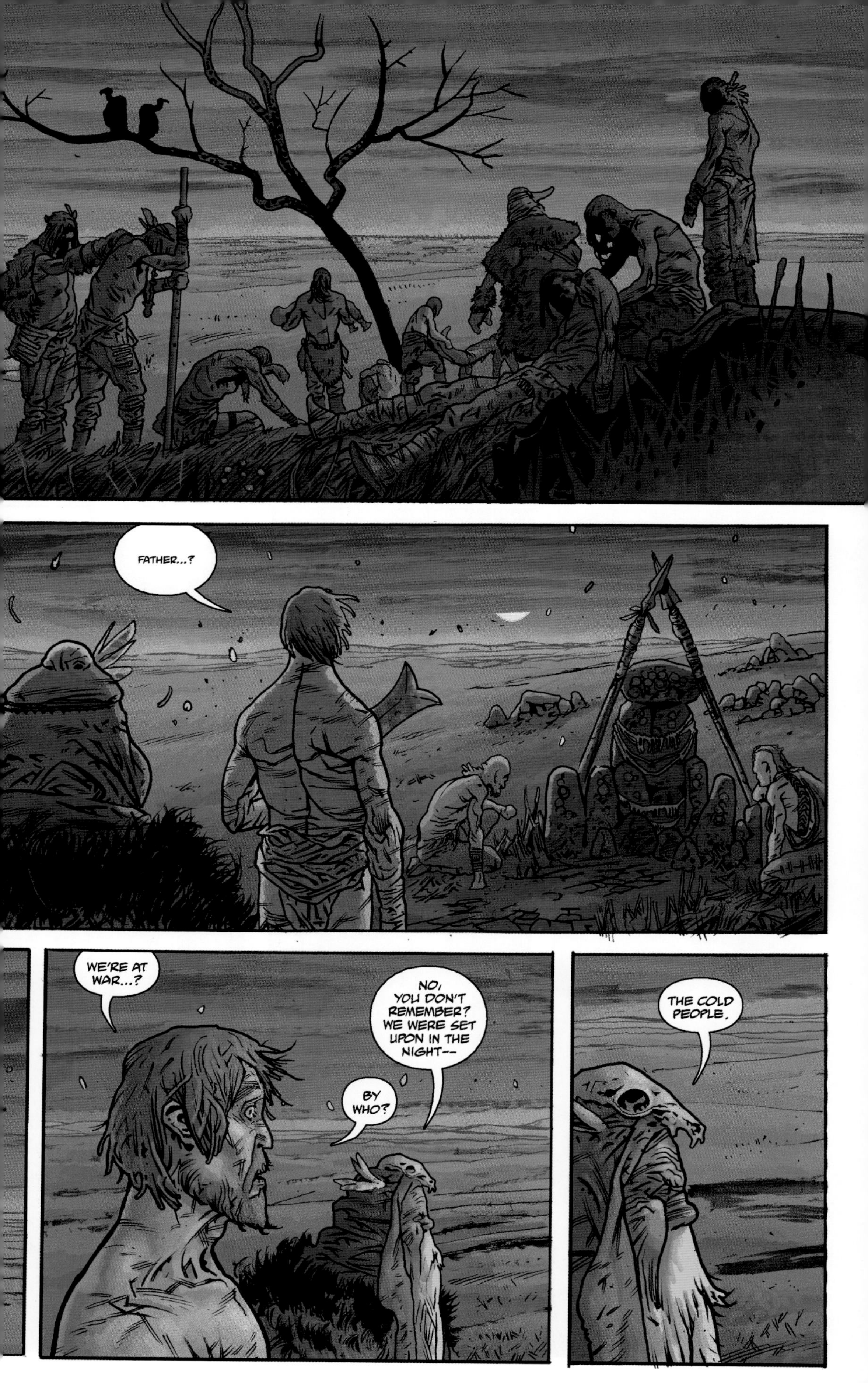
FATHER...?
WE'RE AT WAR...?
NO, YOU DON'T REMEMBER? WE WERE SET UPON IN THE NIGHT--
BY WHO?
THE COLD PEOPLE.

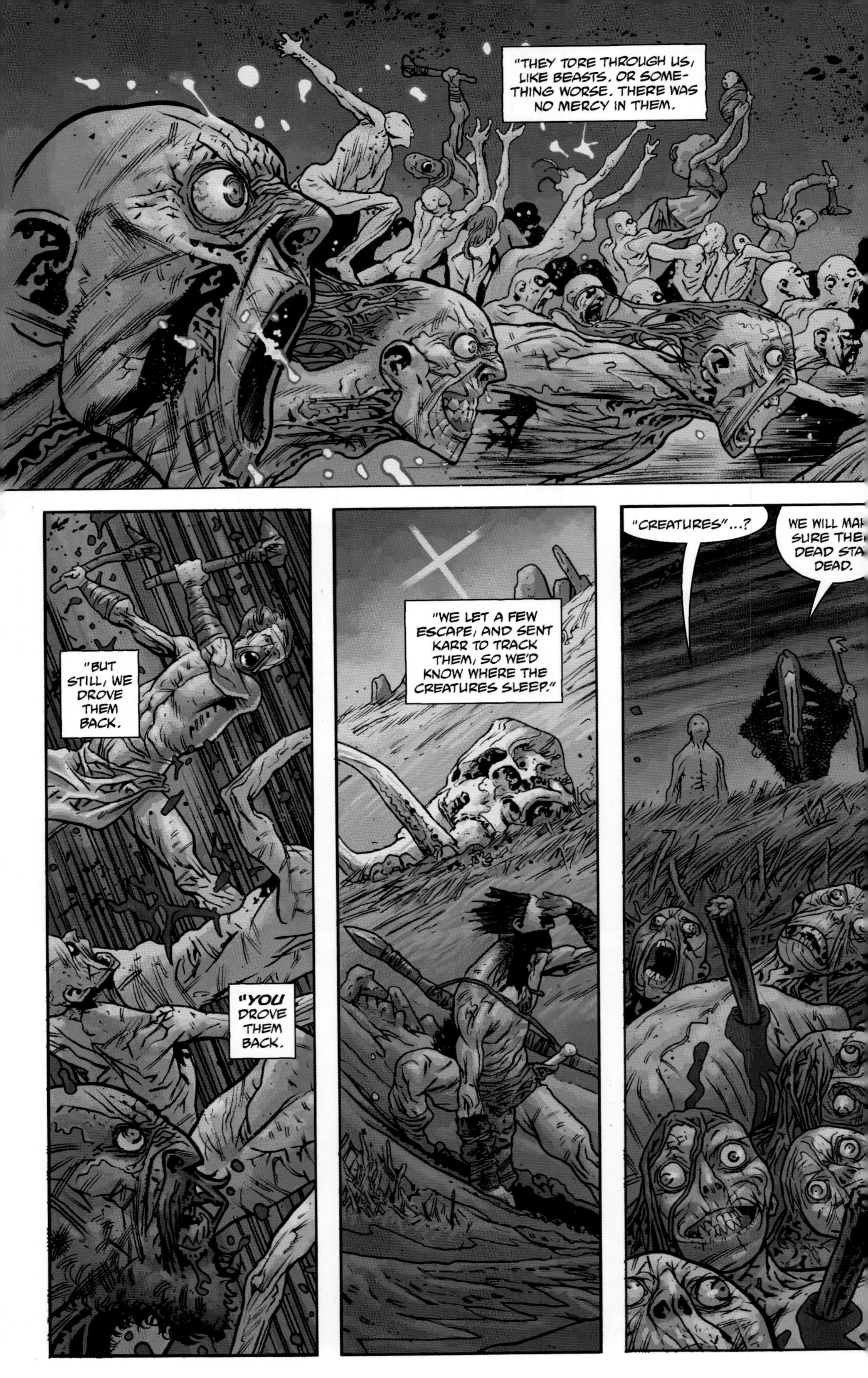
"THEY TORE THROUGH US, LIKE BEASTS. OR SOMETHING WORSE. THERE WAS NO MERCY IN THEM.
"BUT STILL, WE DROVE THEM BACK.
"YOU DROVE THEM BACK.
"WE LET A FEW ESCAPE, AND SENT KARR TO TRACK THEM, SO WE'D KNOW WHERE THE CREATURES SLEEP."
"CREATURES"...?
WE WILL MA SURE THE DEAD STA DEAD.

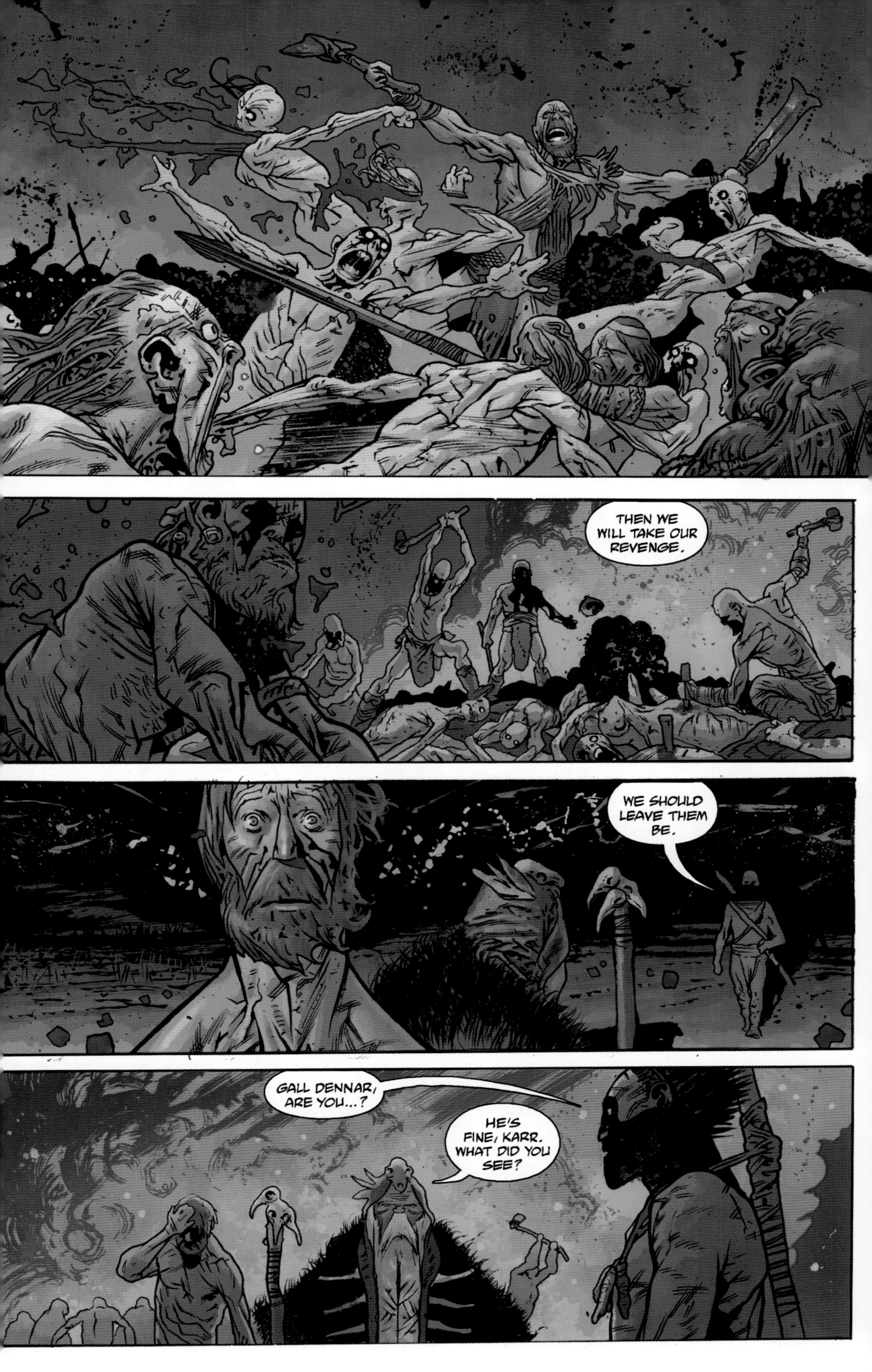
THEN WE WILL TAKE OUR REVENGE.
WE SHOULD LEAVE THEM BE.
GALL DENNAR, ARE YOU...?
HE'S FINE, KARR. WHAT DID YOU SEE?

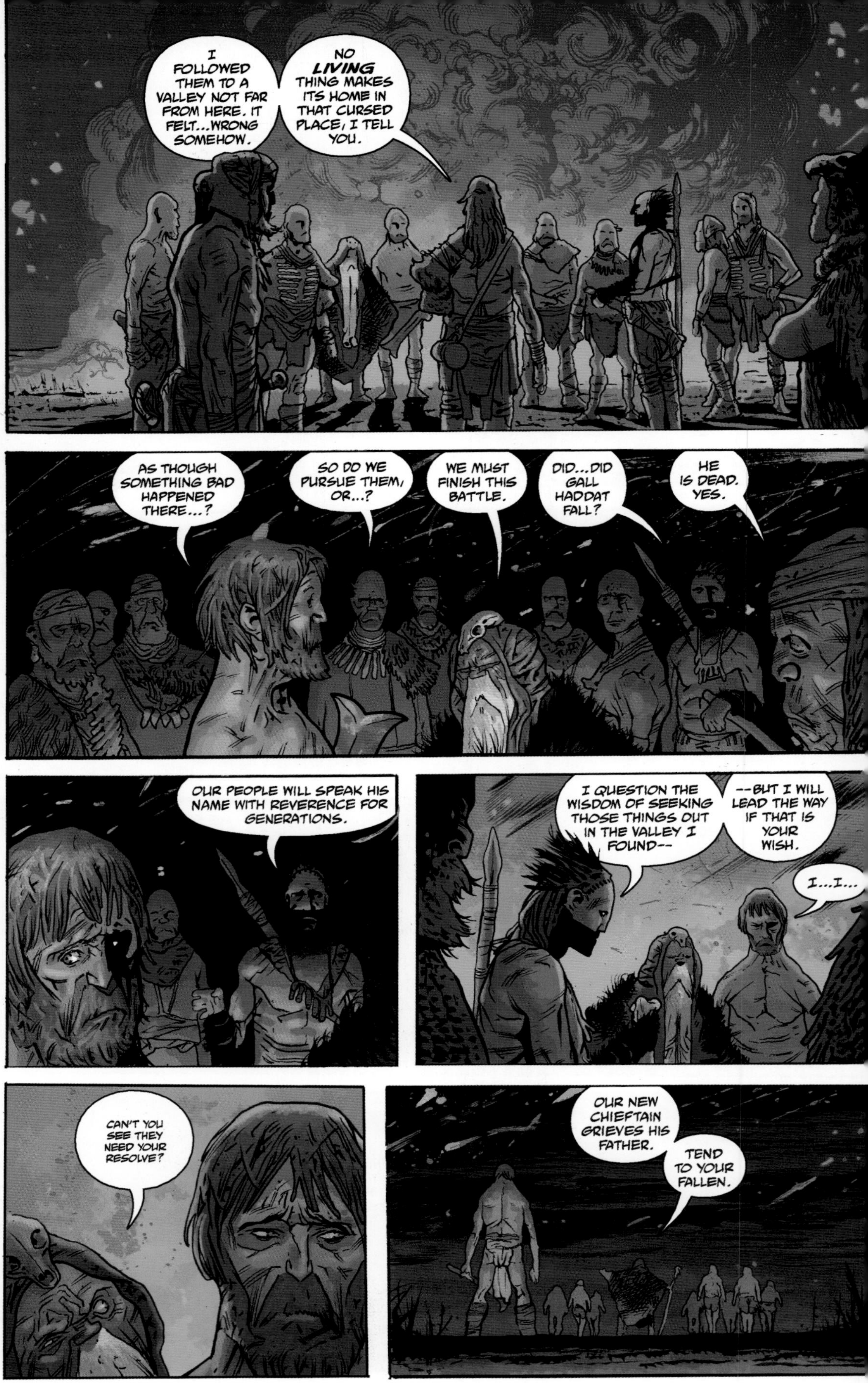
I FOLLOWED THEM TO A VALLEY NOT FAR FROM HERE. IT FELT...WRONG SOMEHOW.
NO LIVING THING MAKES ITS HOME IN THAT CURSED PLACE, I TELL YOU.
AS THOUGH SOMETHING BAD HAPPENED THERE...?
SO DO WE PURSUE THEM, OR...?
WE MUST FINISH THIS BATTLE.
DID...DID GALL HADDAT FALL?
HE IS DEAD. YES.
OUR PEOPLE WILL SPEAK HIS NAME WITH REVERENCE FOR GENERATIONS.
I QUESTION THE WISDOM OF SEEKING THOSE THINGS OUT IN THE VALLEY I FOUND--
--BUT I WILL LEAD THE WAY IF THAT IS YOUR WISH.
I...I...
CAN'T YOU SEE THEY NEED YOUR RESOLVE?
OUR NEW CHIEFTAIN GRIEVES HIS FATHER.
TEND TO YOUR FALLEN.

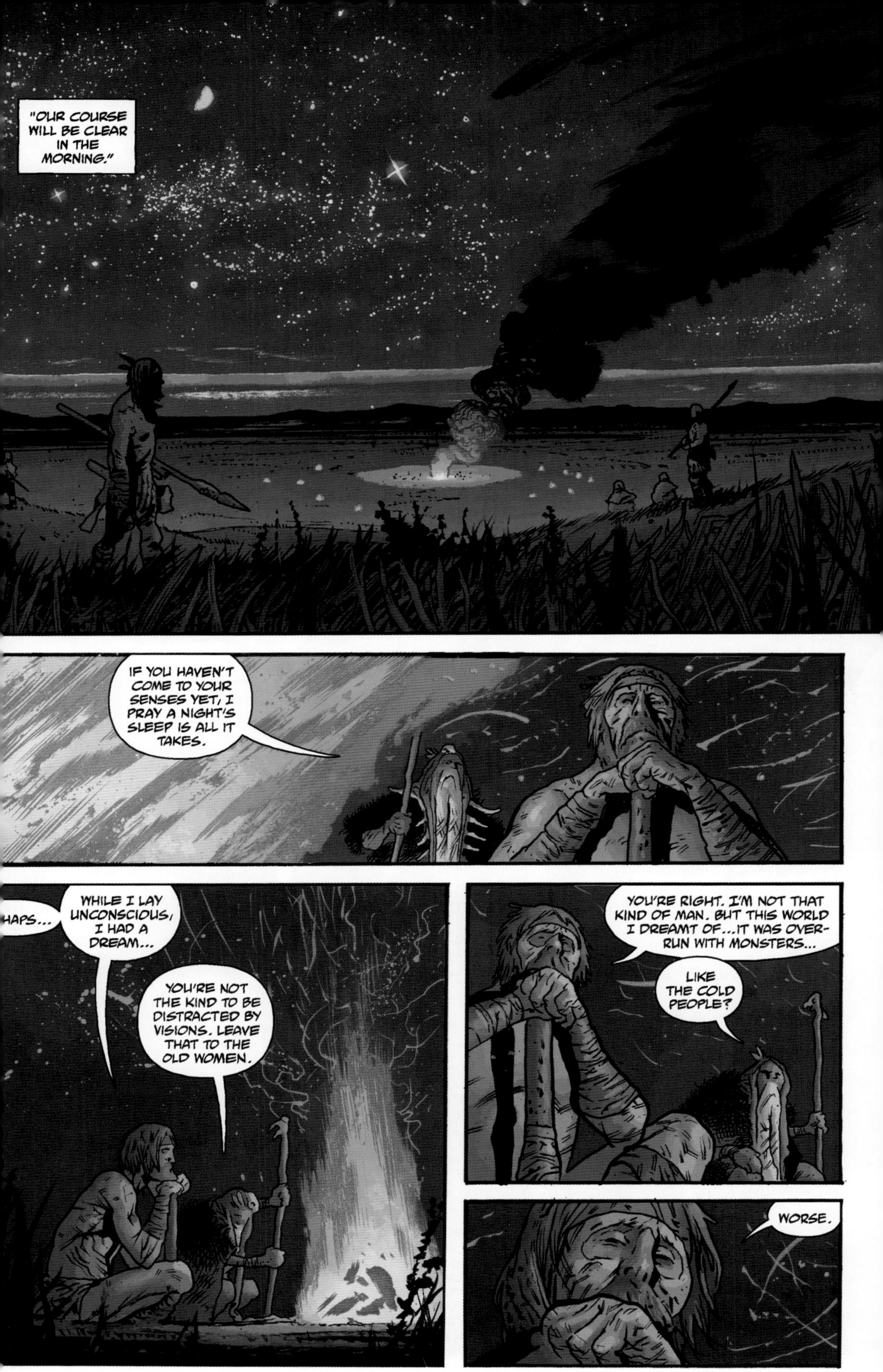

"OUR COURSE WILL BE CLEAR IN THE MORNING."
IF YOU HAVEN'T COME TO YOUR SENSES YET, I PRAY A NIGHT'S SLEEP IS ALL IT TAKES.
HAPS...
WHILE I LAY UNCONSCIOUS, I HAD A DREAM...
YOU'RE NOT THE KIND TO BE DISTRACTED BY VISIONS. LEAVE THAT TO THE OLD WOMEN.
YOU'RE RIGHT. I'M NOT THAT KIND OF MAN. BUT THIS WORLD I DREAMT OF...IT WAS OVER-RUN WITH MONSTERS...
LIKE THE COLD PEOPLE?
WORSE.

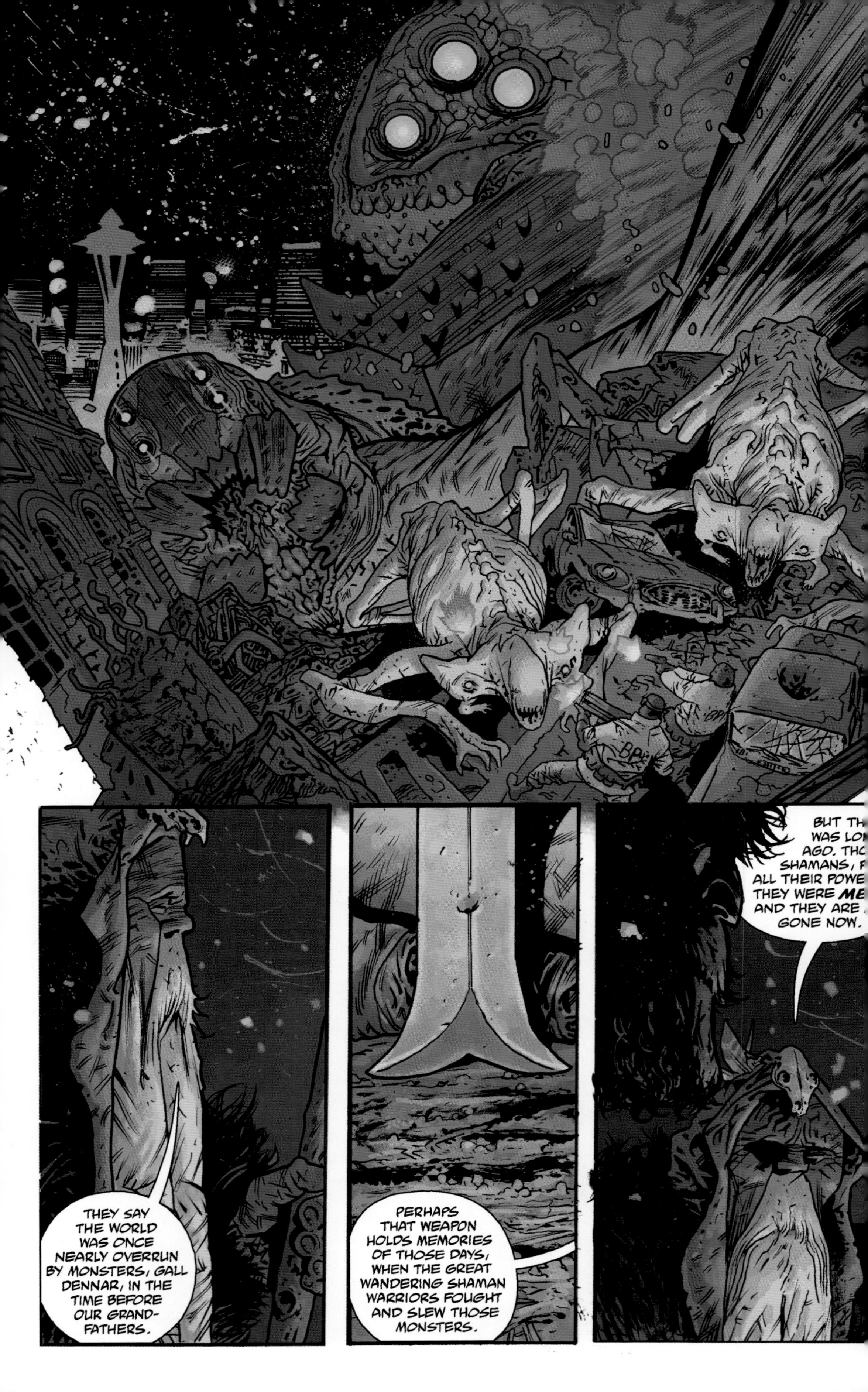
THEY SAY THE WORLD WAS ONCE NEARLY OVERRUN BY MONSTERS, GALL DENNAR, IN THE TIME BEFORE OUR GRAND-FATHERS.
PERHAPS THAT WEAPON HOLDS MEMORIES OF THOSE DAYS, WHEN THE GREAT WANDERING SHAMAN WARRIORS FOUGHT AND SLEW THOSE MONSTERS.
BUT TH WAS LON AGO. THO SHAMANS, F ALL THEIR POWE THEY WERE ME AND THEY ARE GONE NOW.

...AND NOW THE COLD PEOPLE HAVE COME...

PERHAPS THEY'RE THE CHILDREN OF THE SLAIN MONSTERS...MAYBE THEY'LL CALL THEIR MONSTER PARENTS BACK FROM THEIR GRAVES...

WHAT *IS* IS? WHERE DID IT COME FROM?

YOU KNOW AS MUCH AS I DO...

I KNOW IT'S IMPORTANT...

I KNOW IT WAS MY GRAND-FATHER'S...

YOU DON'T REMEMBER THE STORY.

YOUR GRAND-FATHER HAD WANDERED FAR TO THE NORTH...

"...AND AS THE SUN SANK LOW, HE CAME UPON THE RUINS OF A STONE VILLAGE, ONCE HOME TO SOME ANCIENT PEOPLE..."

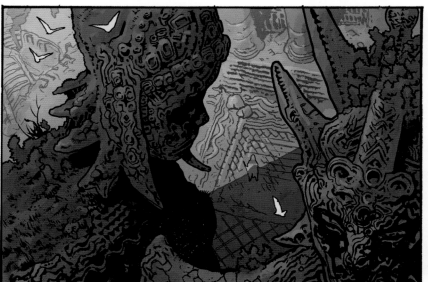

"DEATH HAD CLAIMED THE PLACE LONG AGO.

"YOUR GRANDFATHER COULD NOT KNOW *HOW* DEATH HAD COME, BUT HE STUMBLED UPON THE SCENE OF A STRANGE BATTLE.

"A SINGLE, GREAT WARRIOR HAD KILLED TWENTY OR MORE INHUMAN THINGS...

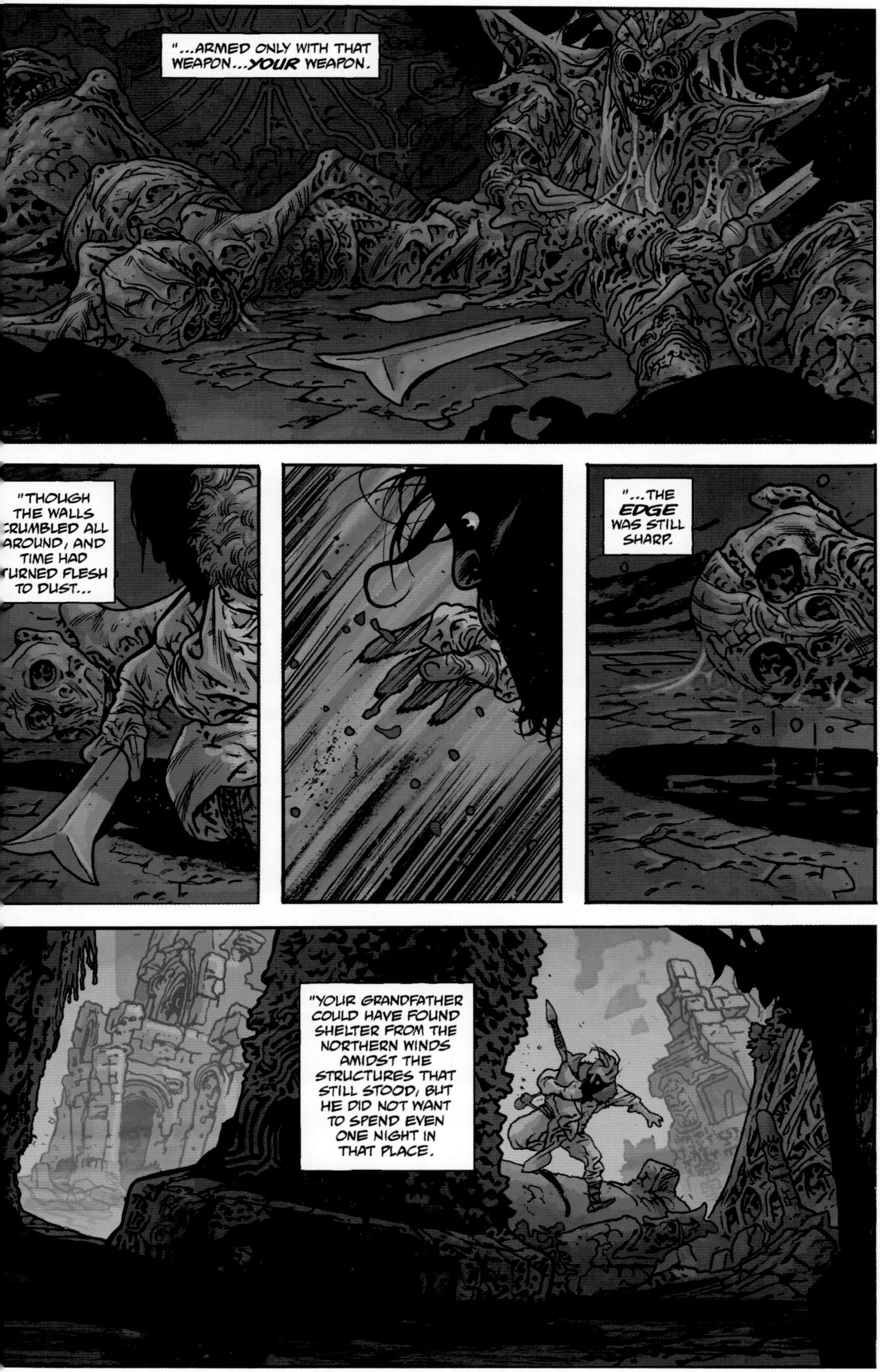
"...ARMED ONLY WITH THAT WEAPON...YOUR WEAPON.
"THOUGH THE WALLS CRUMBLED ALL AROUND, AND TIME HAD TURNED FLESH TO DUST...
"...THE EDGE WAS STILL SHARP.
"YOUR GRANDFATHER COULD HAVE FOUND SHELTER FROM THE NORTHERN WINDS AMIDST THE STRUCTURES THAT STILL STOOD, BUT HE DID NOT WANT TO SPEND EVEN ONE NIGHT IN THAT PLACE.

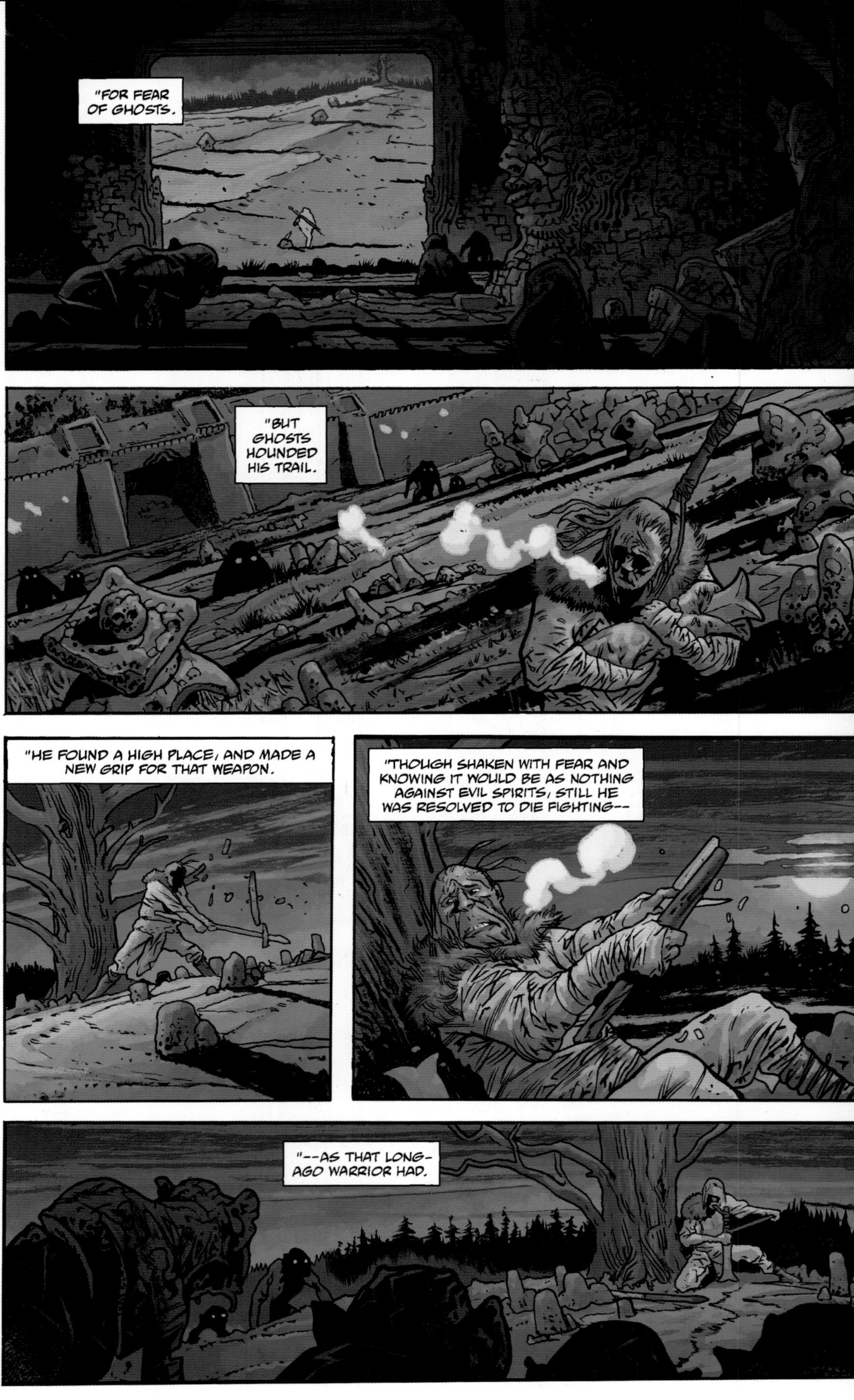
"FOR FEAR OF GHOSTS.
"BUT GHOSTS HOUNDED HIS TRAIL.
"HE FOUND A HIGH PLACE, AND MADE A NEW GRIP FOR THAT WEAPON.
"THOUGH SHAKEN WITH FEAR AND KNOWING IT WOULD BE AS NOTHING AGAINST EVIL SPIRITS, STILL HE WAS RESOLVED TO DIE FIGHTING--
"--AS THAT LONG-AGO WARRIOR HAD.

"THEN, AS DEATH CLOSED AROUND HIM, THE WARRIOR'S SPIRIT CAME TO HIM AND ENTERED INTO HIS ARM, AND THAT WEAPON.

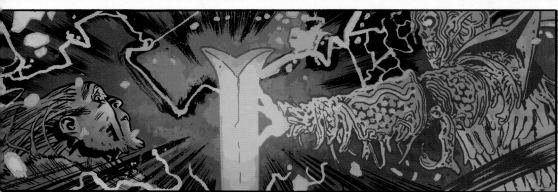

AND YOUR GRAND-FATHER WAS *NOT* AFRAID TO STAND HIS GROUND.

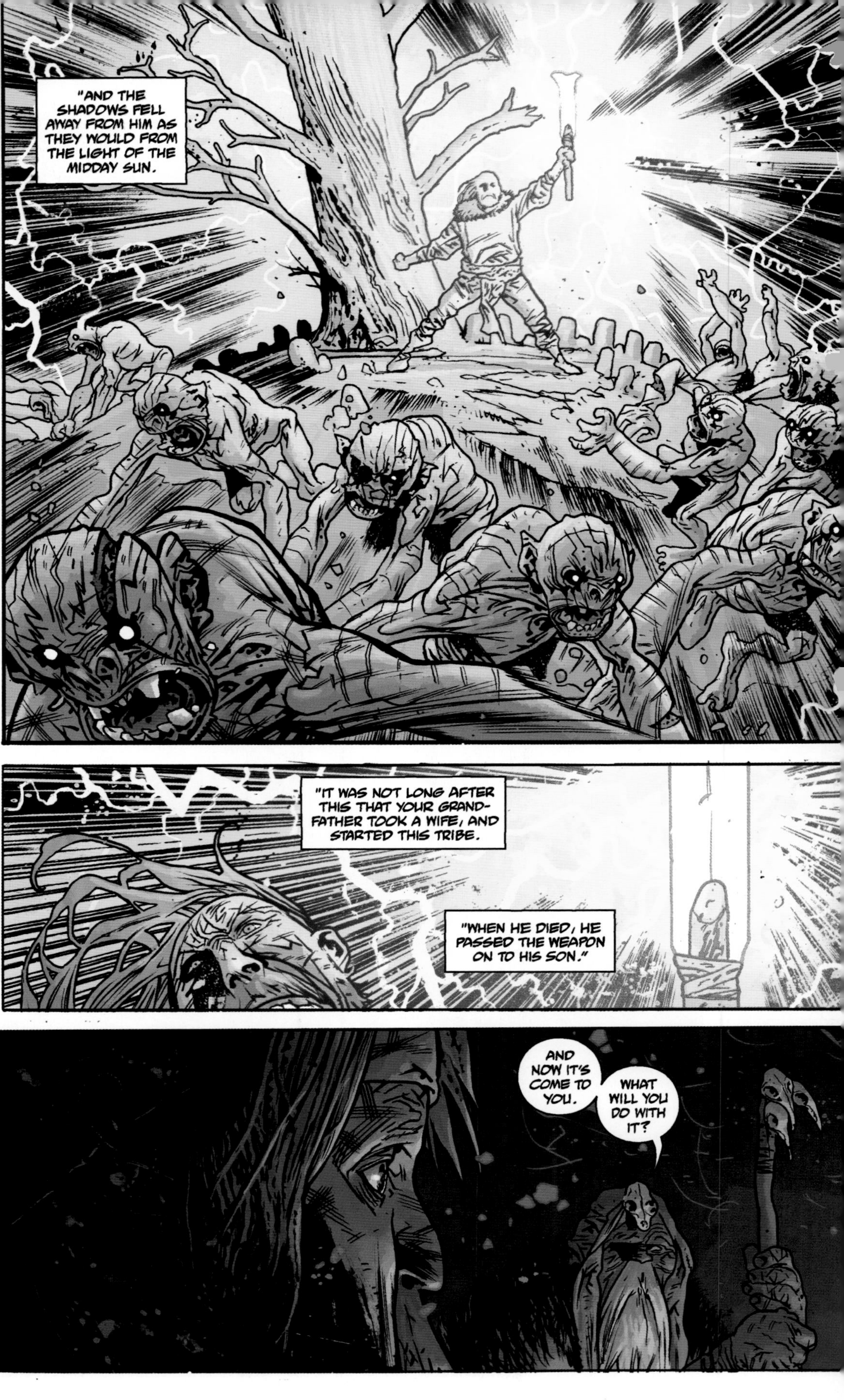
"AND THE SHADOWS FELL AWAY FROM HIM AS THEY WOULD FROM THE LIGHT OF THE MIDDAY SUN.
"IT WAS NOT LONG AFTER THIS THAT YOUR GRAND-FATHER TOOK A WIFE, AND STARTED THIS TRIBE.
"WHEN HE DIED, HE PASSED THE WEAPON ON TO HIS SON."
AND NOW IT'S COME TO YOU.
WHAT WILL YOU DO WITH IT?

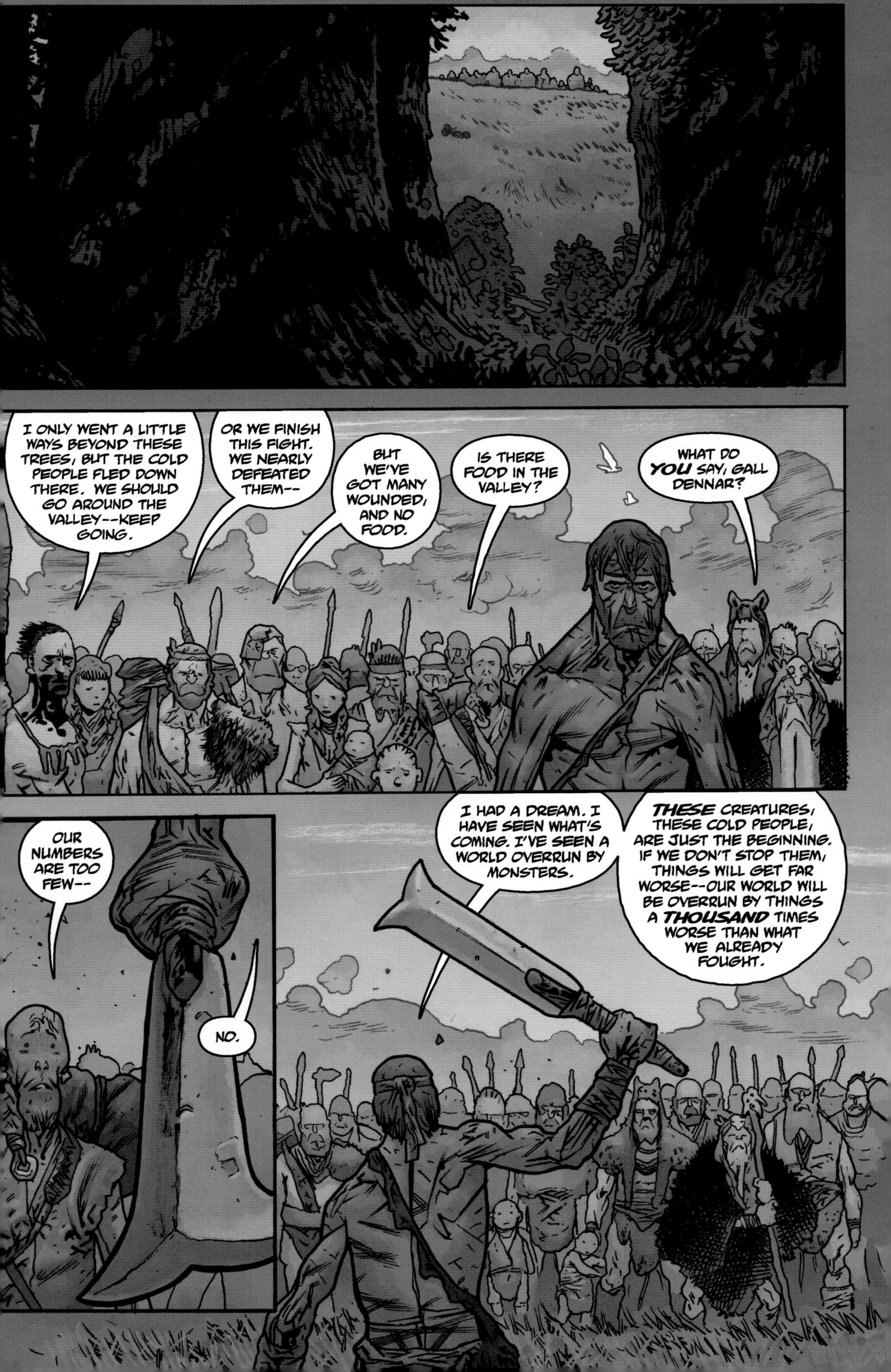
I ONLY WENT A LITTLE WAYS BEYOND THESE TREES, BUT THE COLD PEOPLE FLED DOWN THERE. WE SHOULD GO AROUND THE VALLEY--KEEP GOING.
OR WE FINISH THIS FIGHT. WE NEARLY DEFEATED THEM--
BUT WE'VE GOT MANY WOUNDED, AND NO FOOD.
IS THERE FOOD IN THE VALLEY?
WHAT DO YOU SAY, GALL DENNAR?
OUR NUMBERS ARE TOO FEW--
NO.
I HAD A DREAM. I HAVE SEEN WHAT'S COMING. I'VE SEEN A WORLD OVERRUN BY MONSTERS.
THESE CREATURES, THESE COLD PEOPLE, ARE JUST THE BEGINNING. IF WE DON'T STOP THEM, THINGS WILL GET FAR WORSE--OUR WORLD WILL BE OVERRUN BY THINGS A THOUSAND TIMES WORSE THAN WHAT WE ALREADY FOUGHT.

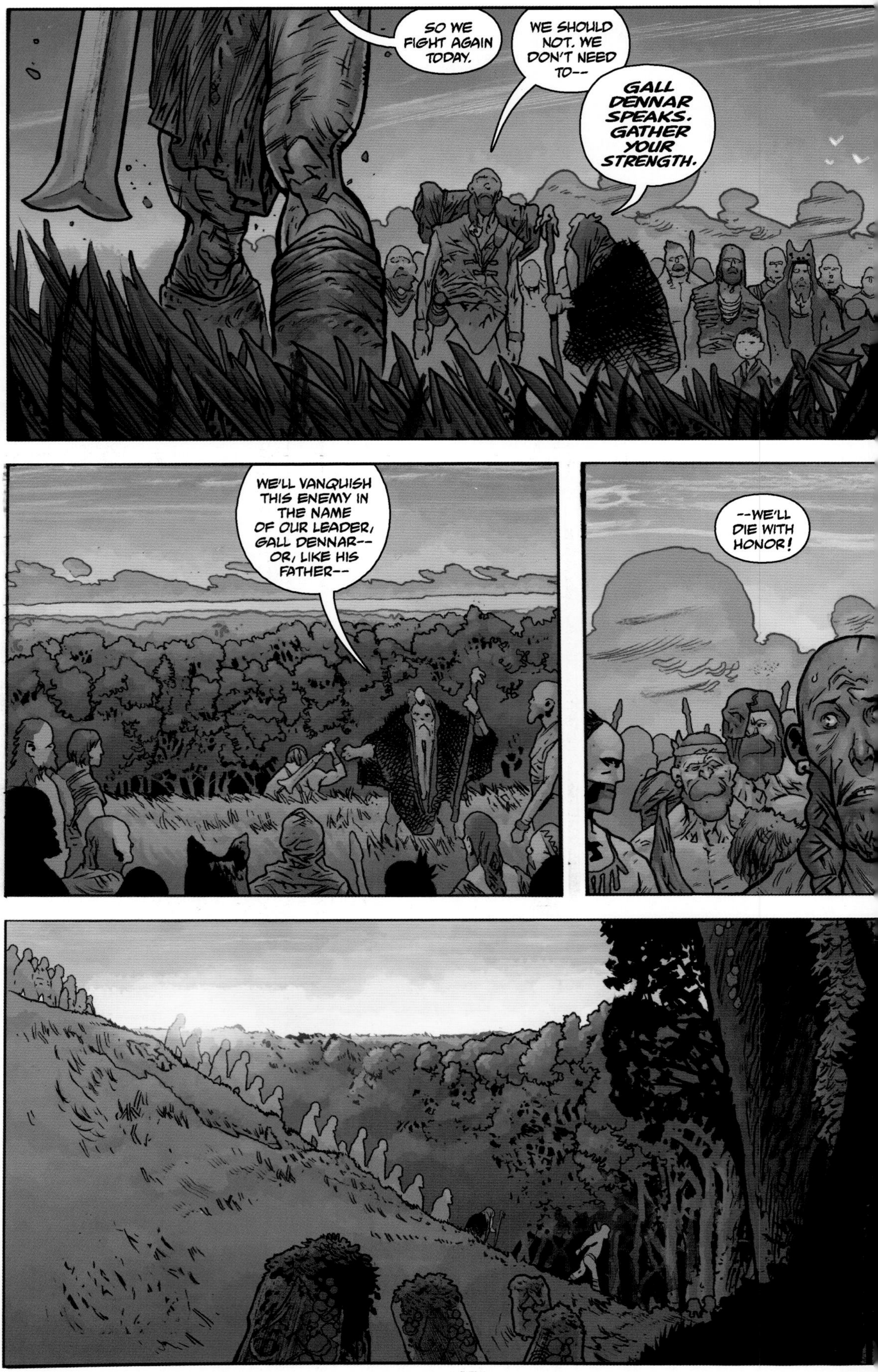
SO WE FIGHT AGAIN TODAY.
WE SHOULD NOT. WE DON'T NEED TO--
GALL DENNAR SPEAKS. GATHER YOUR STRENGTH.
WE'LL VANQUISH THIS ENEMY IN THE NAME OF OUR LEADER, GALL DENNAR-- OR, LIKE HIS FATHER--
--WE'LL DIE WITH HONOR!

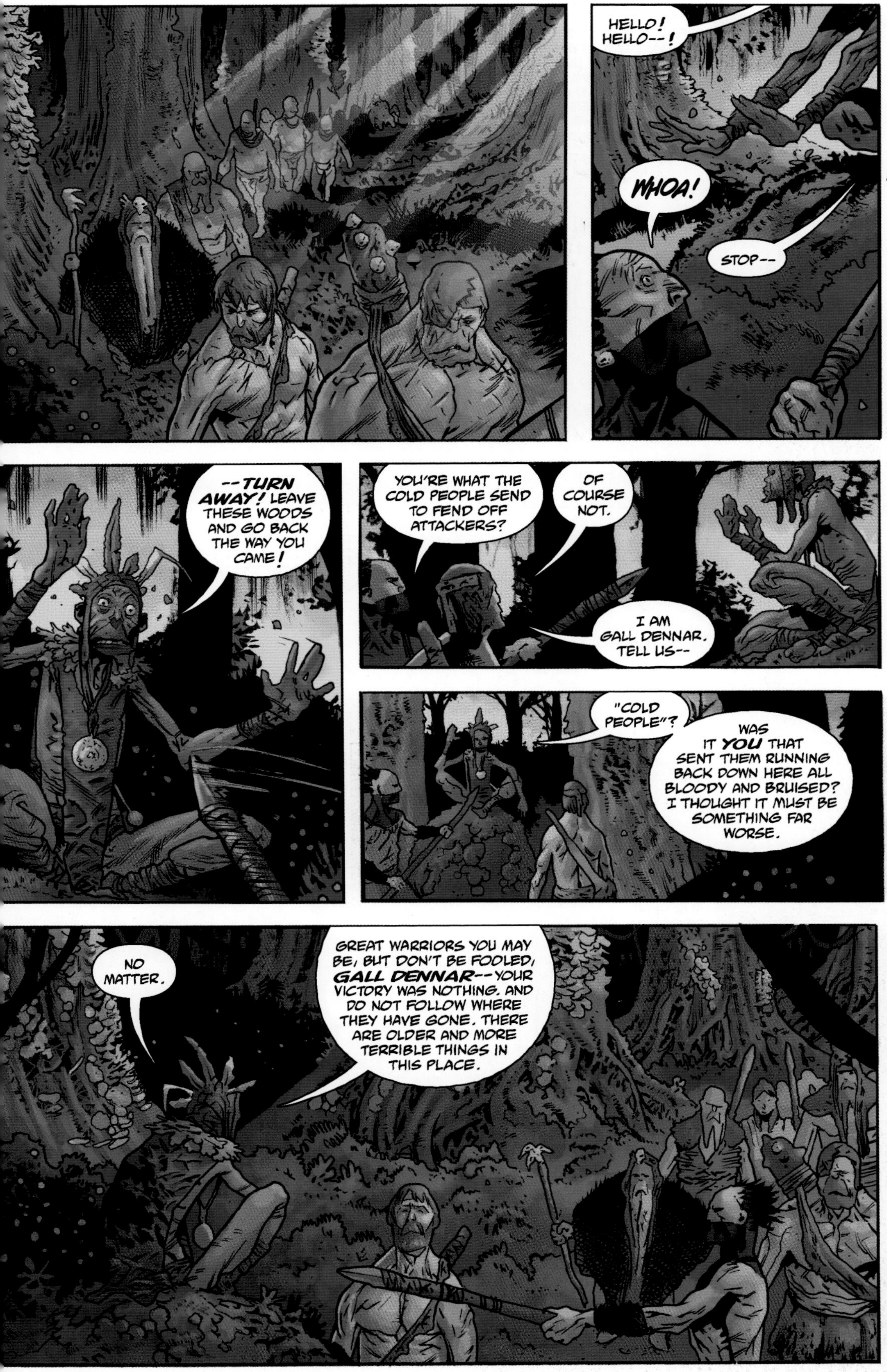
HELLO! HELLO--!
WHOA!
STOP--
--TURN AWAY! LEAVE THESE WOODS AND GO BACK THE WAY YOU CAME!
YOU'RE WHAT THE COLD PEOPLE SEND TO FEND OFF ATTACKERS?
OF COURSE NOT.
I AM GALL DENNAR. TELL US--
"COLD PEOPLE"?
WAS IT YOU THAT SENT THEM RUNNING BACK DOWN HERE ALL BLOODY AND BRUISED? I THOUGHT IT MUST BE SOMETHING FAR WORSE.
NO MATTER.
GREAT WARRIORS YOU MAY BE, BUT DON'T BE FOOLED, GALL DENNAR--YOUR VICTORY WAS NOTHING. AND DO NOT FOLLOW WHERE THEY HAVE GONE. THERE ARE OLDER AND MORE TERRIBLE THINGS IN THIS PLACE.

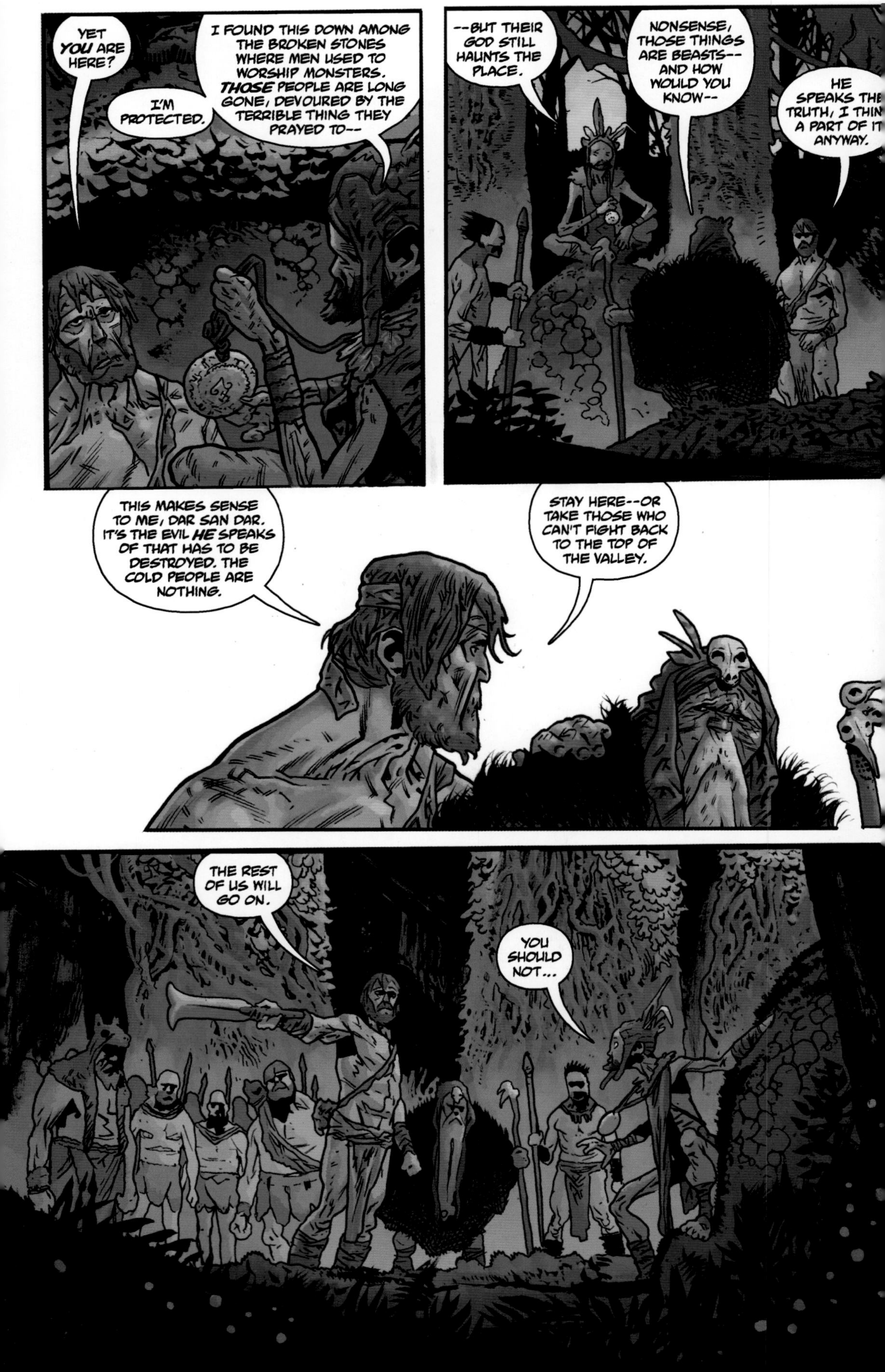
YET YOU ARE HERE?
I'M PROTECTED.
I FOUND THIS DOWN AMONG THE BROKEN STONES WHERE MEN USED TO WORSHIP MONSTERS. THOSE PEOPLE ARE LONG GONE, DEVOURED BY THE TERRIBLE THING THEY PRAYED TO--
--BUT THEIR GOD STILL HAUNTS THE PLACE.
NONSENSE, THOSE THINGS ARE BEASTS-- AND HOW WOULD YOU KNOW--
HE SPEAKS THE TRUTH, I THINK A PART OF IT ANYWAY.
THIS MAKES SENSE TO ME, DAR SAN DAR. IT'S THE EVIL HE SPEAKS OF THAT HAS TO BE DESTROYED. THE COLD PEOPLE ARE NOTHING.
STAY HERE--OR TAKE THOSE WHO CAN'T FIGHT BACK TO THE TOP OF THE VALLEY.
THE REST OF US WILL GO ON.
YOU SHOULD NOT...

...BUT YOU ARE BRAVE. I'LL SHOW YOU THE WAY--AND I WILL GIVE YOU THIS.

BEWARE, THOUGH.

IT ONLY PROTECTS YOU FROM THE SPIRITS AT WORK HERE, THE THINGS THAT POISON THE SOUL.

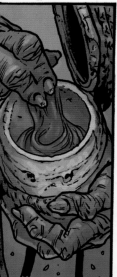

"THOSE YOU CALL THE 'COLD PEOPLE' WERE COMMON MEN AND WOMEN ONCE. THE SPIRITS MADE THEM WHAT THEY ARE NOW.

"THIS SIGN HAS LEFT ME FREE IN A VALLEY OF MADNESS.

"BUT IT CAN'T PROTECT YOU FROM THE GRIP OF REAL MONSTERS."

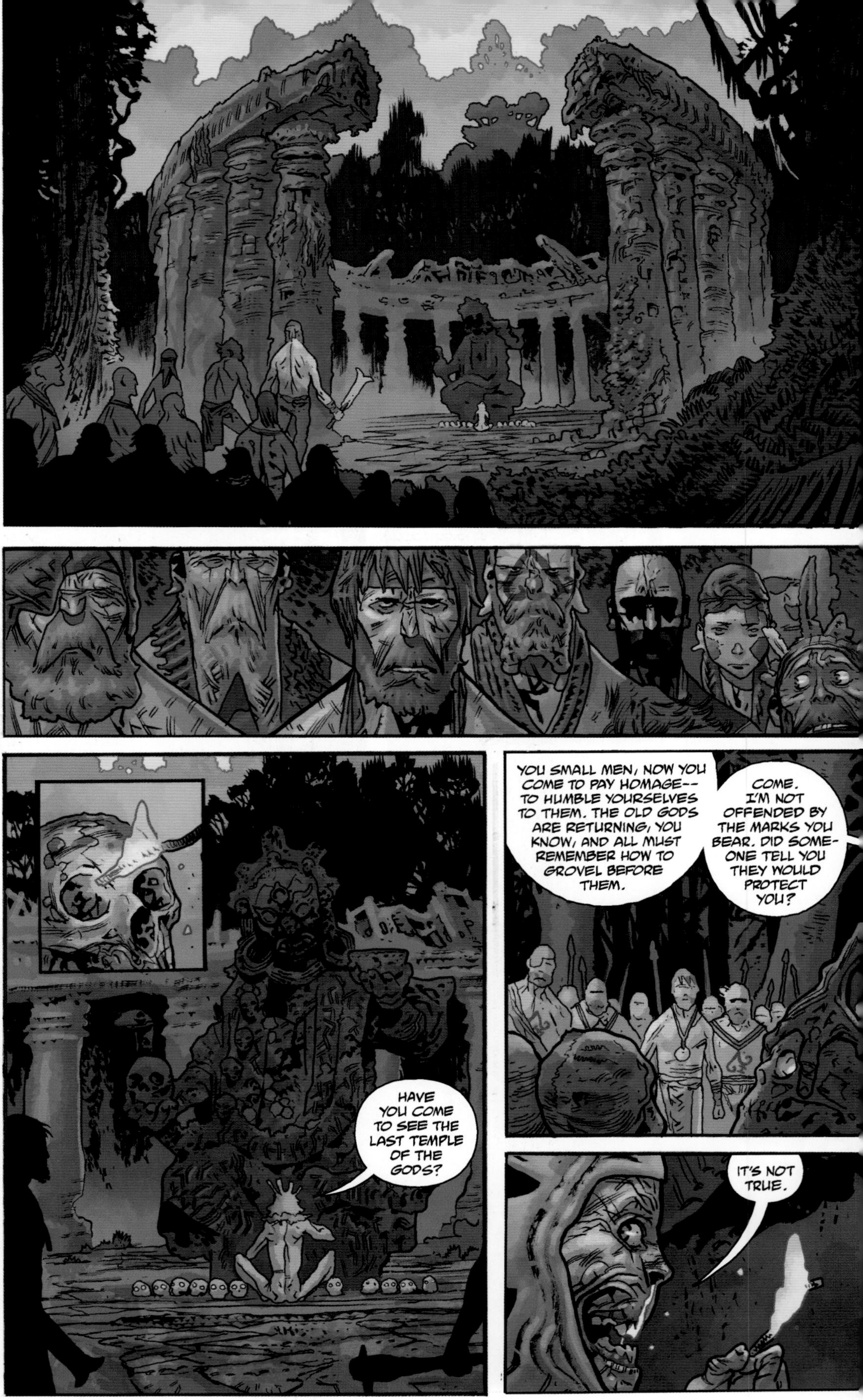
HAVE YOU COME TO SEE THE LAST TEMPLE OF THE GODS?
YOU SMALL MEN, NOW YOU COME TO PAY HOMAGE-- TO HUMBLE YOURSELVES TO THEM. THE OLD GODS ARE RETURNING, YOU KNOW, AND ALL MUST REMEMBER HOW TO GROVEL BEFORE THEM.
COME. I'M NOT OFFENDED BY THE MARKS YOU BEAR. DID SOMEONE TELL YOU THEY WOULD PROTECT YOU?
IT'S NOT TRUE.

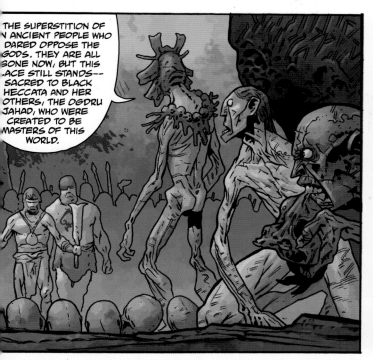

THE SUPERSTITION OF AN ANCIENT PEOPLE WHO DARED OPPOSE THE GODS. THEY ARE ALL GONE NOW, BUT THIS PLACE STILL STANDS-- SACRED TO BLACK HECCATA AND HER OTHERS, THE OGDRU JAHAD, WHO WERE CREATED TO BE MASTERS OF THIS WORLD.

LONG AGO WERE THEY DRIVEN AWAY, BUT COULD NOT BE DESTROYED-- THEY ONLY SLUMBER.

ETH UMM RAHAAB EG. AS IT WAS IN THE BEGINNING, IT WILL BE AGAIN.

WE, THE *CHILDREN* OF THE OLD GODS, REMAIN--

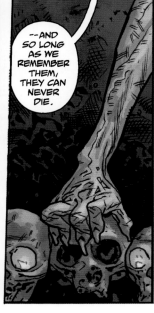

--AND SO LONG AS WE REMEMBER THEM, THEY CAN NEVER DIE.

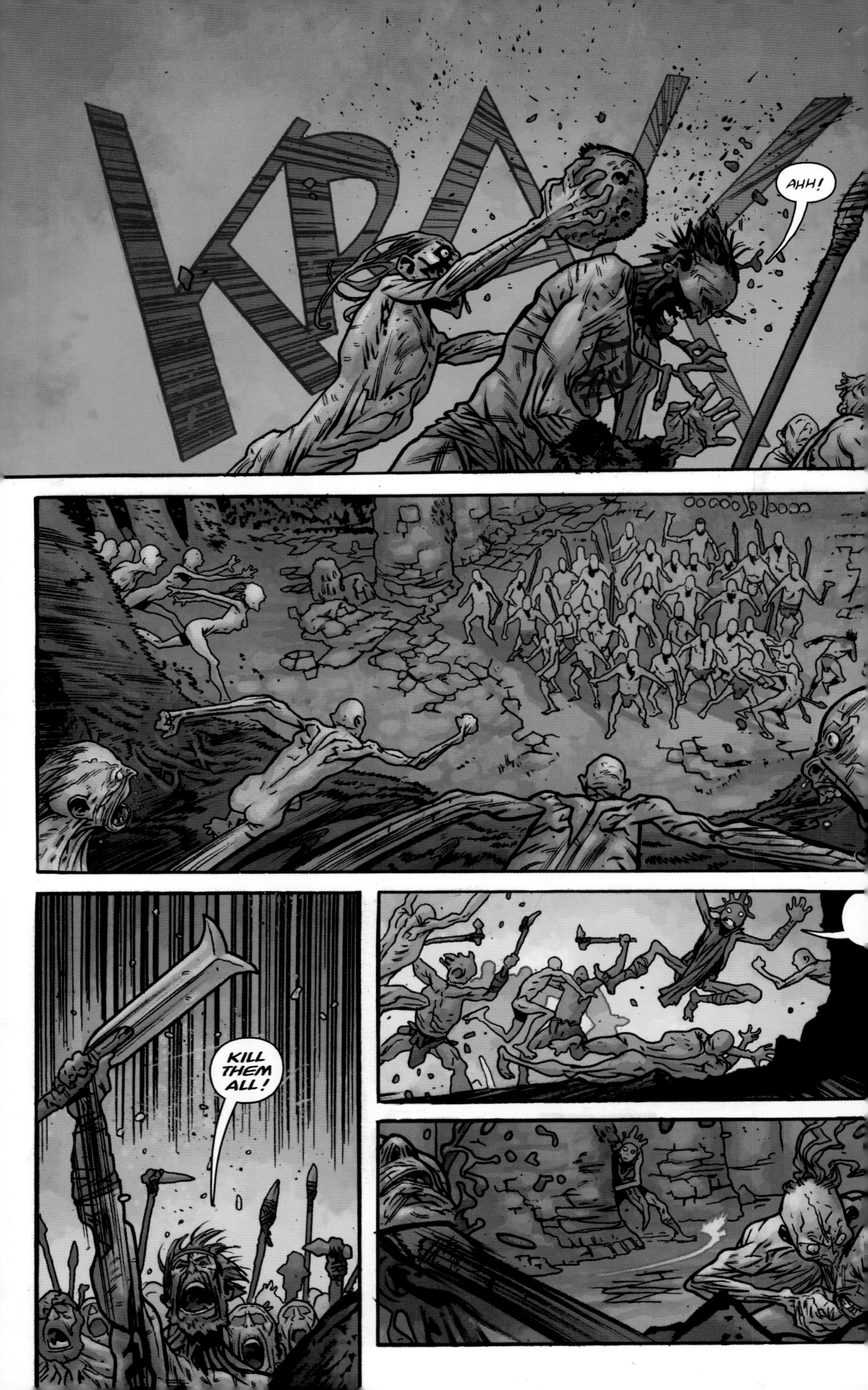
KRAK
AHH!
KILL THEM ALL!

HA! YES! SPLATTER BLOOD, WARM AND COLD, UPON THE SACRED STONES! ALL BLOOD IS THEIRS--

--THE GLORY OF THE TRUE GODS!

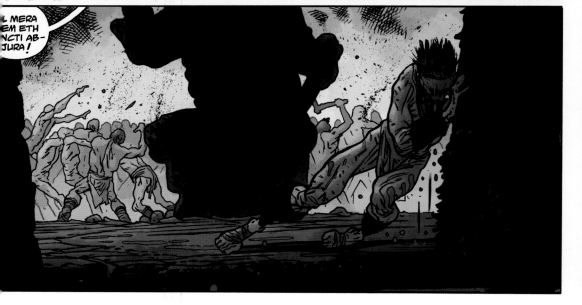

L MERA EM ETH NCTI AB- JURA!

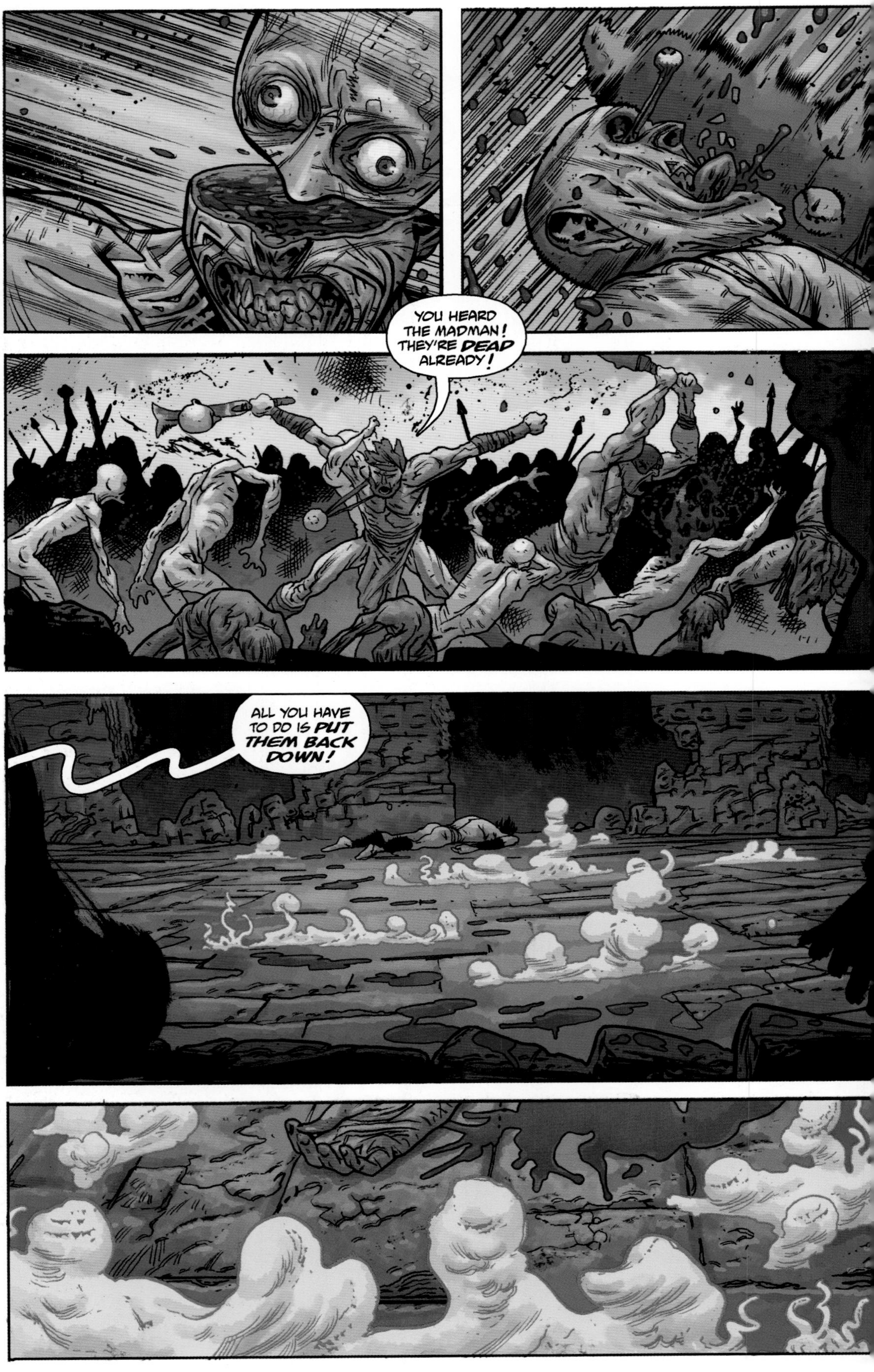
YOU HEARD THE MADMAN! THEY'RE **DEAD** ALREADY!
ALL YOU HAVE TO DO IS **PUT THEM BACK DOWN!**

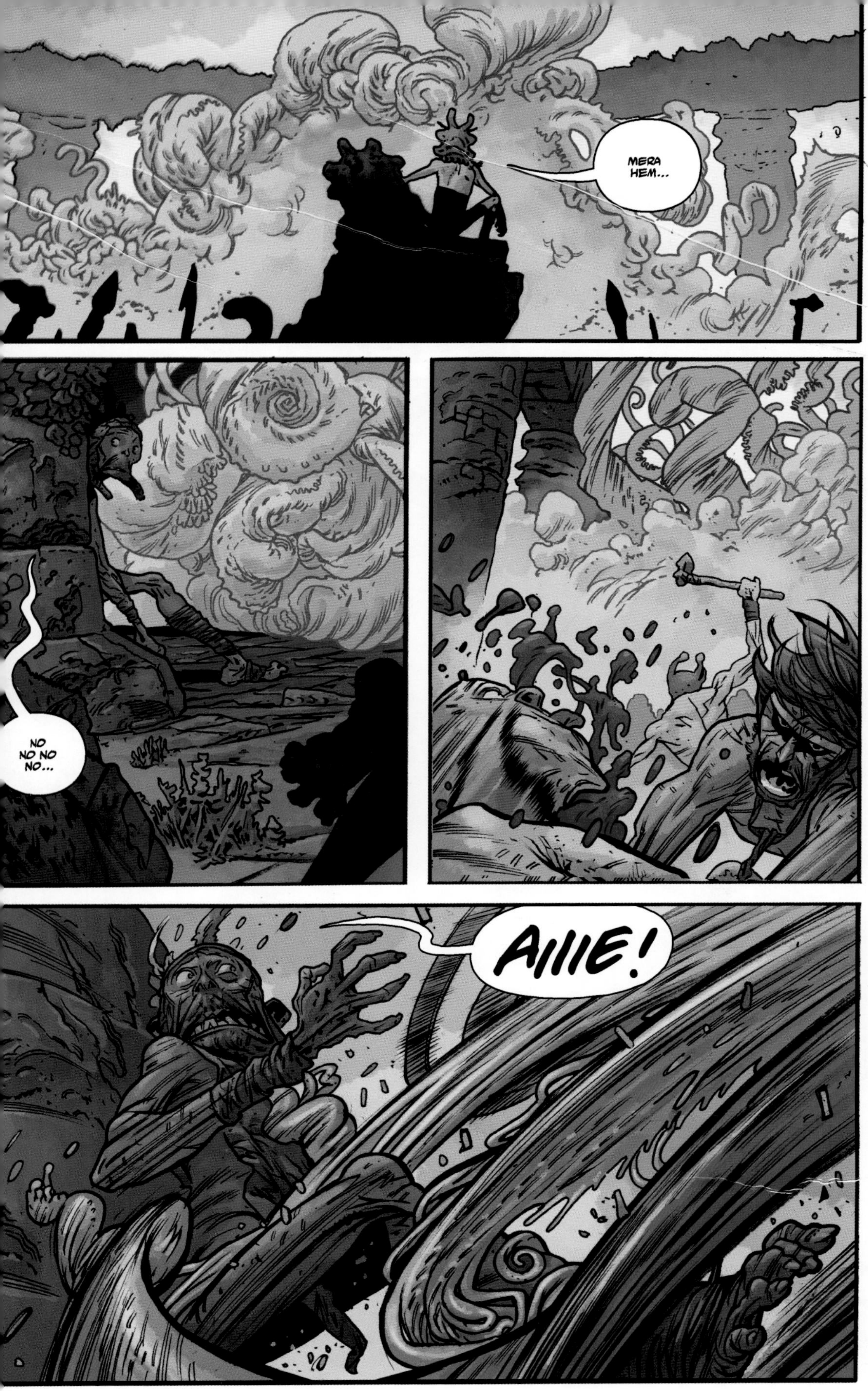
MERA HEM...
NO NO NO NO...
AIIIE!

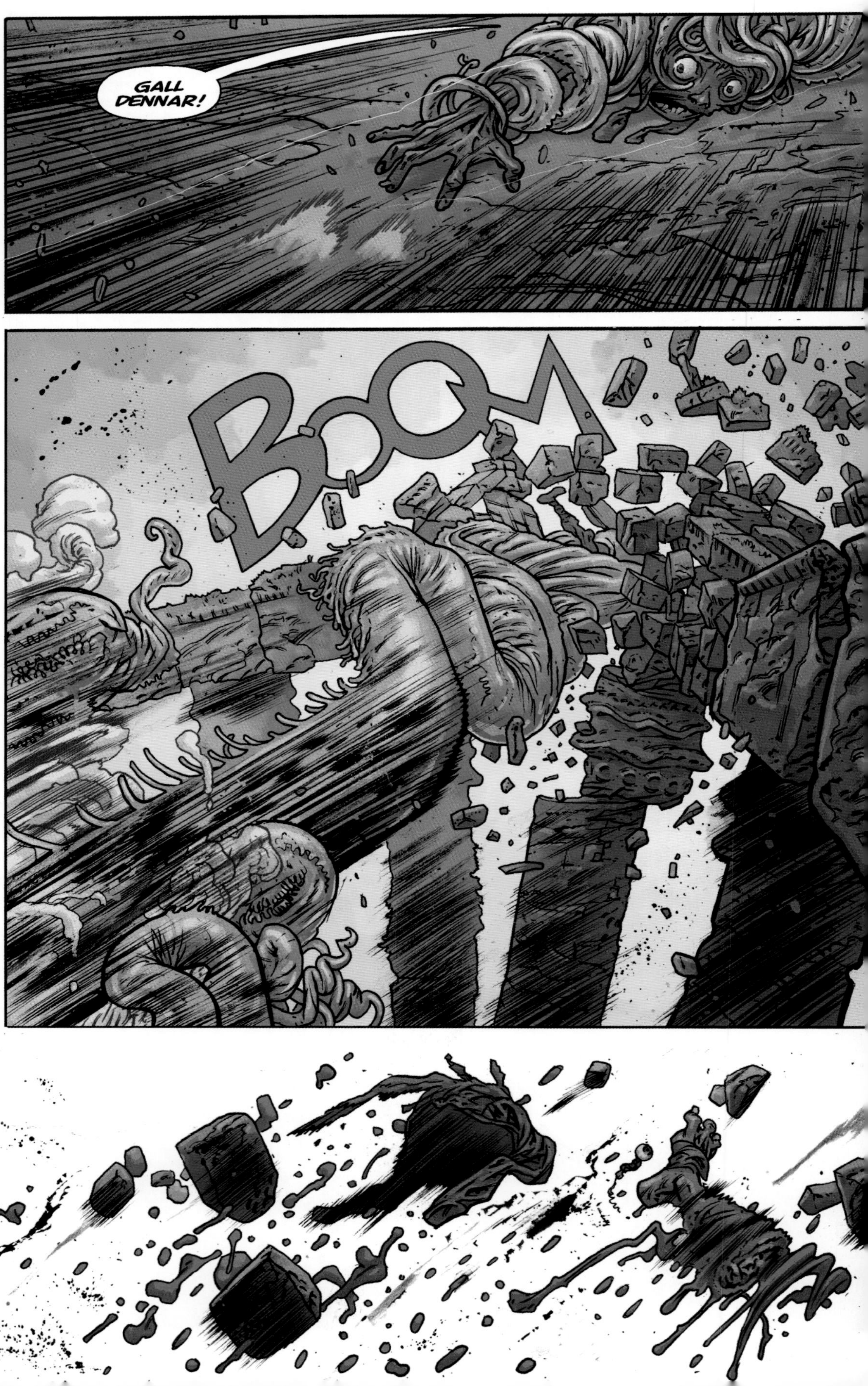
GALL DENNAR!
BOOM

CHOP

!

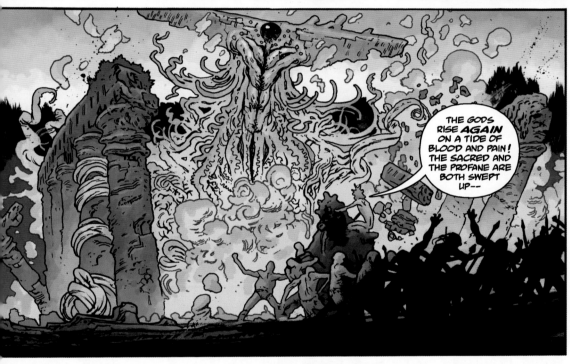

THE GODS RISE *AGAIN* ON A TIDE OF BLOOD AND PAIN! THE SACRED AND THE PROFANE ARE BOTH SWEPT UP--

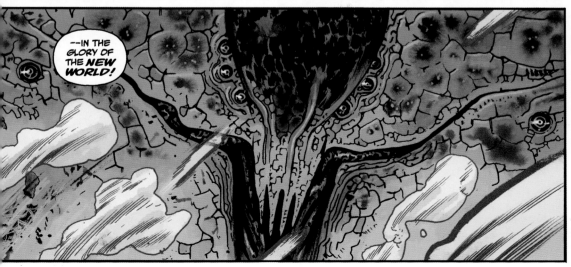

--IN THE GLORY OF THE *NEW WORLD!*

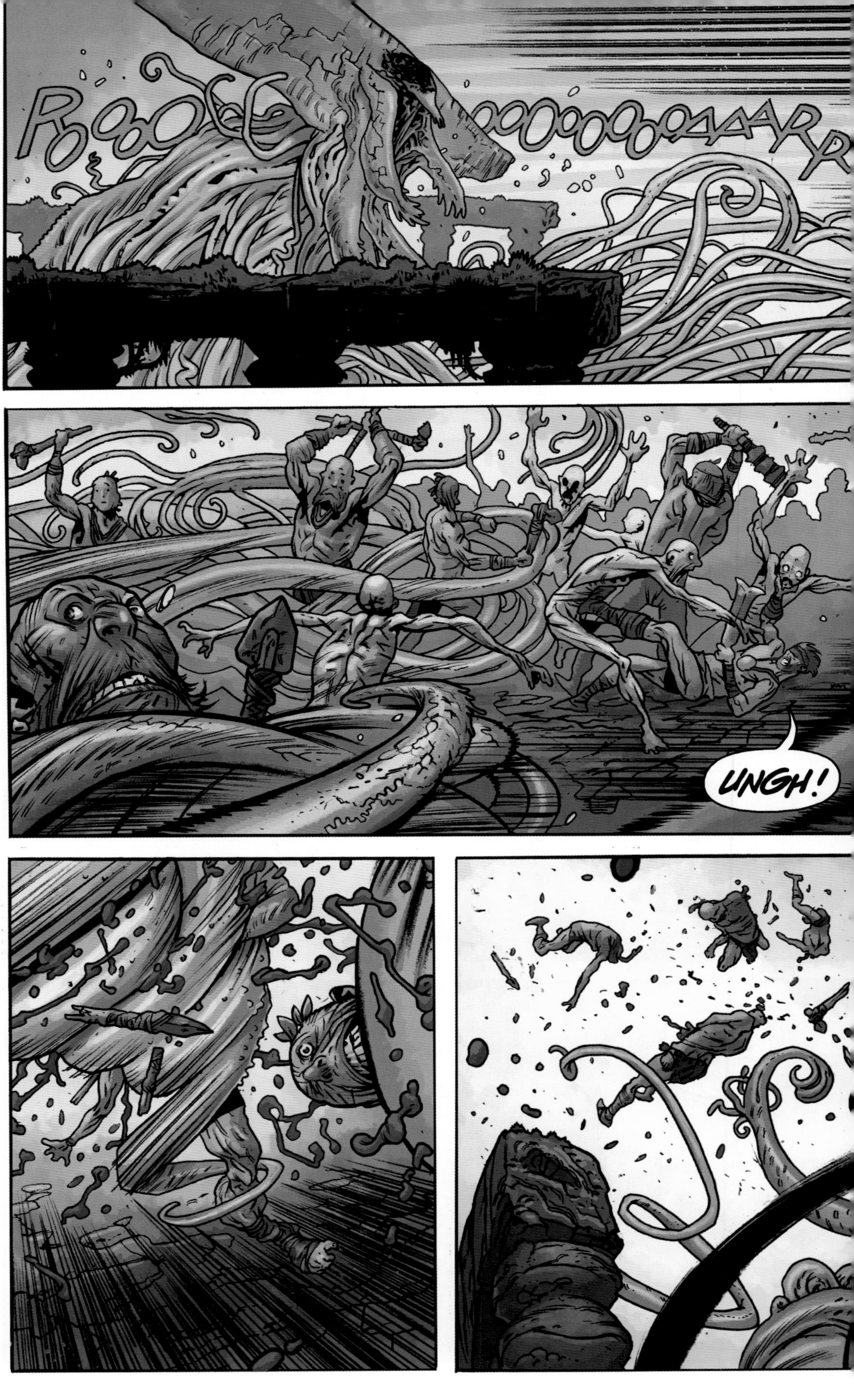
ROOOOOOOOOOOOOOOOOOOAAARR
UNGH!

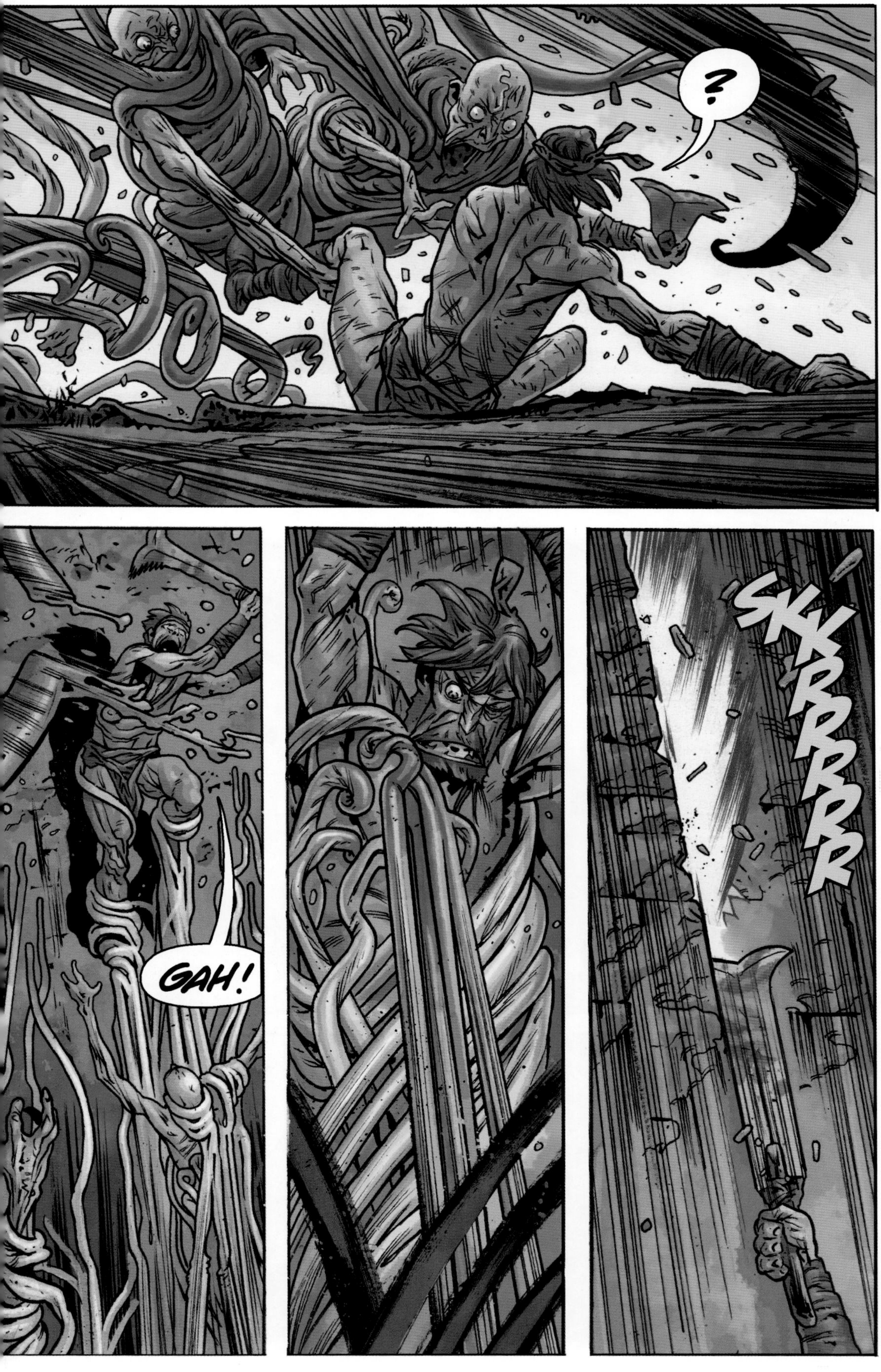
?
GAH!
SKRRRRRR

AHHH!

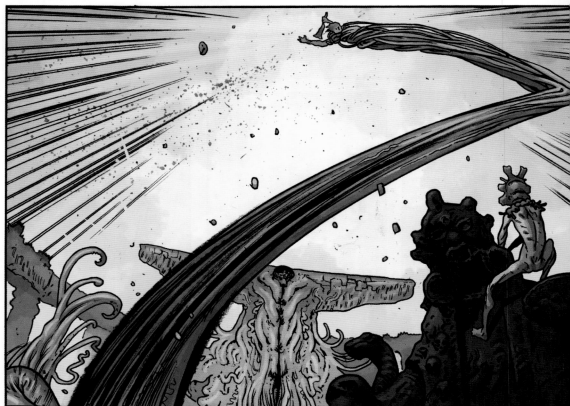

RISE! *RISE!* MERA HEM UTH DANI HECCATA! *WAKE* AND CALL FORTH THE NEW RACE!

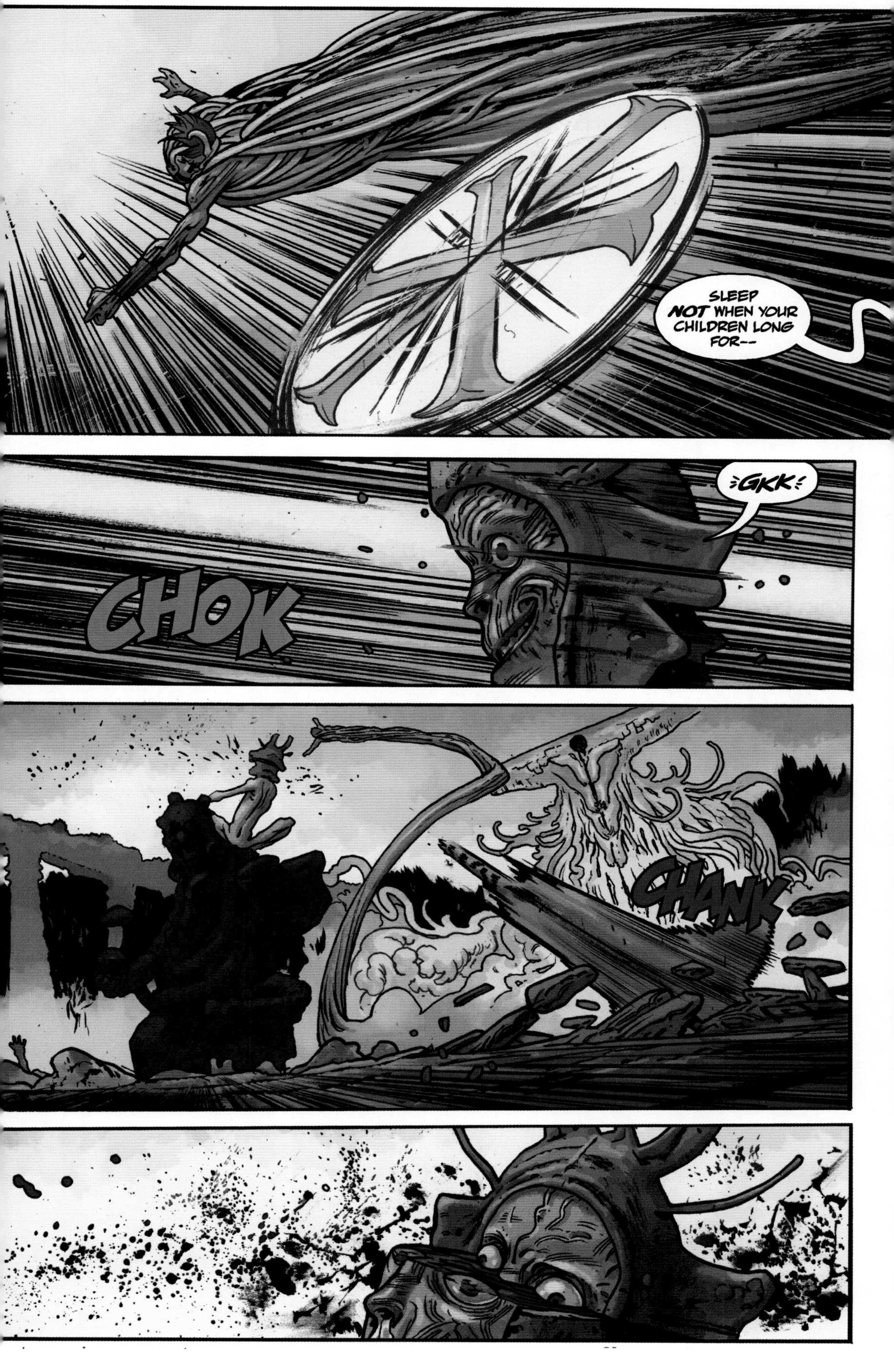
SLEEP NOT WHEN YOUR CHILDREN LONG FOR--
CHOK
GKK
CHANK

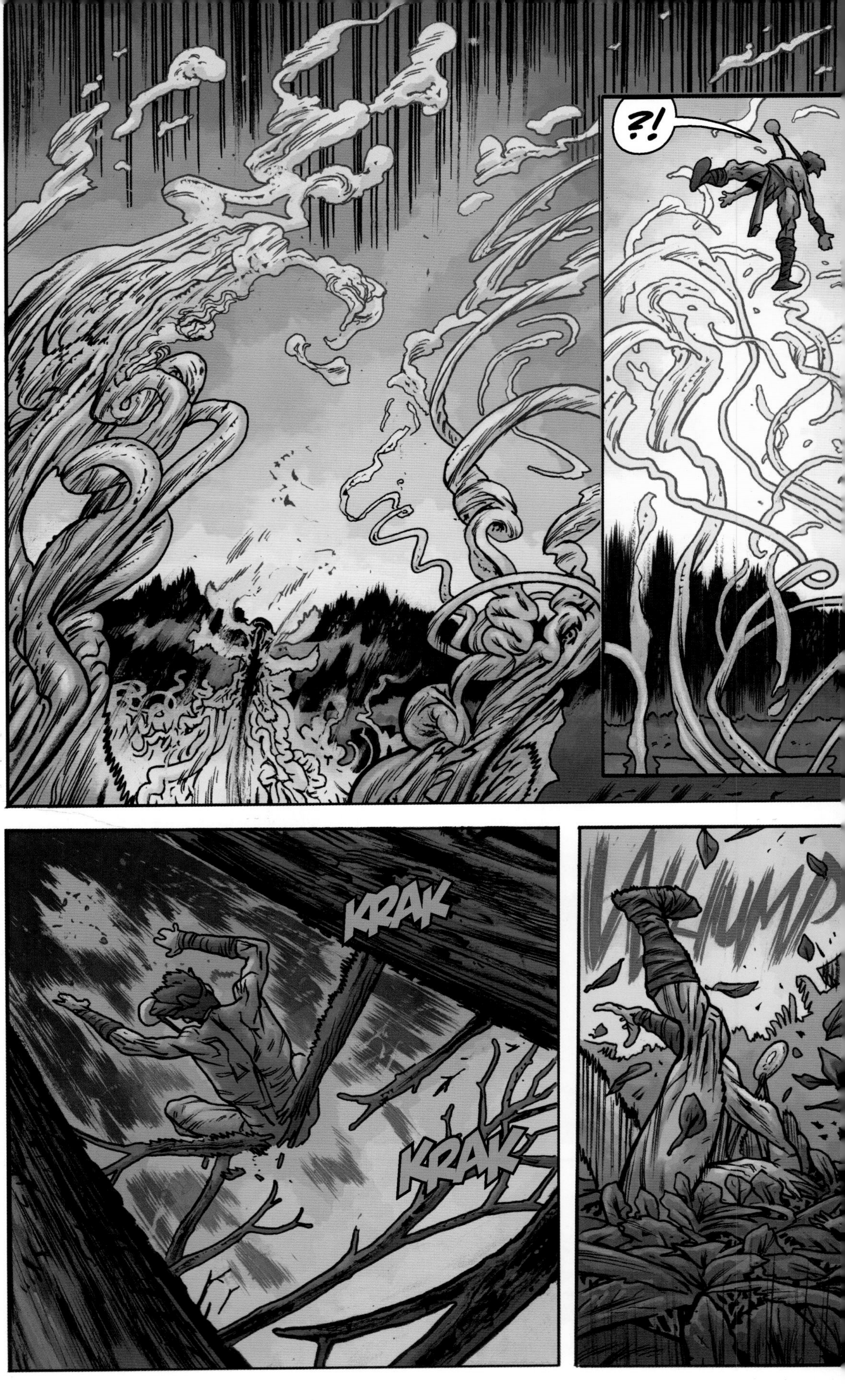
?!
KRAK
KRAK

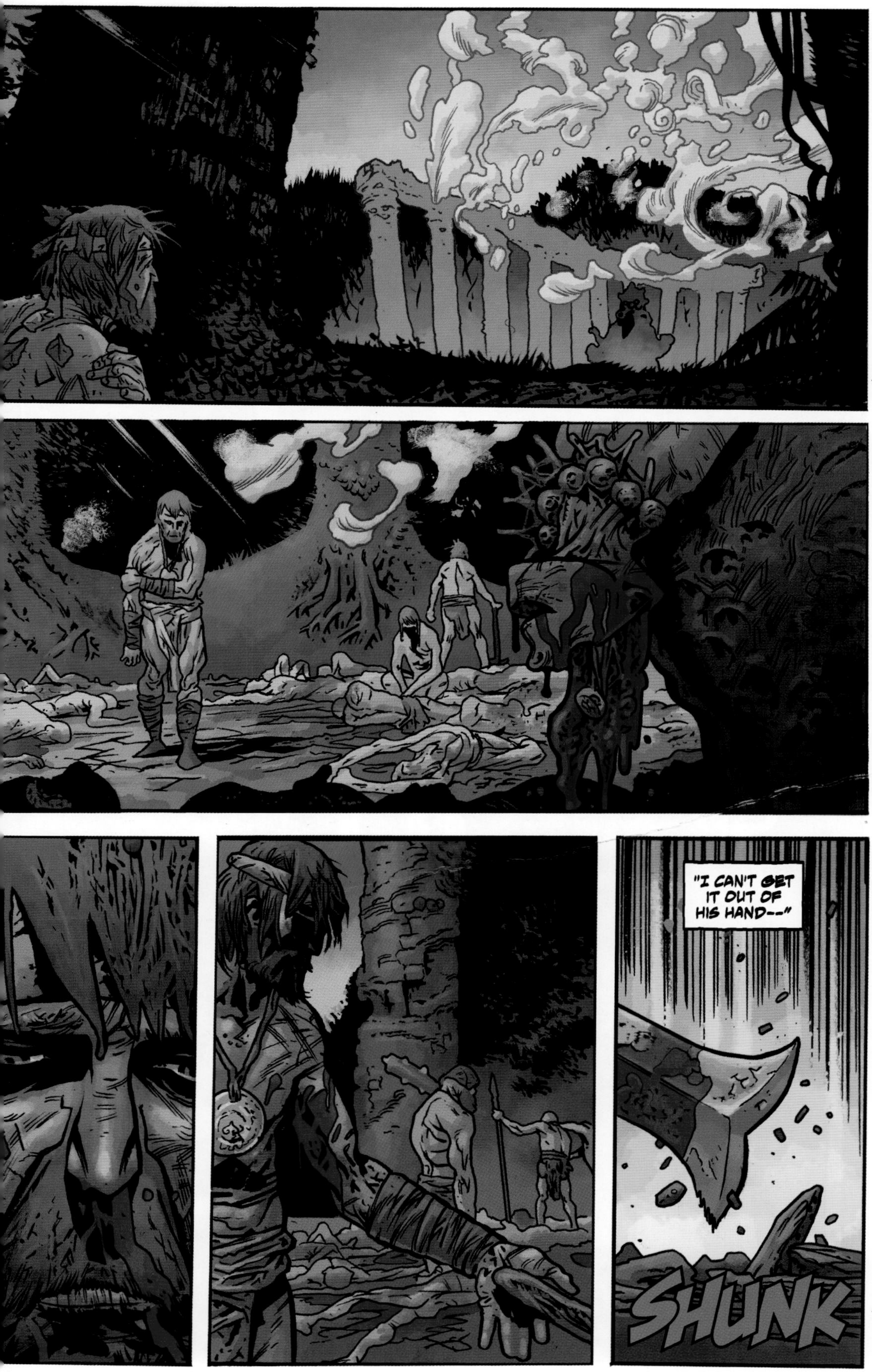
"I CAN'T GET IT OUT OF HIS HAND--"
SHUNK

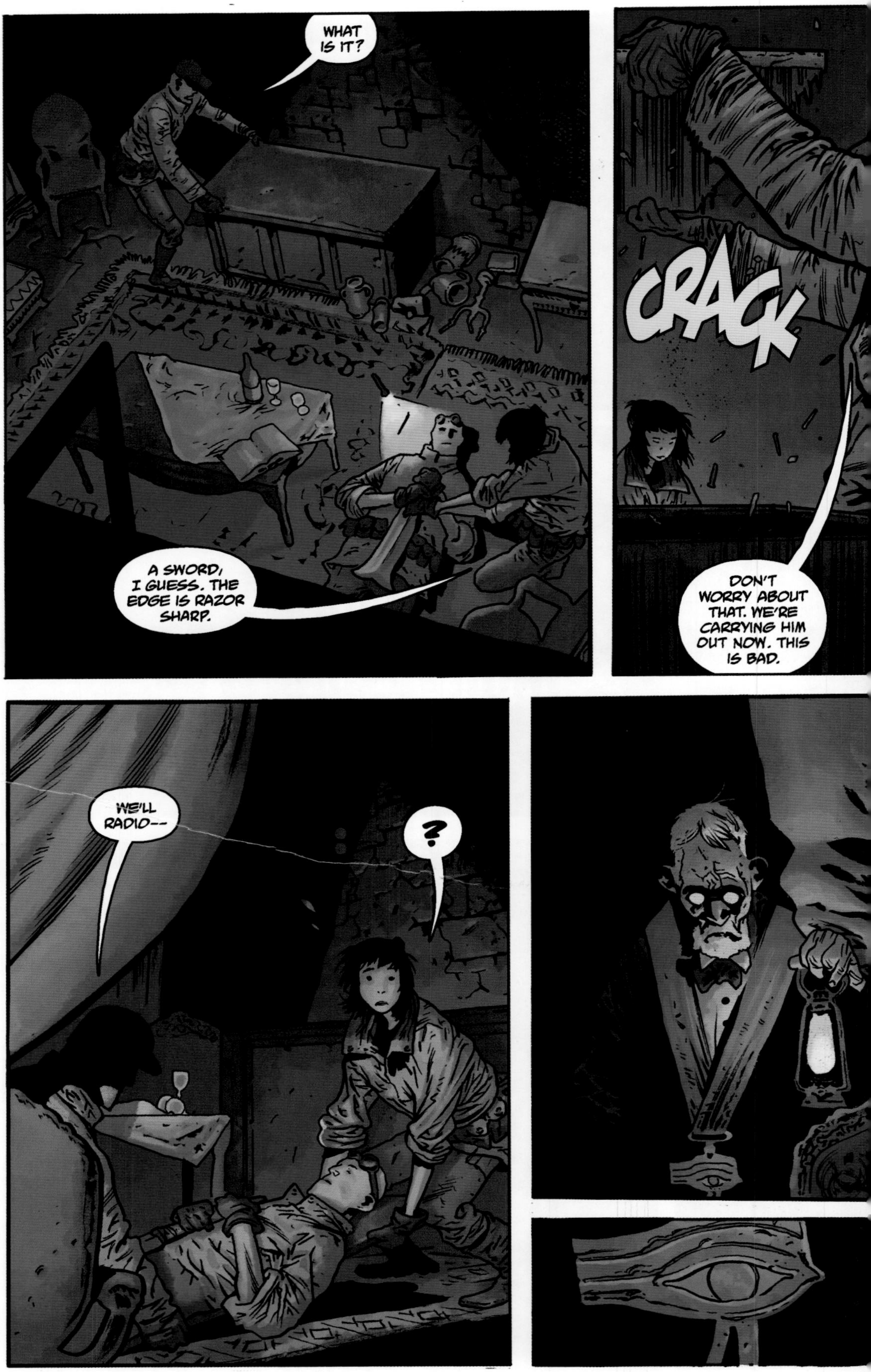
WHAT IS IT?
A SWORD, I GUESS. THE EDGE IS RAZOR SHARP.
CRACK
DON'T WORRY ABOUT THAT. WE'RE CARRYING HIM OUT NOW. THIS IS BAD.
WE'LL RADIO--
?

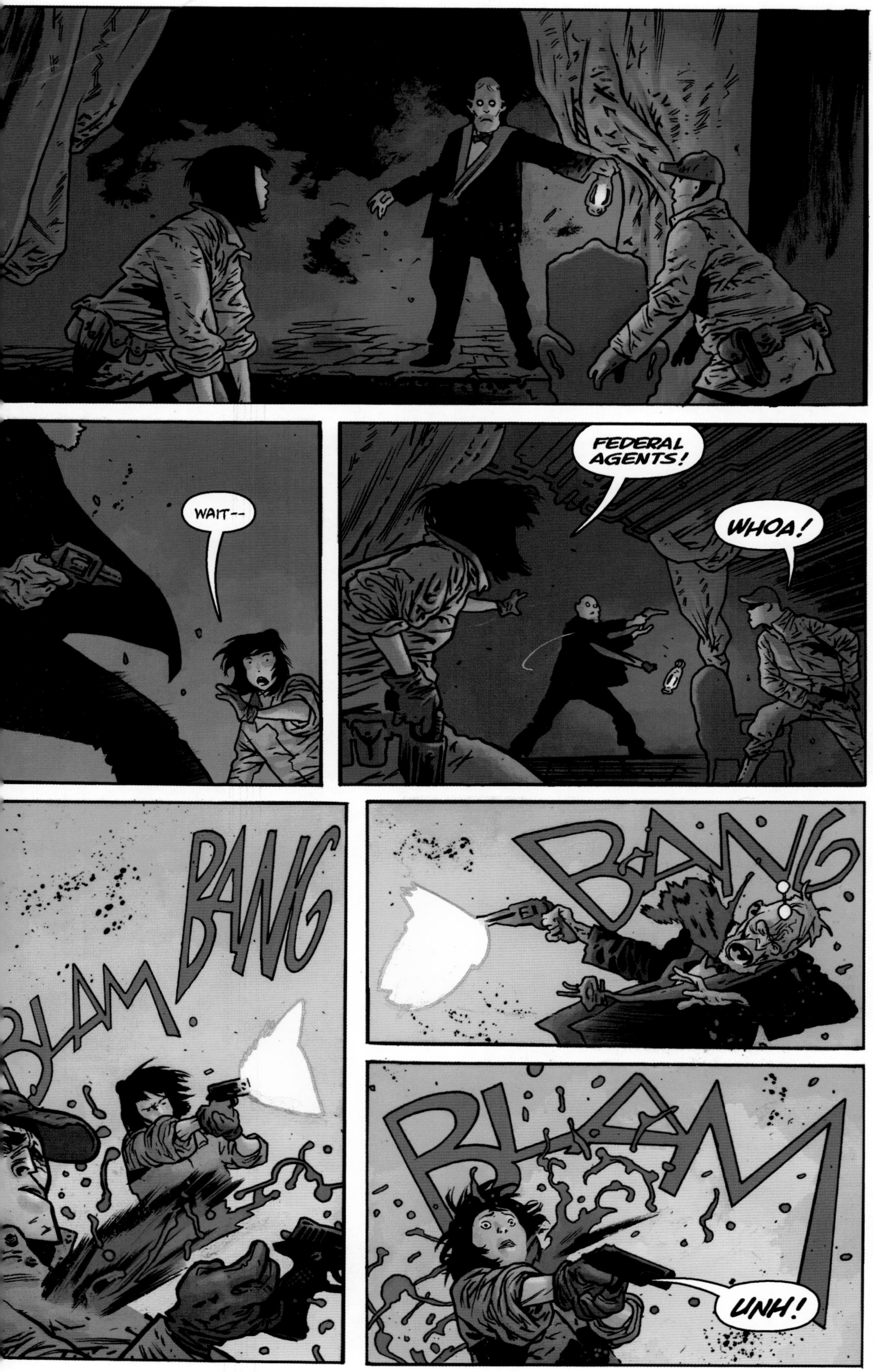
WAIT--
FEDERAL AGENTS!
WHOA!
BLAM
BANG
BANG
BLAM
UNH!

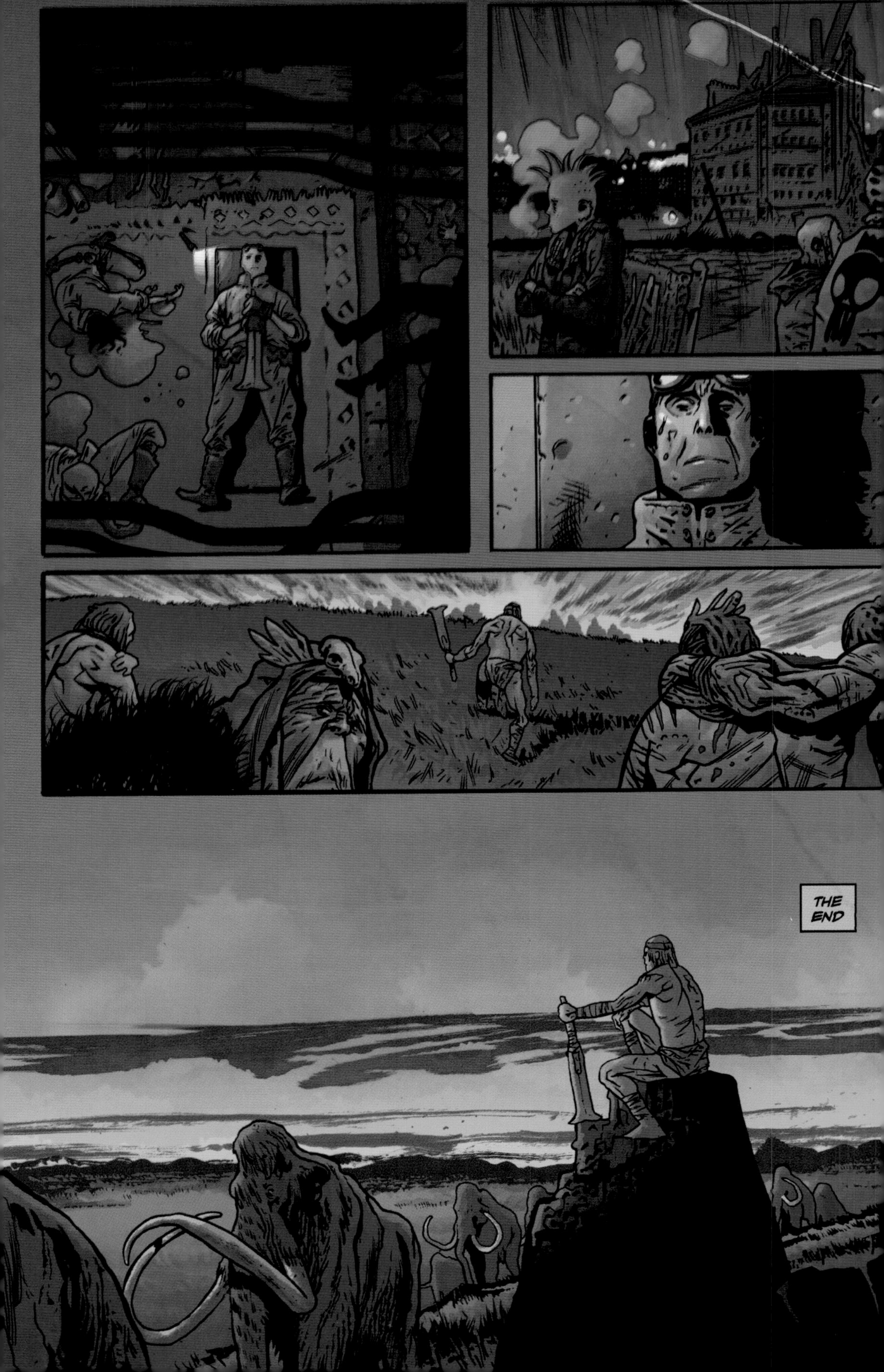
THE END

B.P.R.D.™

SKETCHBOOK

Notes by Scott Allie

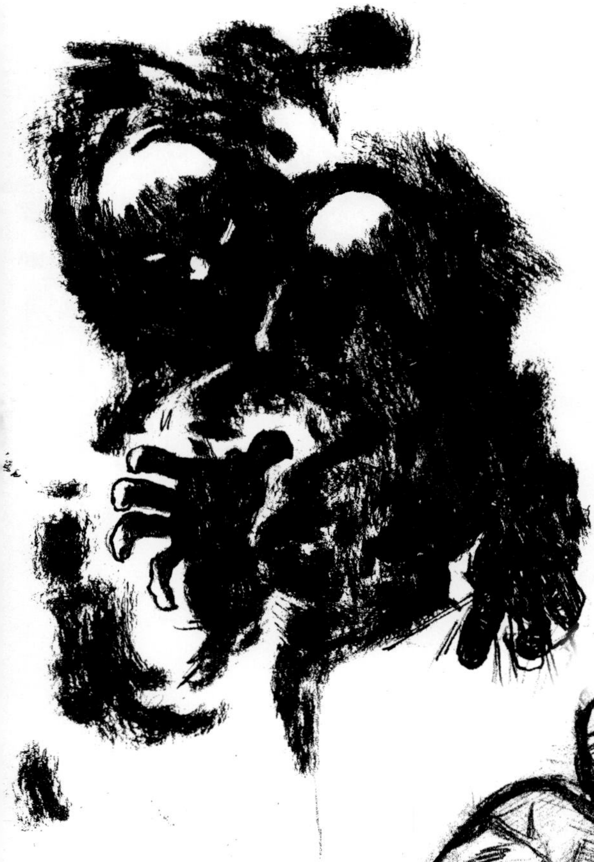

Jason Latour warms up for *The Pickens County Horror*. Agent Vaughn first appeared drawn by Guy Davis in "Casualties," collected in *B.P.R.D.: Being Human*.

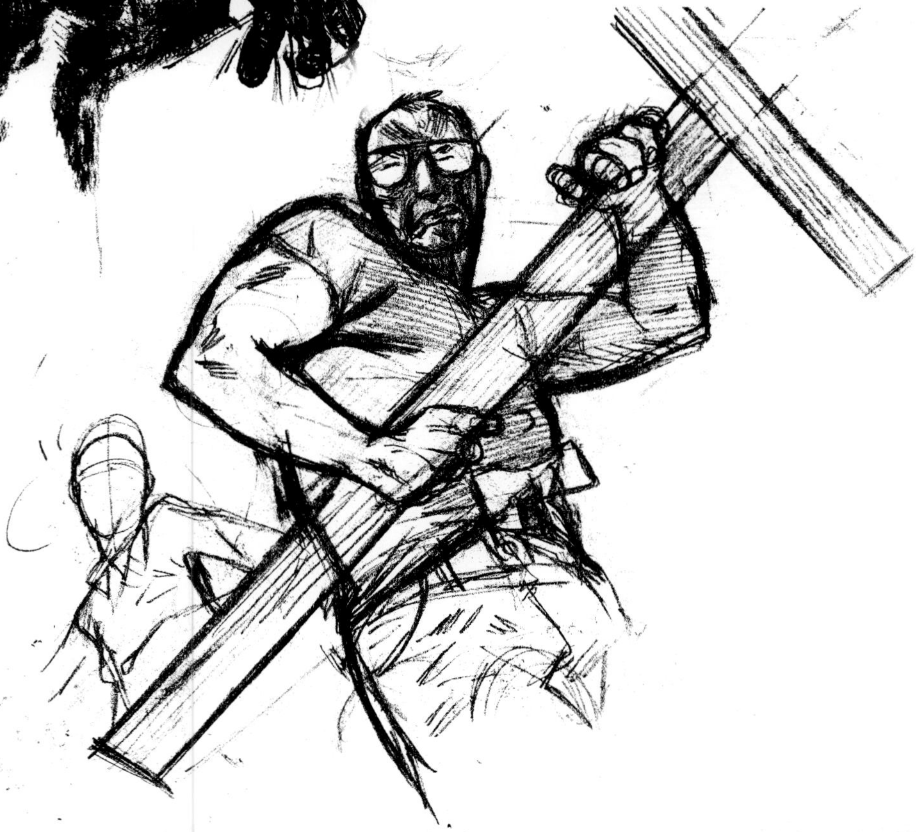

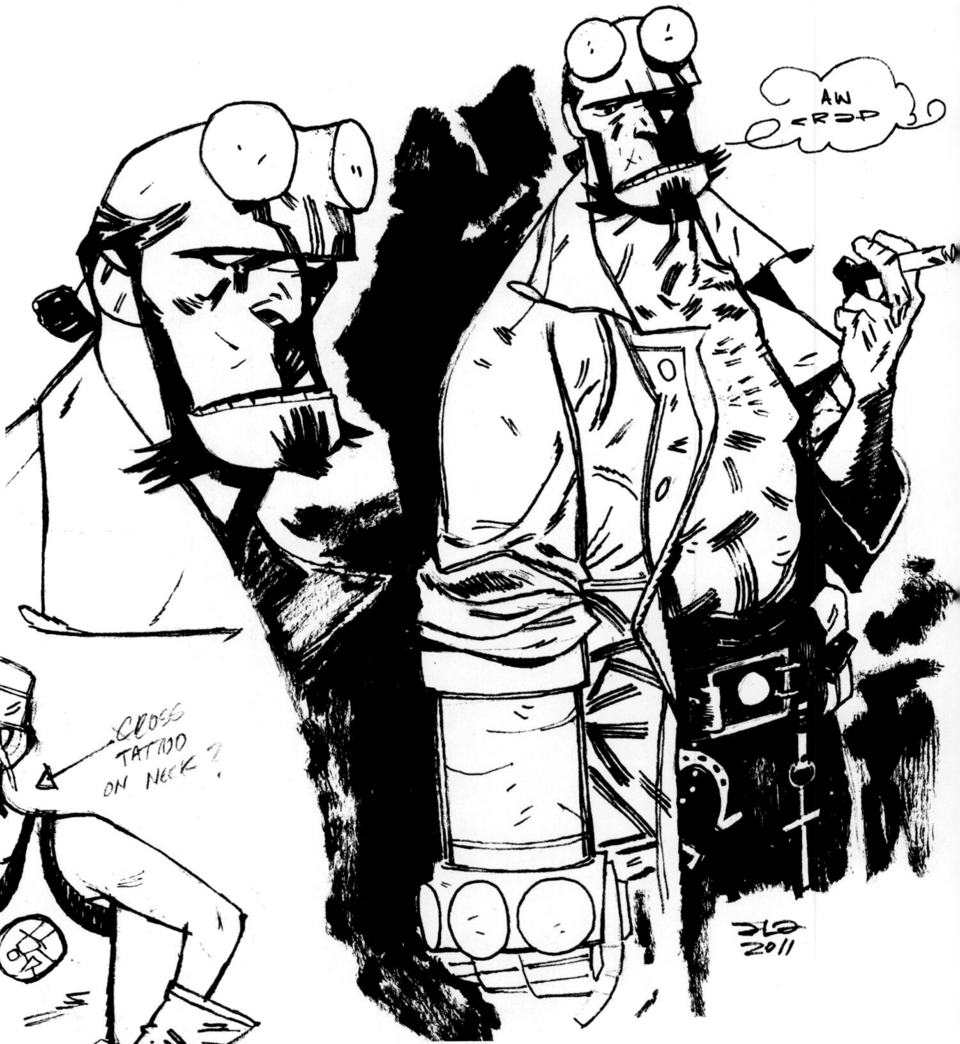
AW CRAP

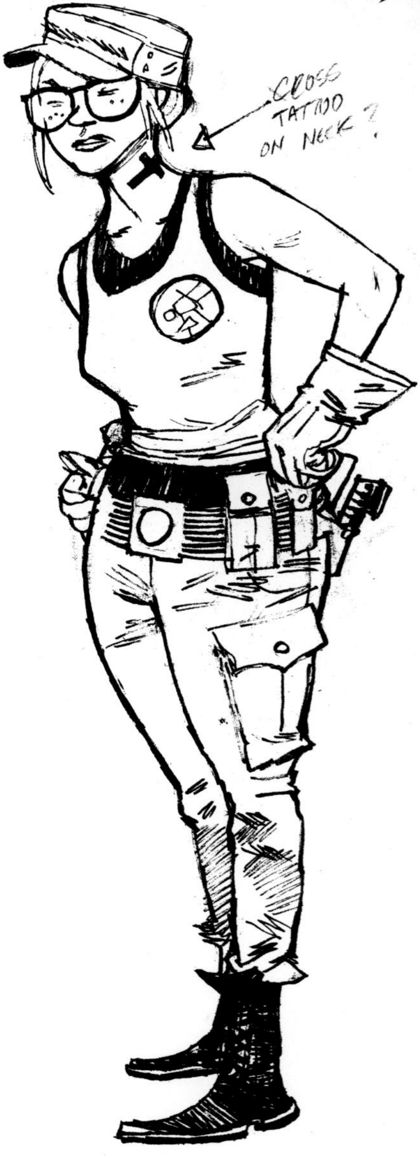
CROSS TATTOO ON NECK ?

An unused design for Agent Peters. At first, knowing only that the story featured vampires, Jason wanted to give her an attitude: "I like to think she retained a touch of that in the final story, but I'm glad we lost the way too on-the-nose cross tattoo."

Above: Practicing for Hellboy's scene.

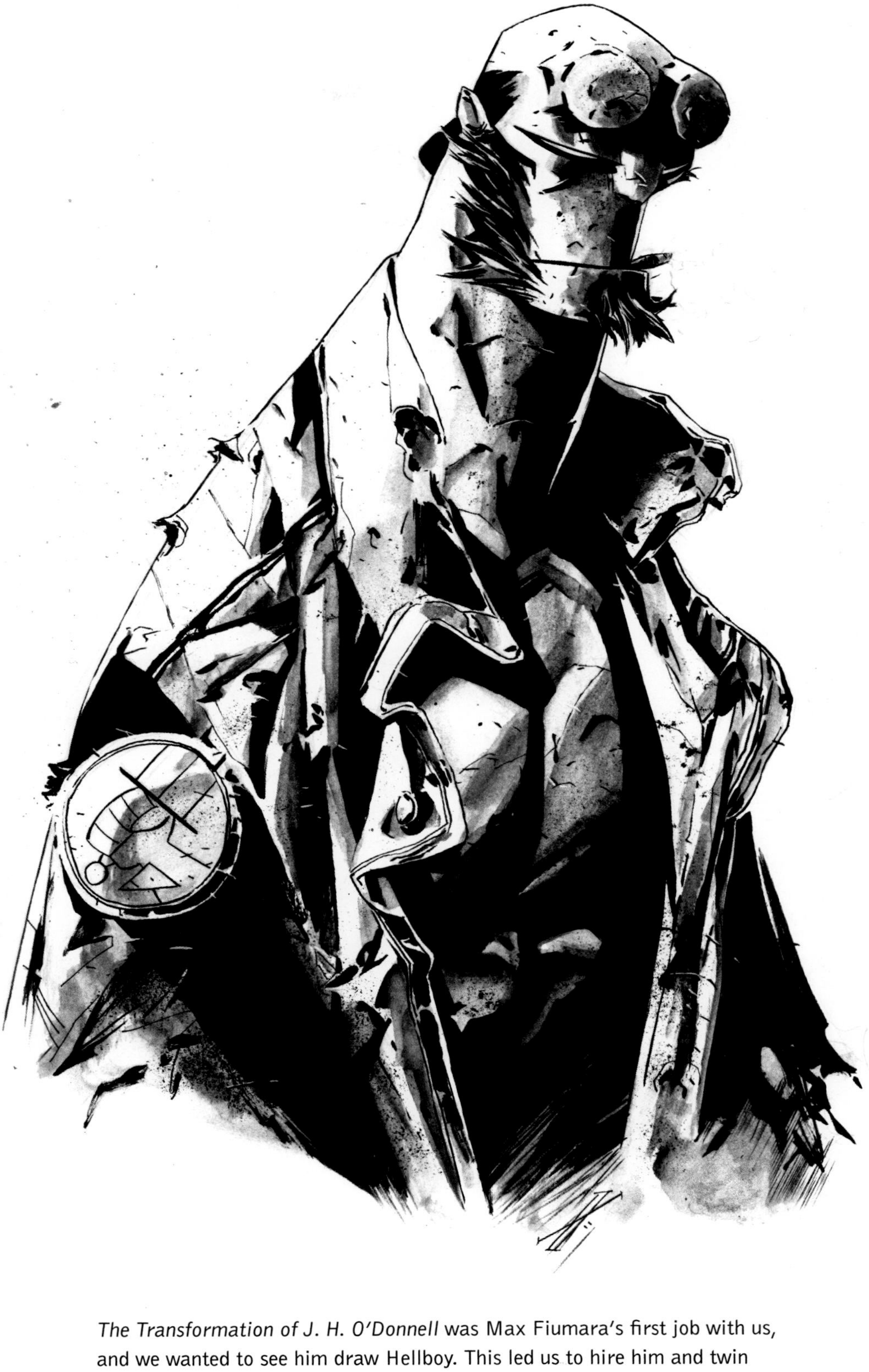

The Transformation of J. H. O'Donnell was Max Fiumara's first job with us, and we wanted to see him draw Hellboy. This led us to hire him and twin brother Sebastián as the regular artists on our *Abe Sapien* series.

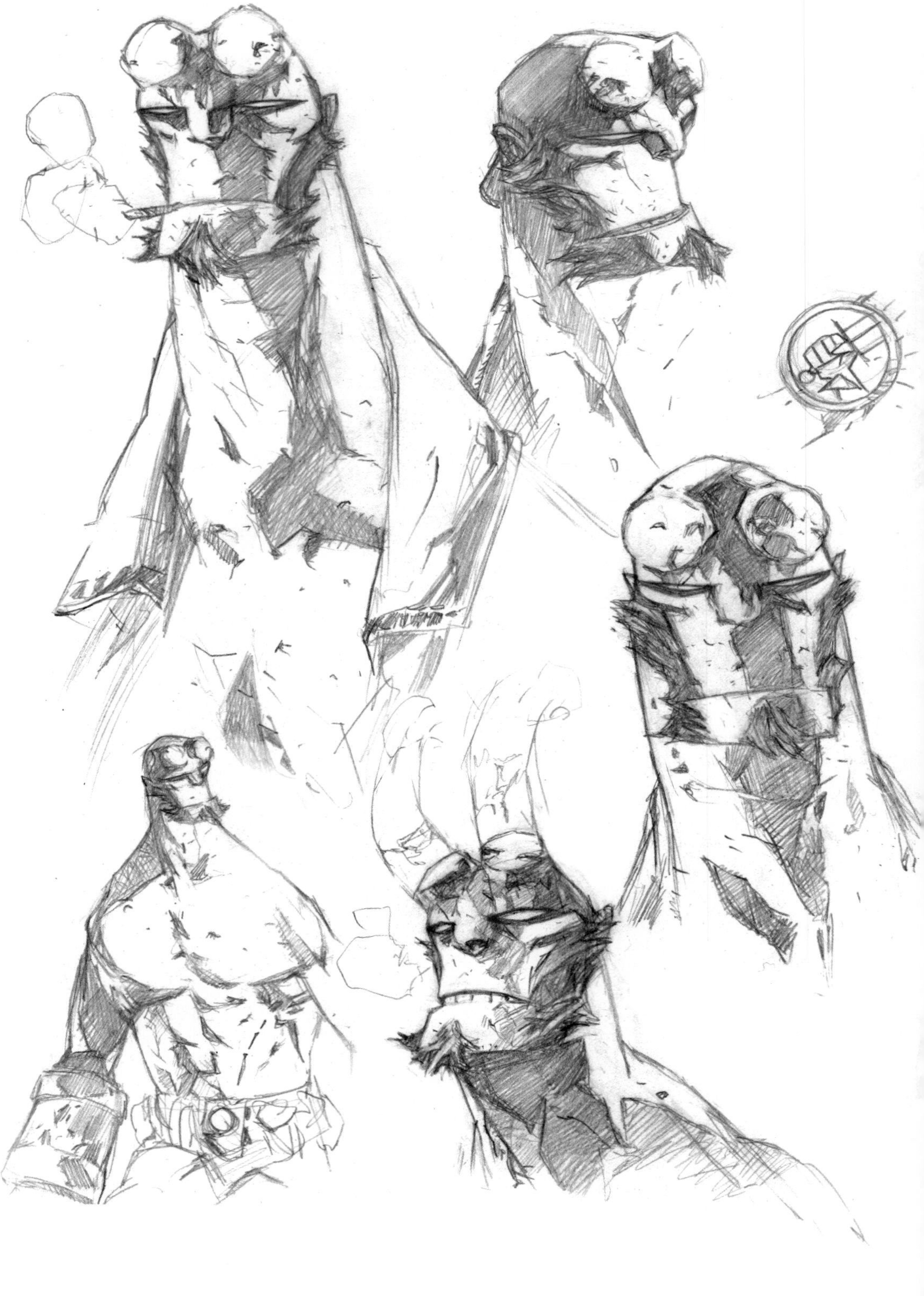

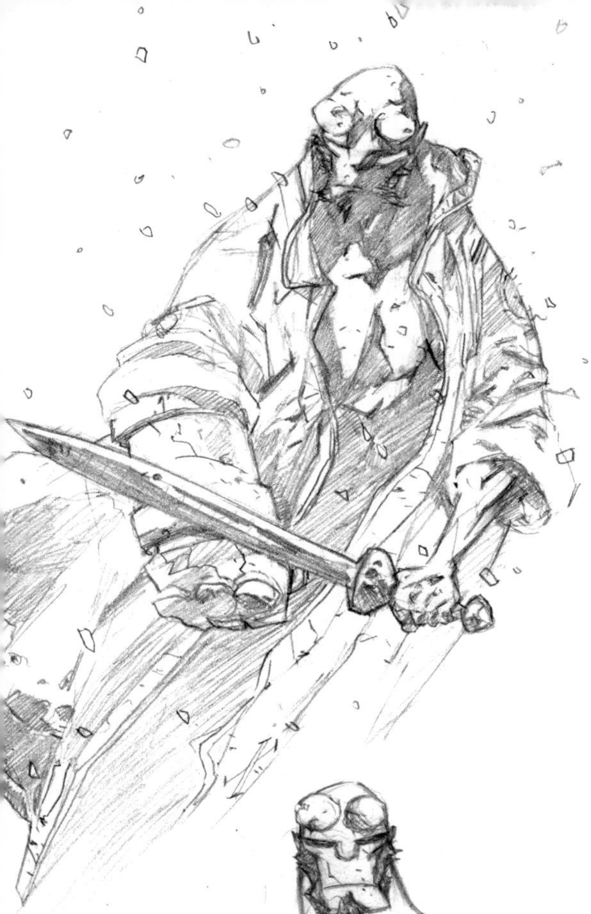
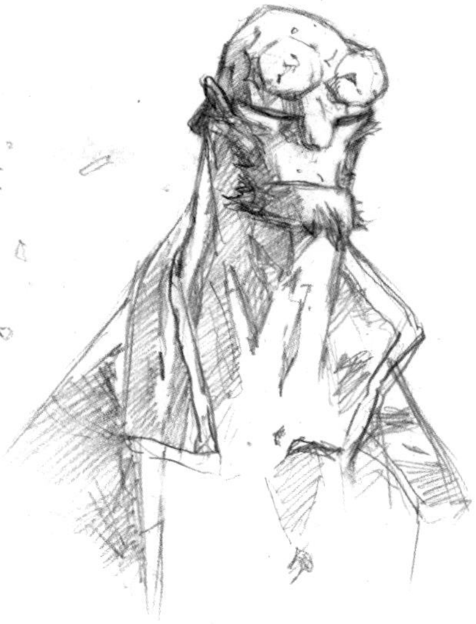
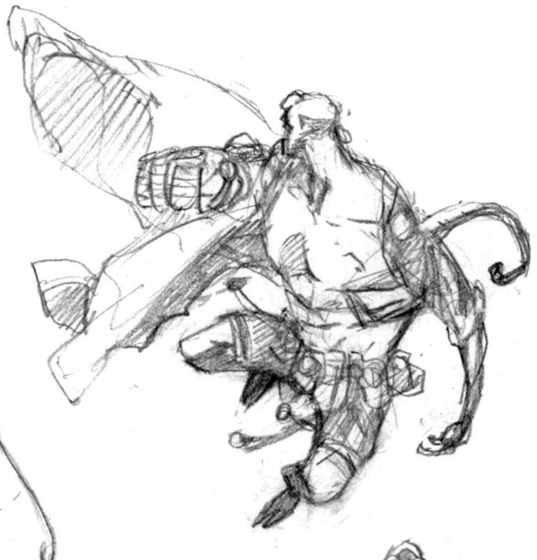
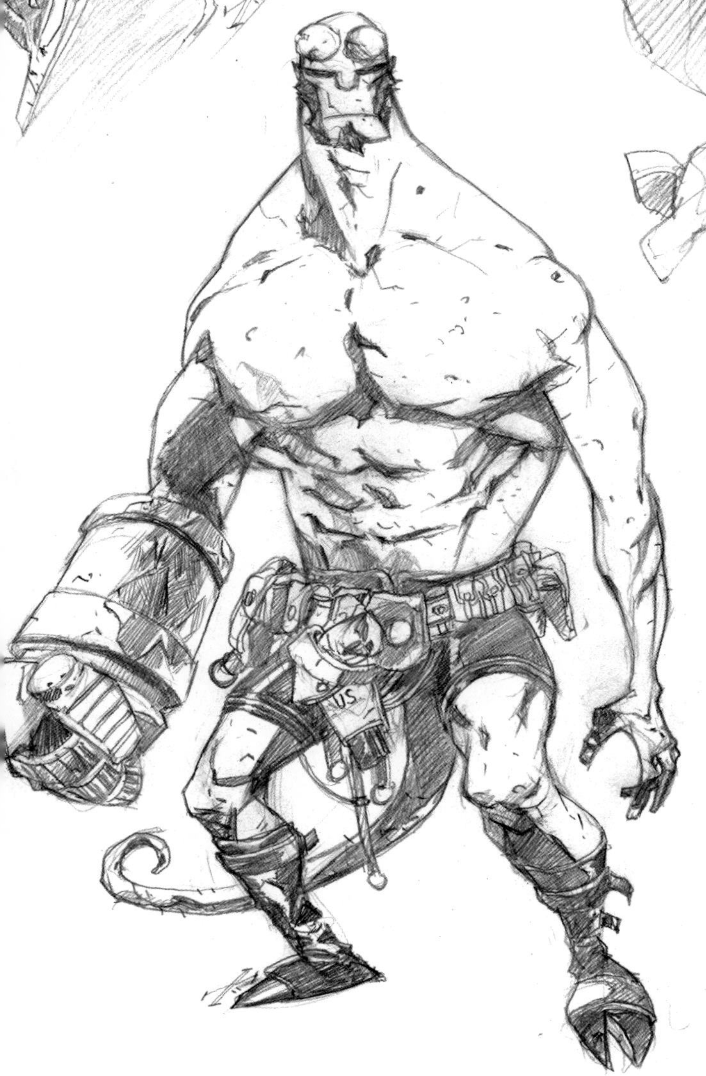
U.S.
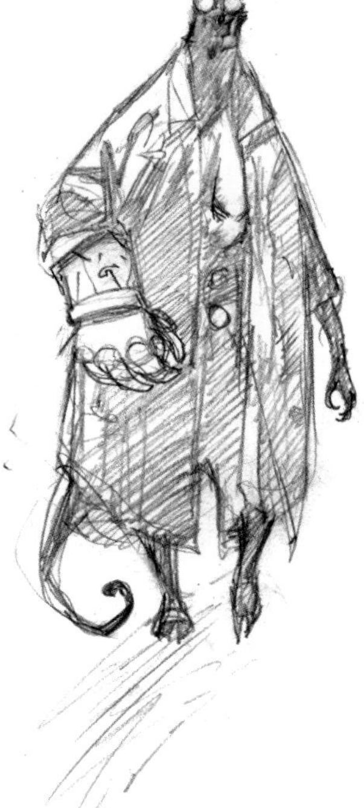

Max adapted a handful of characters from previous stories. Agent Raskin appeared years earlier in the Mignola-drawn Hellboy stories "Dr. Carp's Experiment" and "The Ghoul, " while Agent Nichols was making his first appearance in the James Harren–drawn story *The Long Death* around the time Max was drawing this. With no printed version of Nichols available, we passed penciled pages back and forth between the artists to keep Nichols consistent.

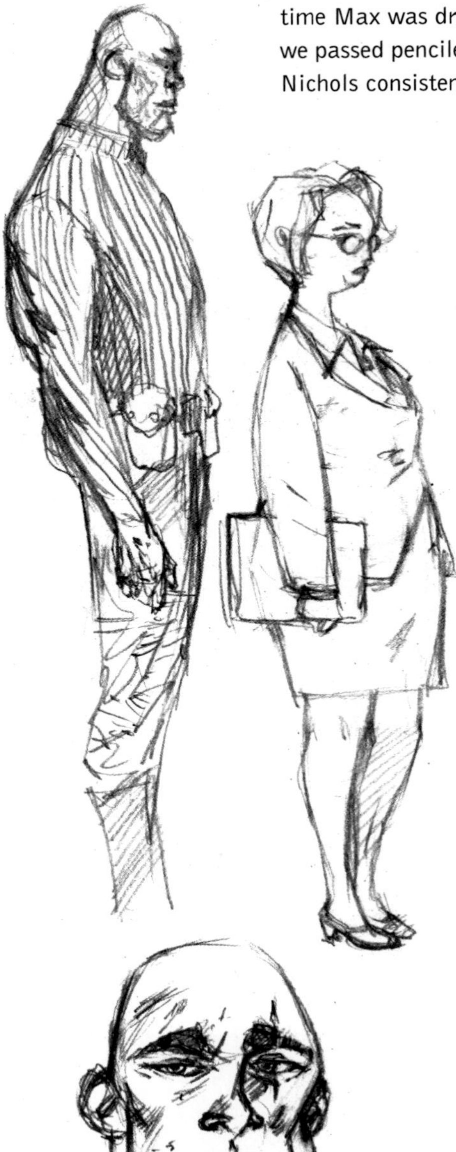

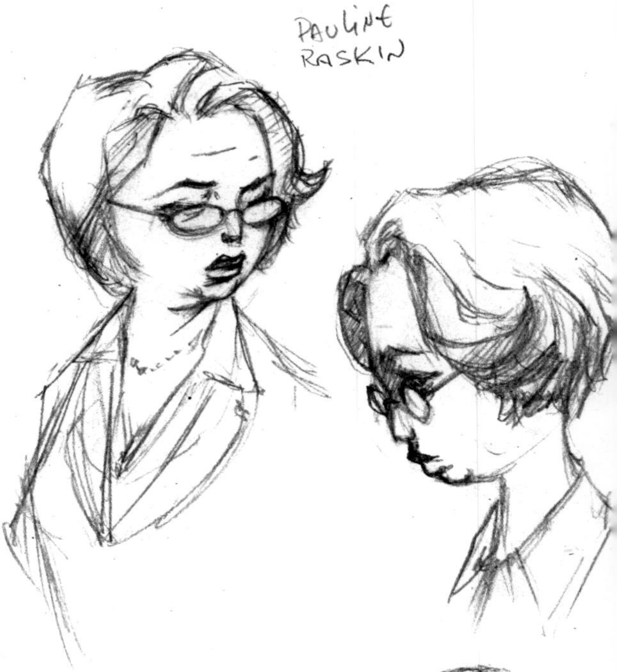
PAULINE
RASKIN

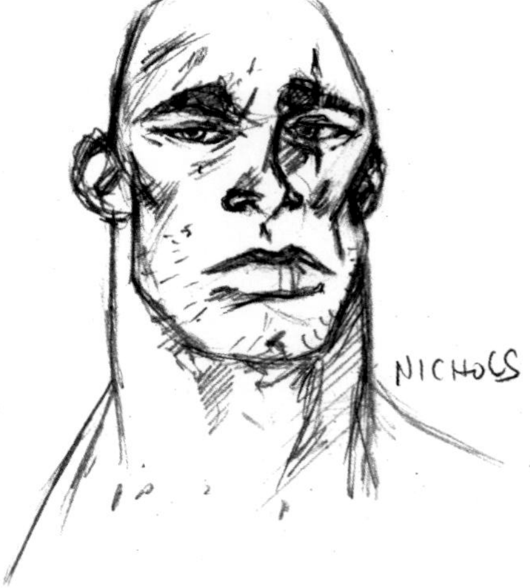
NICHOLS

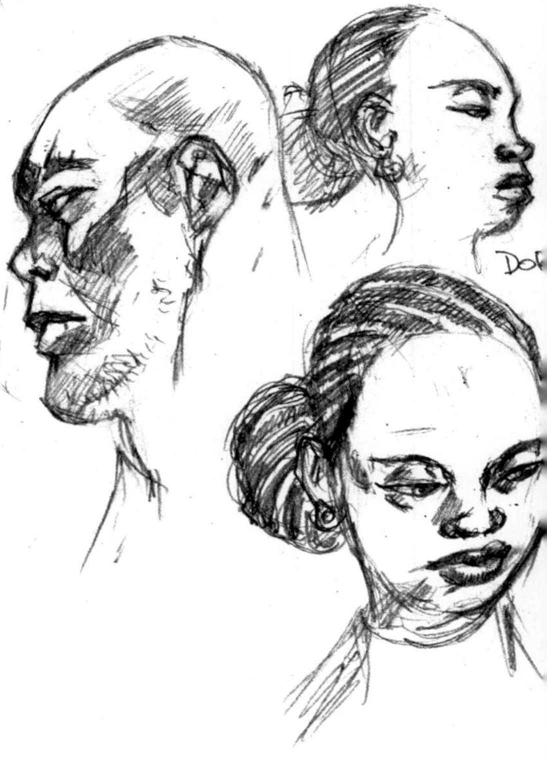

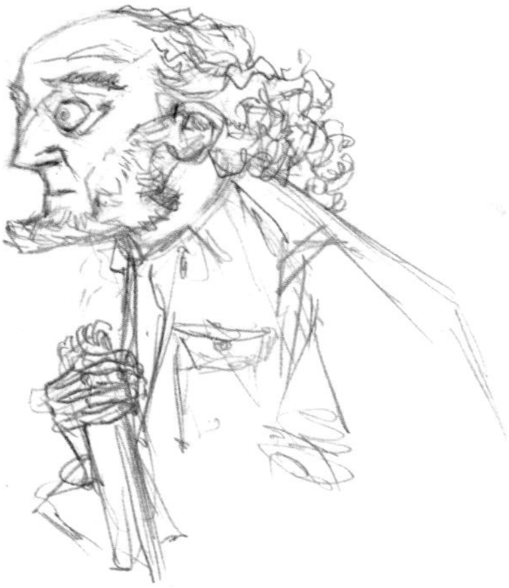

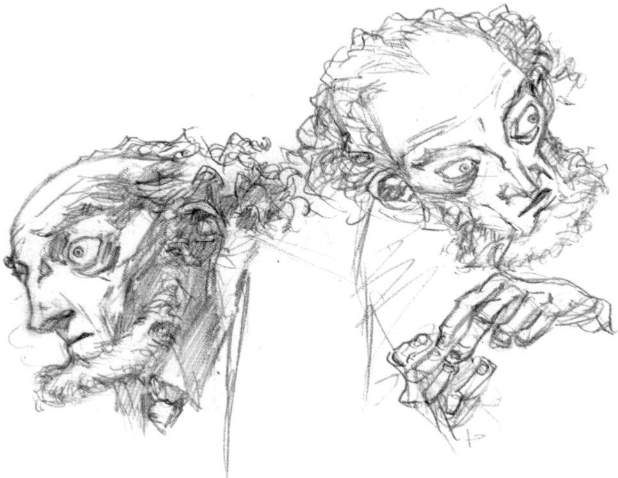

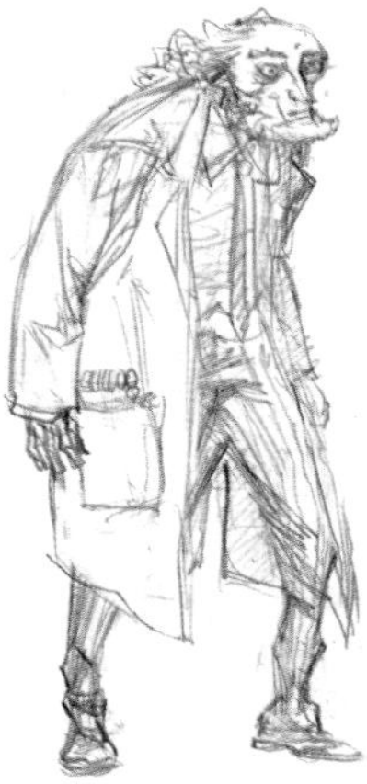

Professor O'Donnell had been established by Guy Davis, but Max created a younger version. Divizia and the minotaur are Max's own designs, and the bugs came from designs by Mike with Max putting his spin on them (following pages).

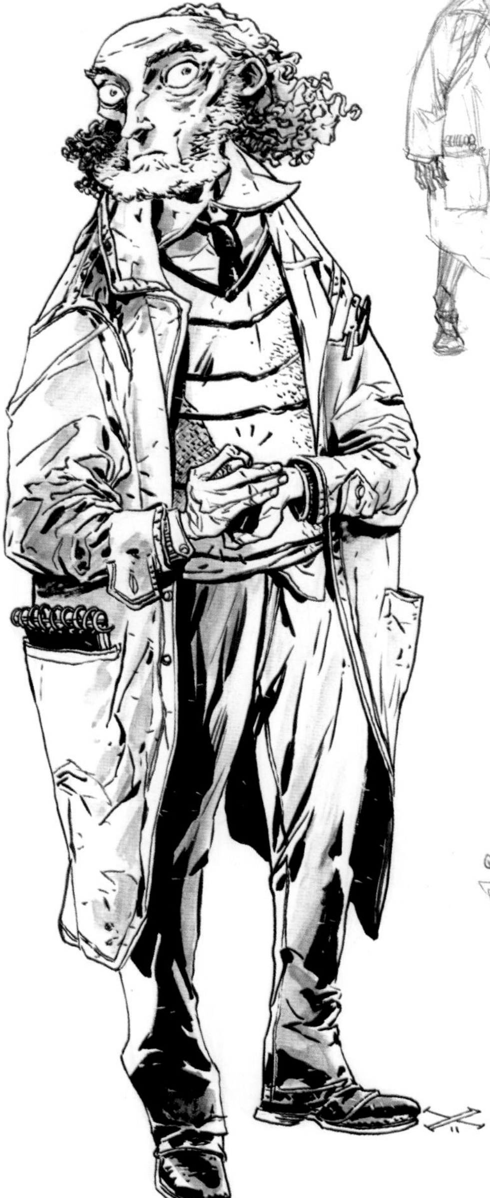

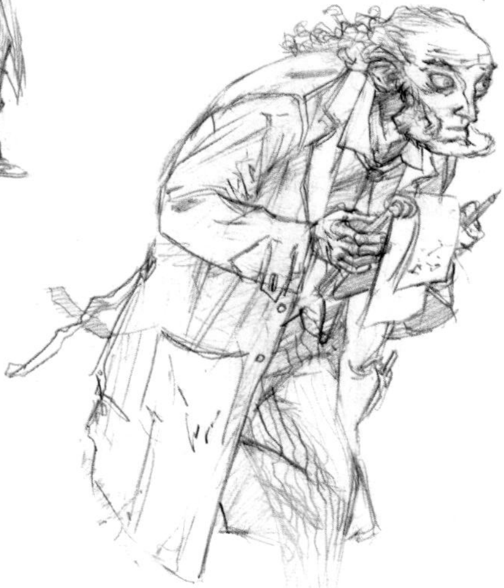

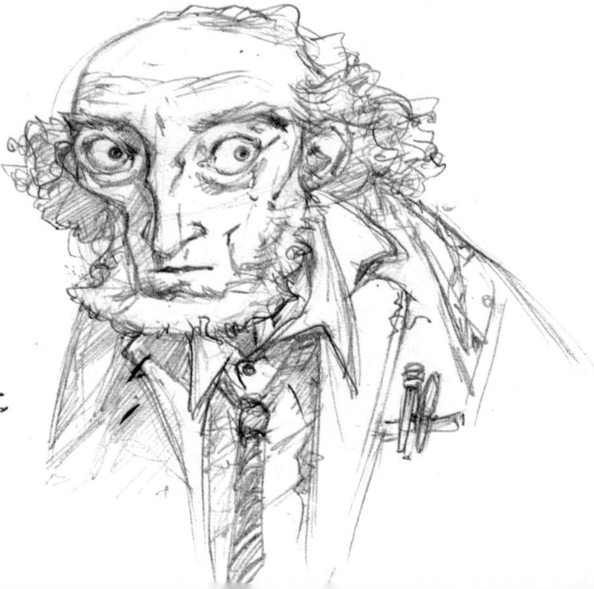

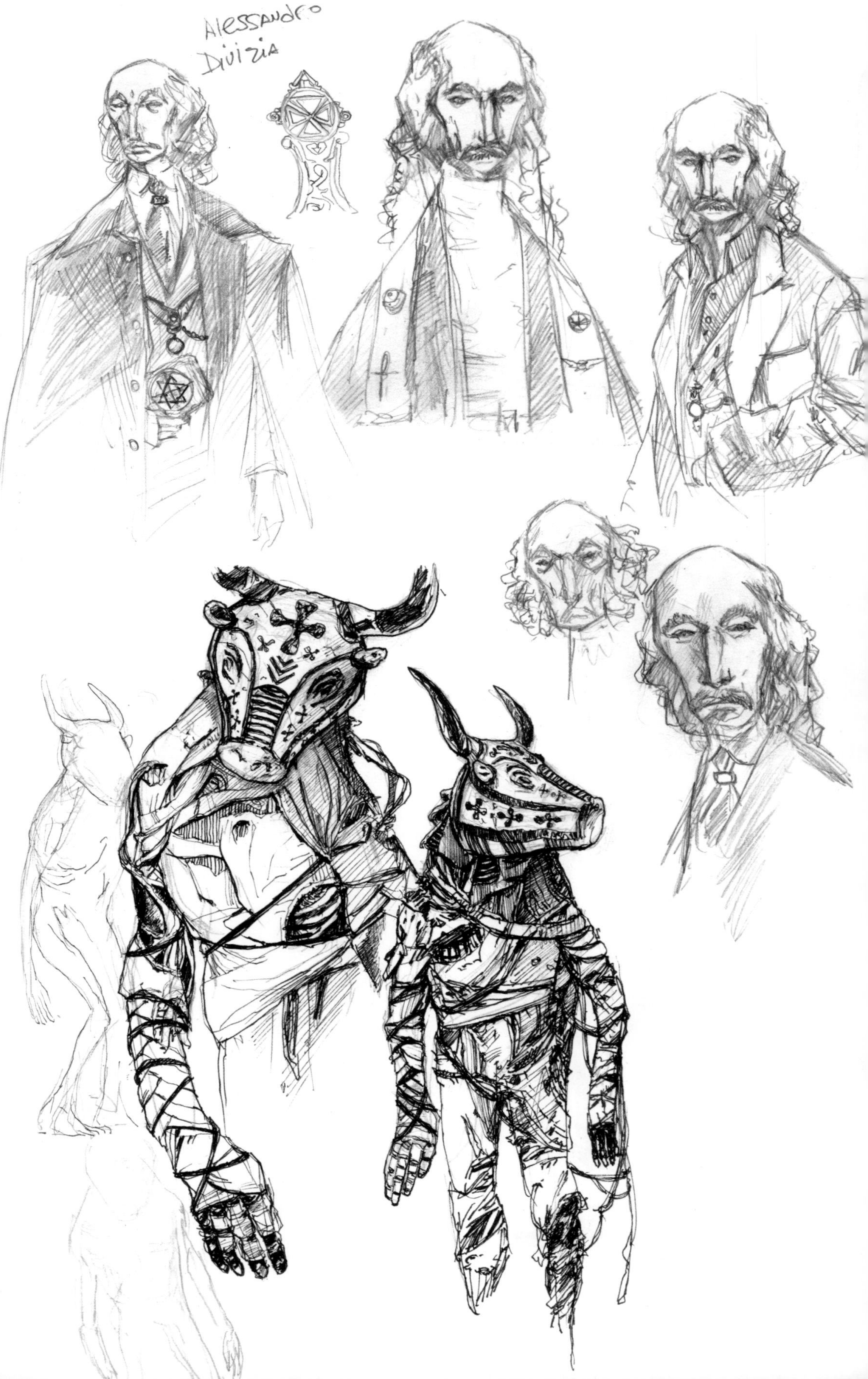
Alessandro
Divizia

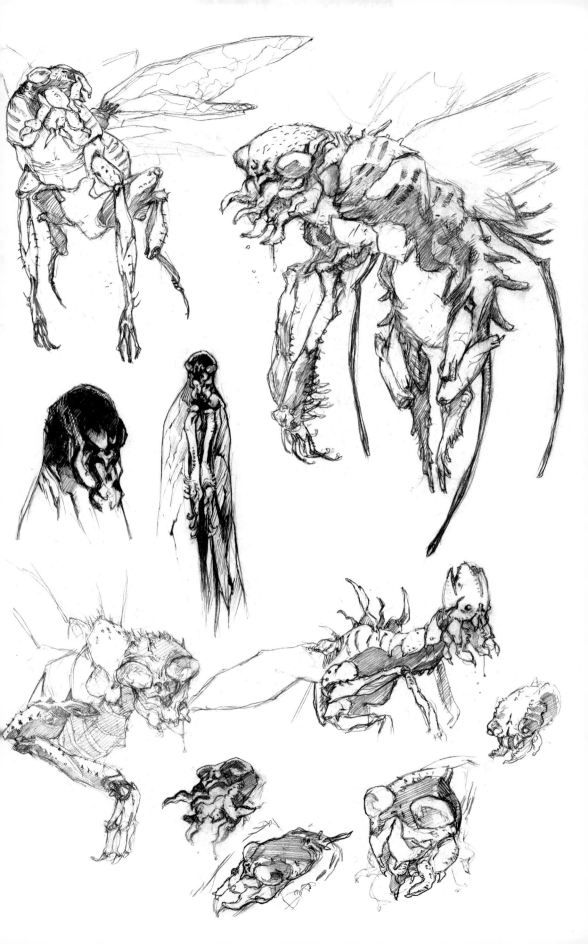

Mike had long threatened to do a caveman comic, at times planning on writing it himself, at times with John Arcudi. He had a lot of sketchbook material to give James Harren for *The Abyss of Time*.

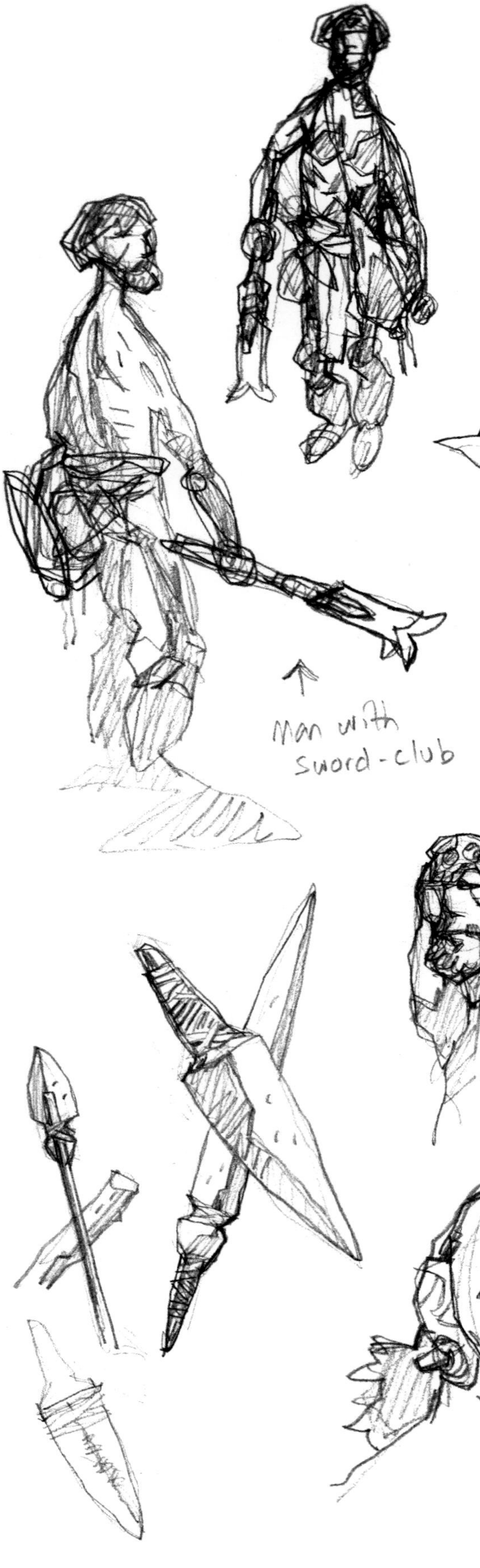
man with
sword-club

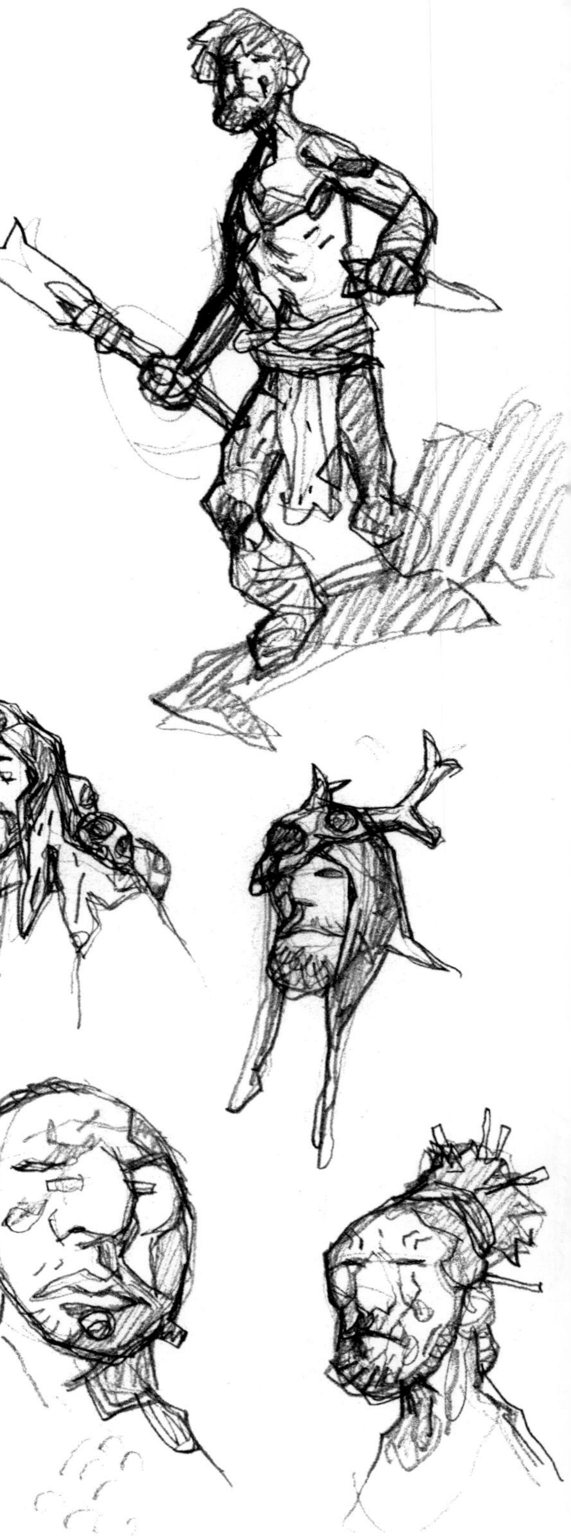

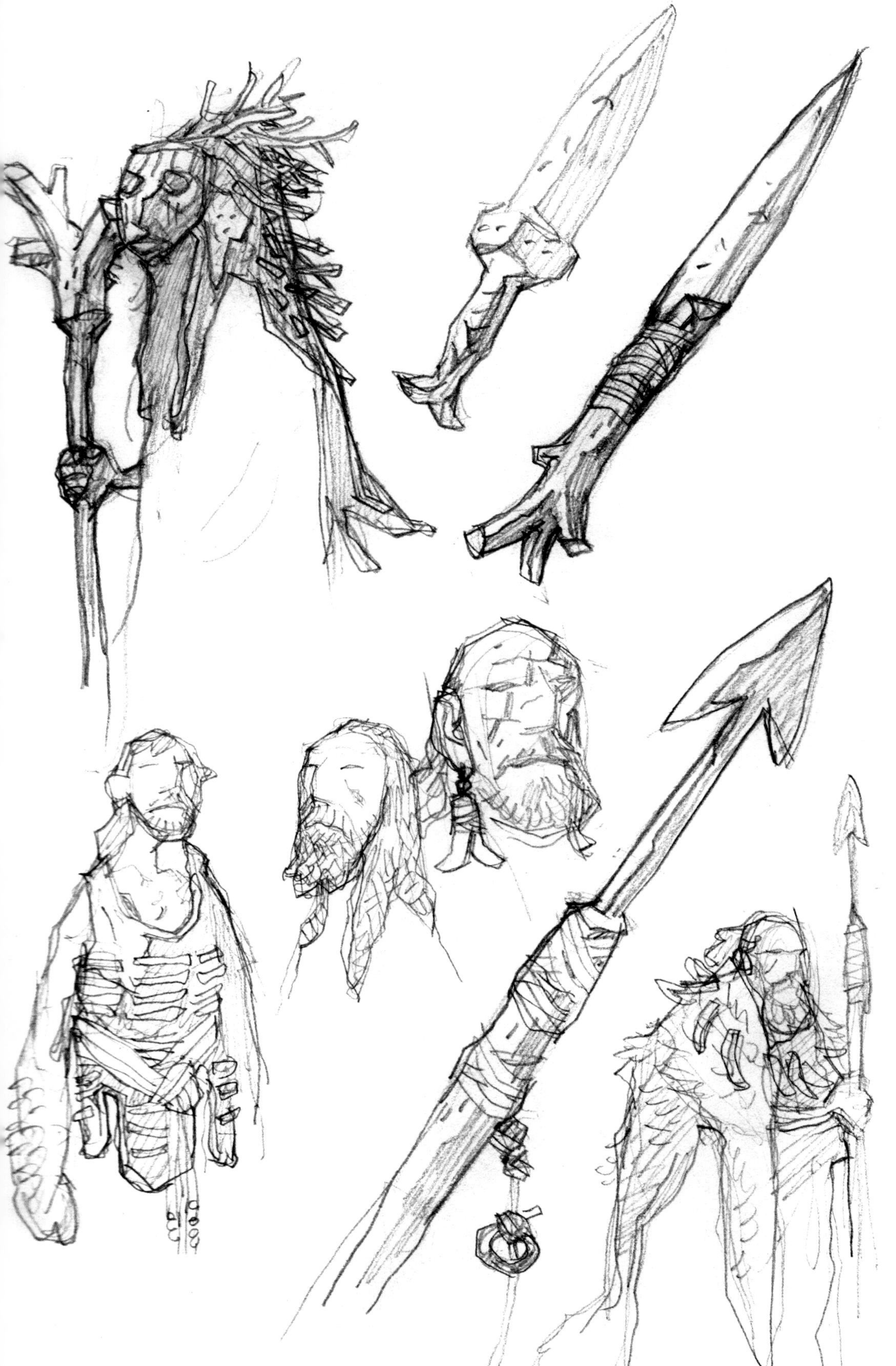

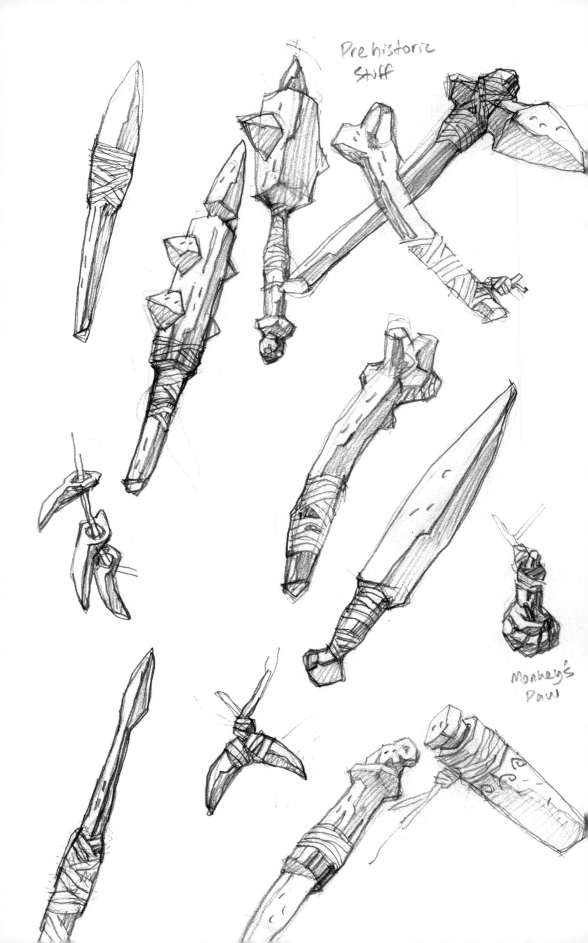

Prehistoric
Stuff

Monkey's
Paw

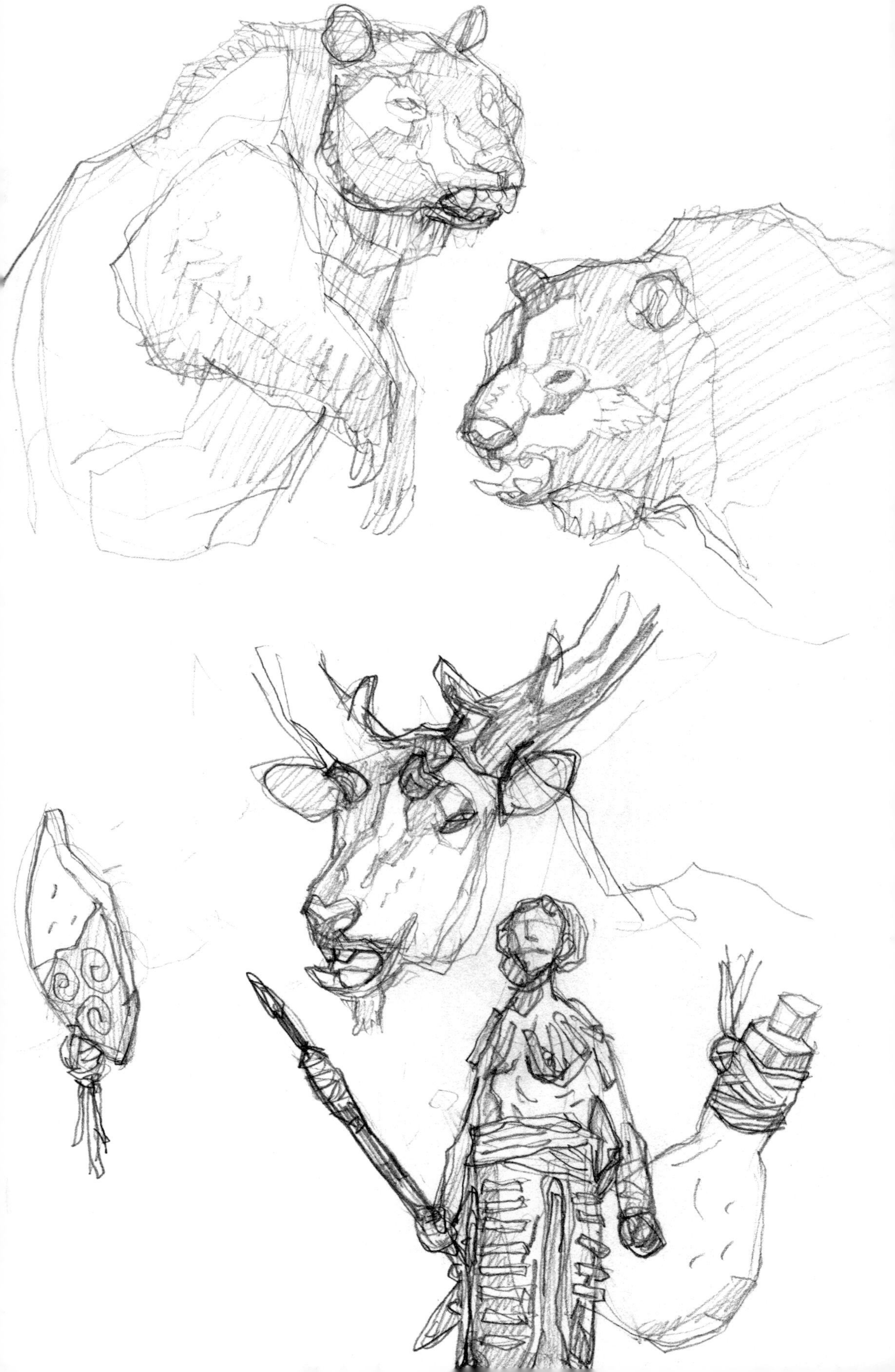

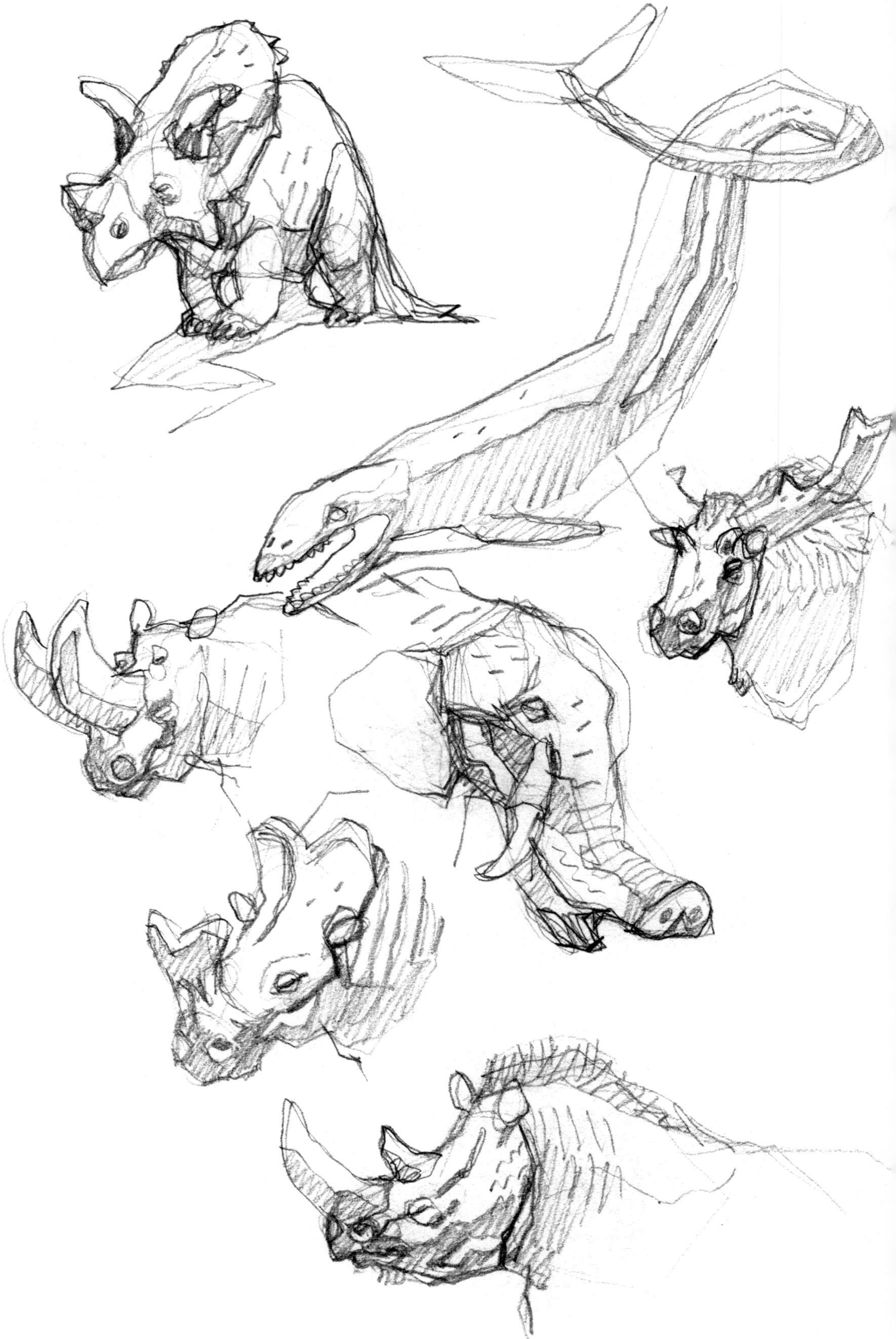

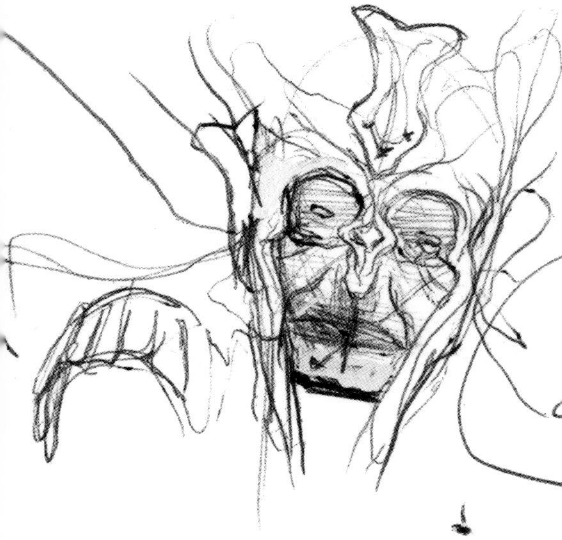

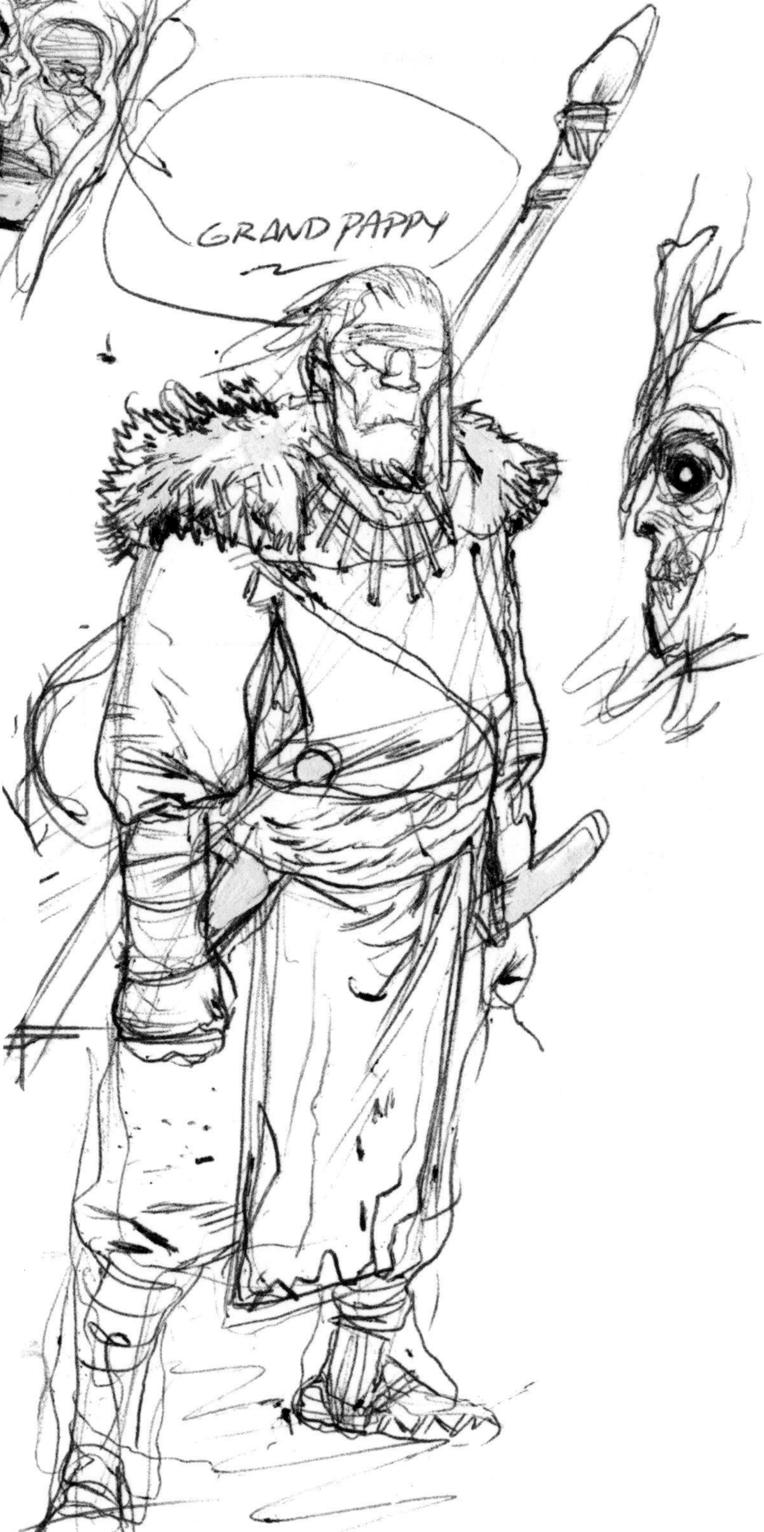
GRAND PAPPY

Having fallen in love with James's work on *The Devil Does Not Jest* and *The Long Death*, we gave him a lot of room to design the details of the story himself.

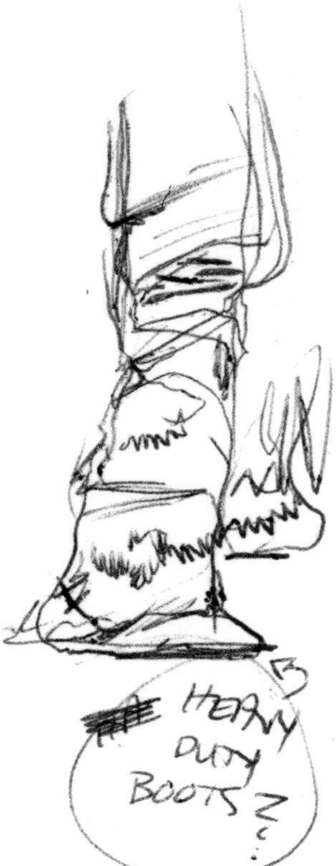
HEAVY DUTY BOOTS ?

For a long time we called this story *B.P.R.D.: Caveman*, until it was time to announce it, when we came up with the actual title.

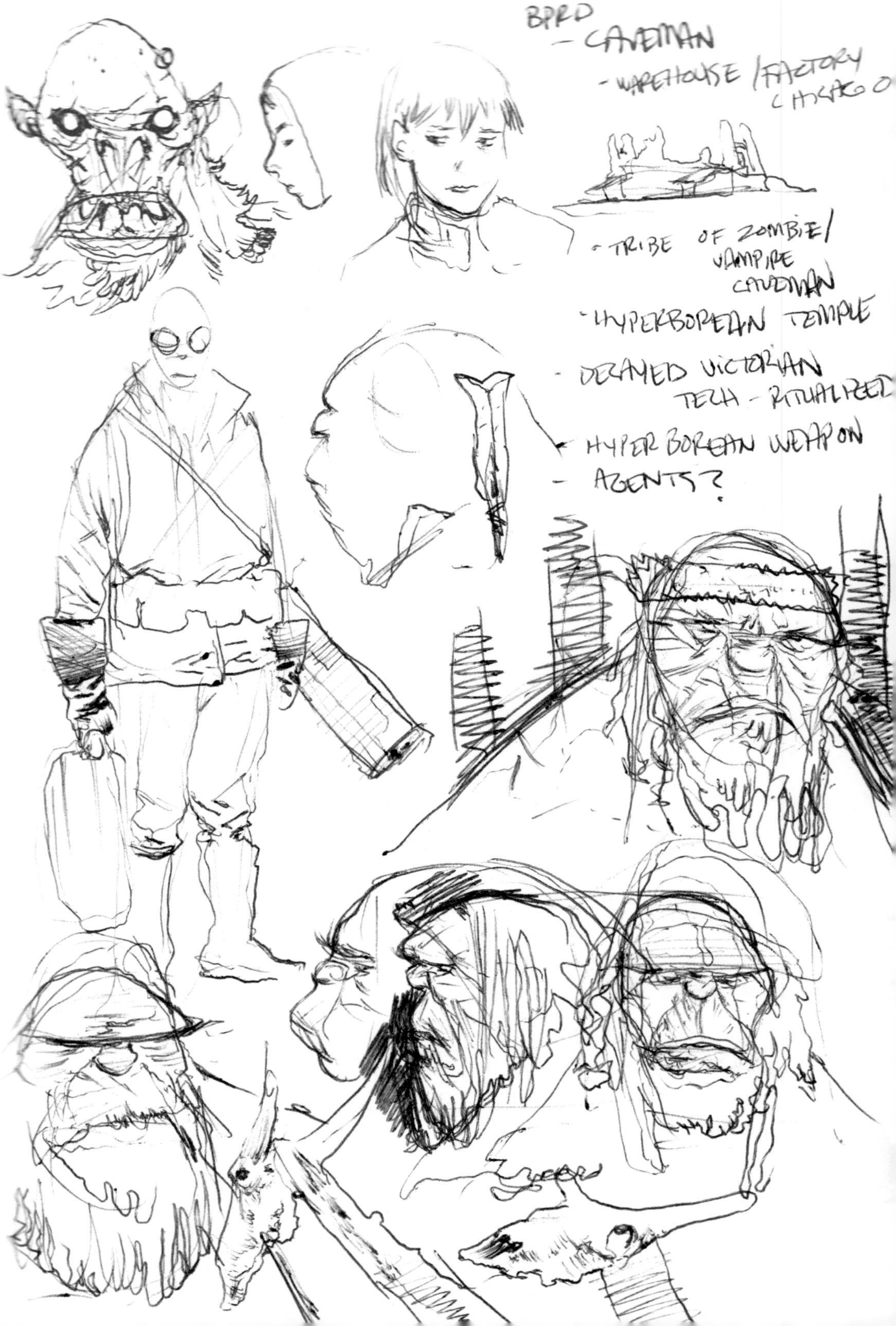
BPRD
- CAVEMAN
- WAREHOUSE / FACTORY
CHICAGO
- TRIBE OF ZOMBIE / VAMPIRE CAVEMAN
- HYPERBOREAN TEMPLE
- DERANGED VICTORIAN TECH - RITUALIZED
- HYPER BOREAN WEAPON
- AGENTS?

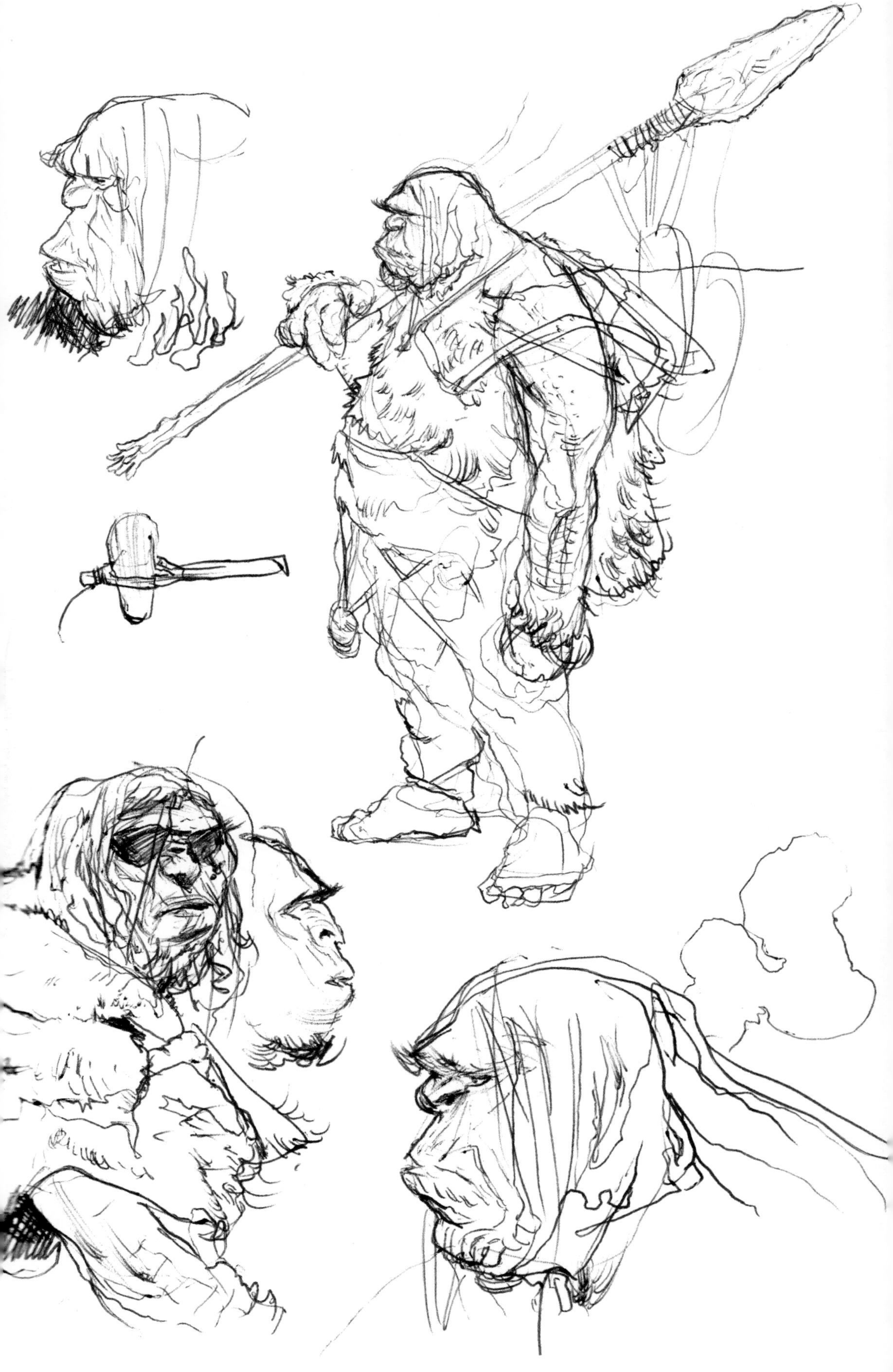

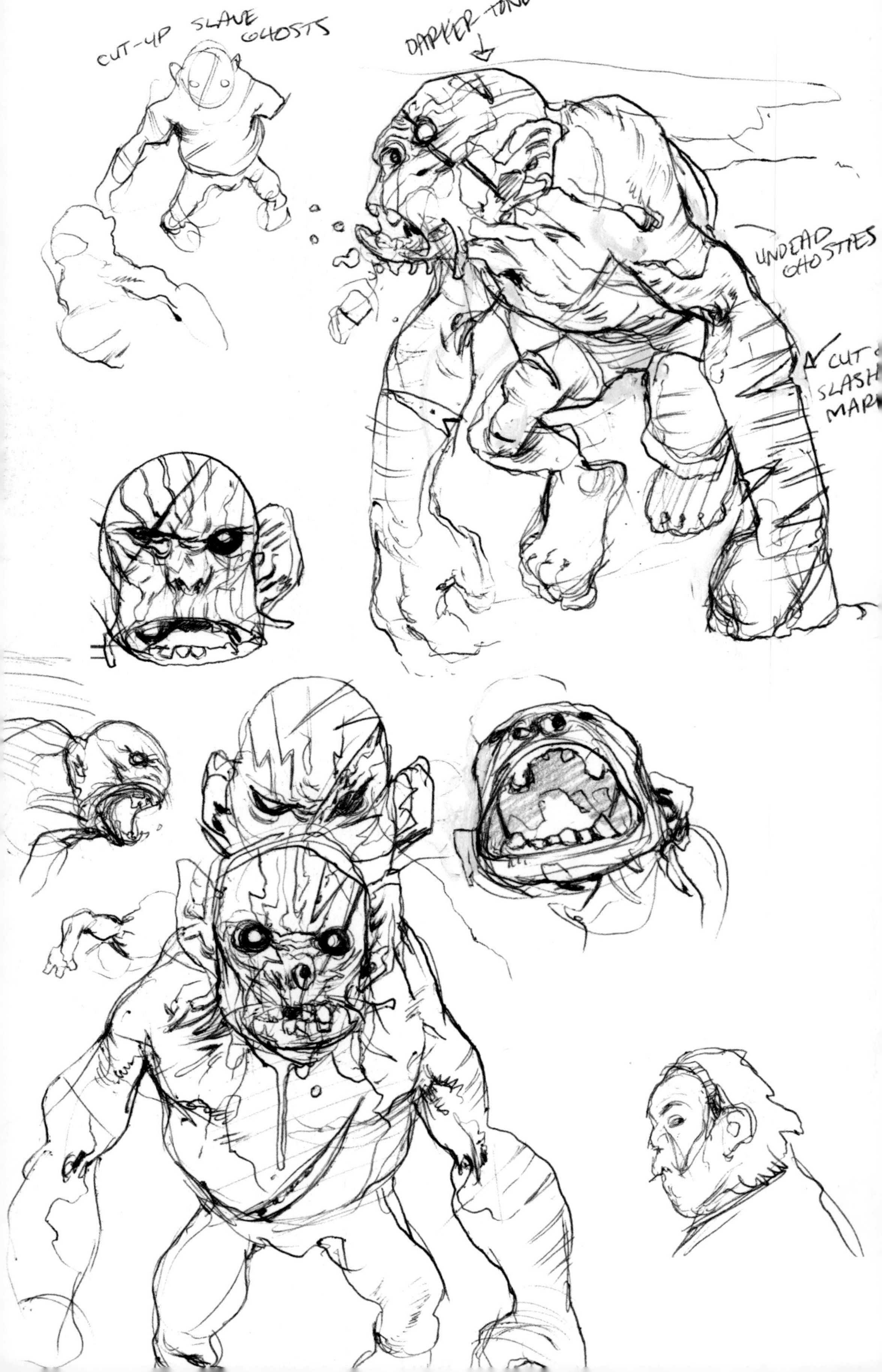
CUT-UP SLAVE GHOSTS
DARKER TONE
UNDEAD GHOSTIES
CUT
SLASH
MAR

We love James's wild imagination, but sometimes we need him to rein it in, as with the Cold People, whose initial designs were more inhuman than fit the story.

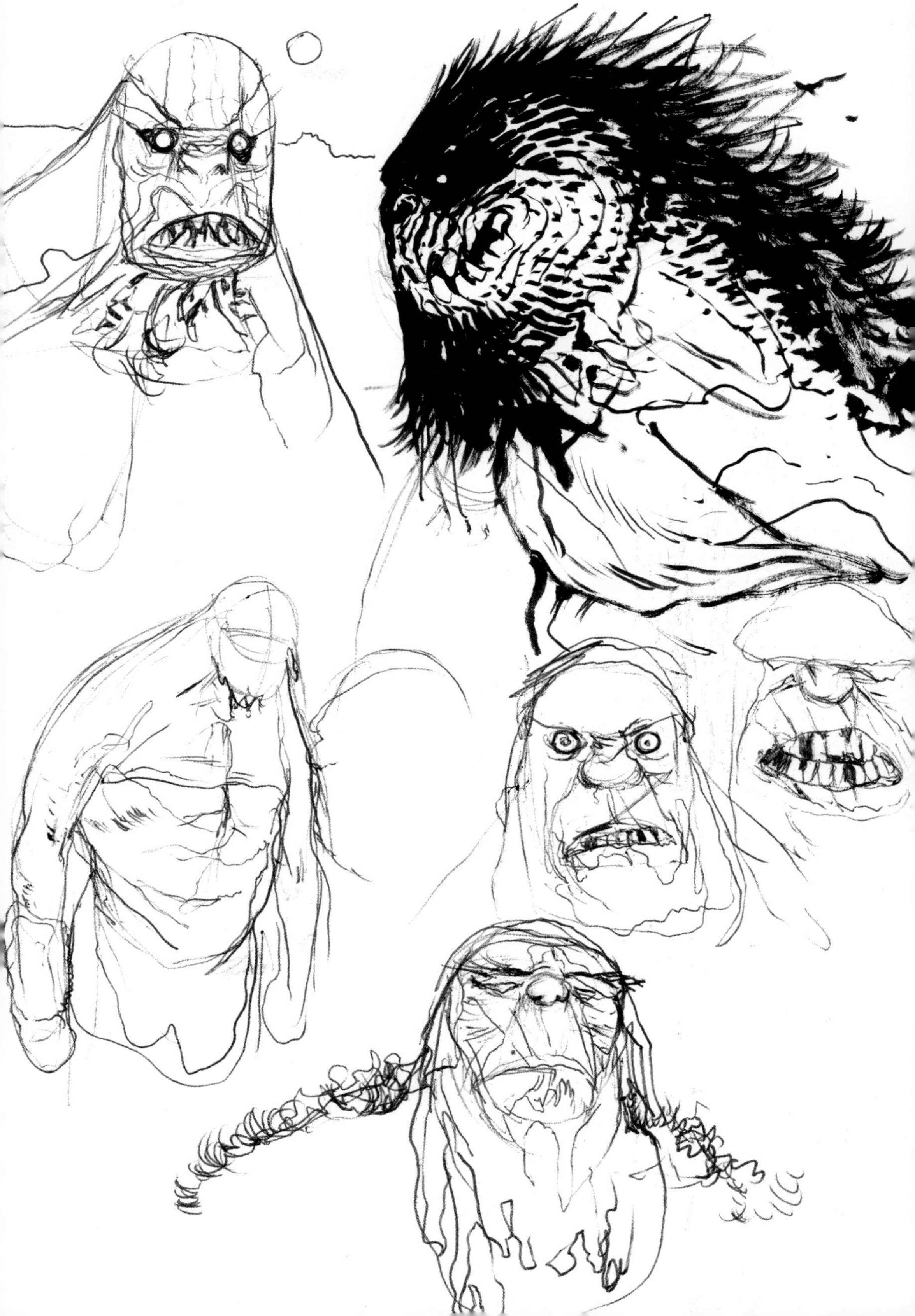

His Ogdru Hem
was perfect.

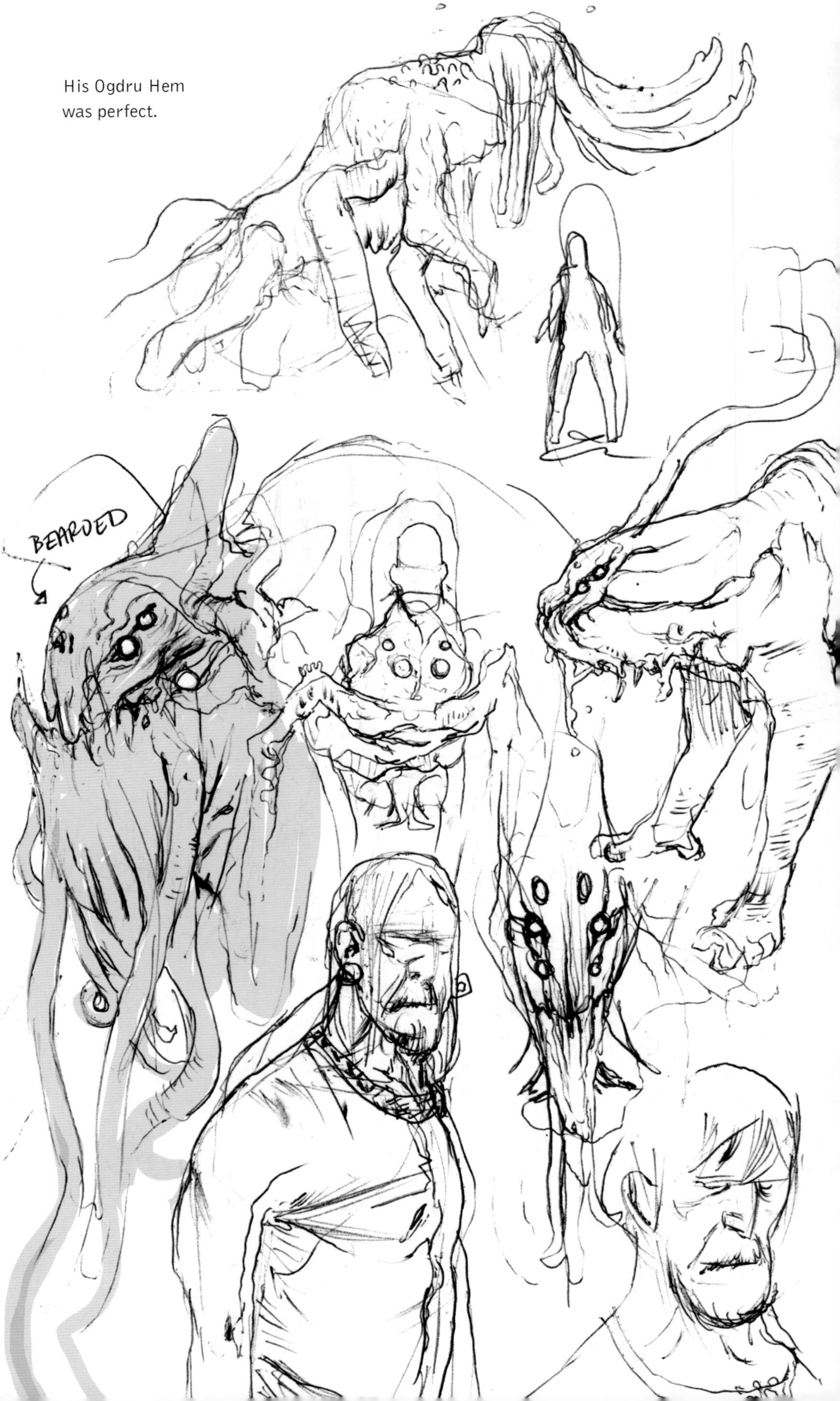
BEARDED

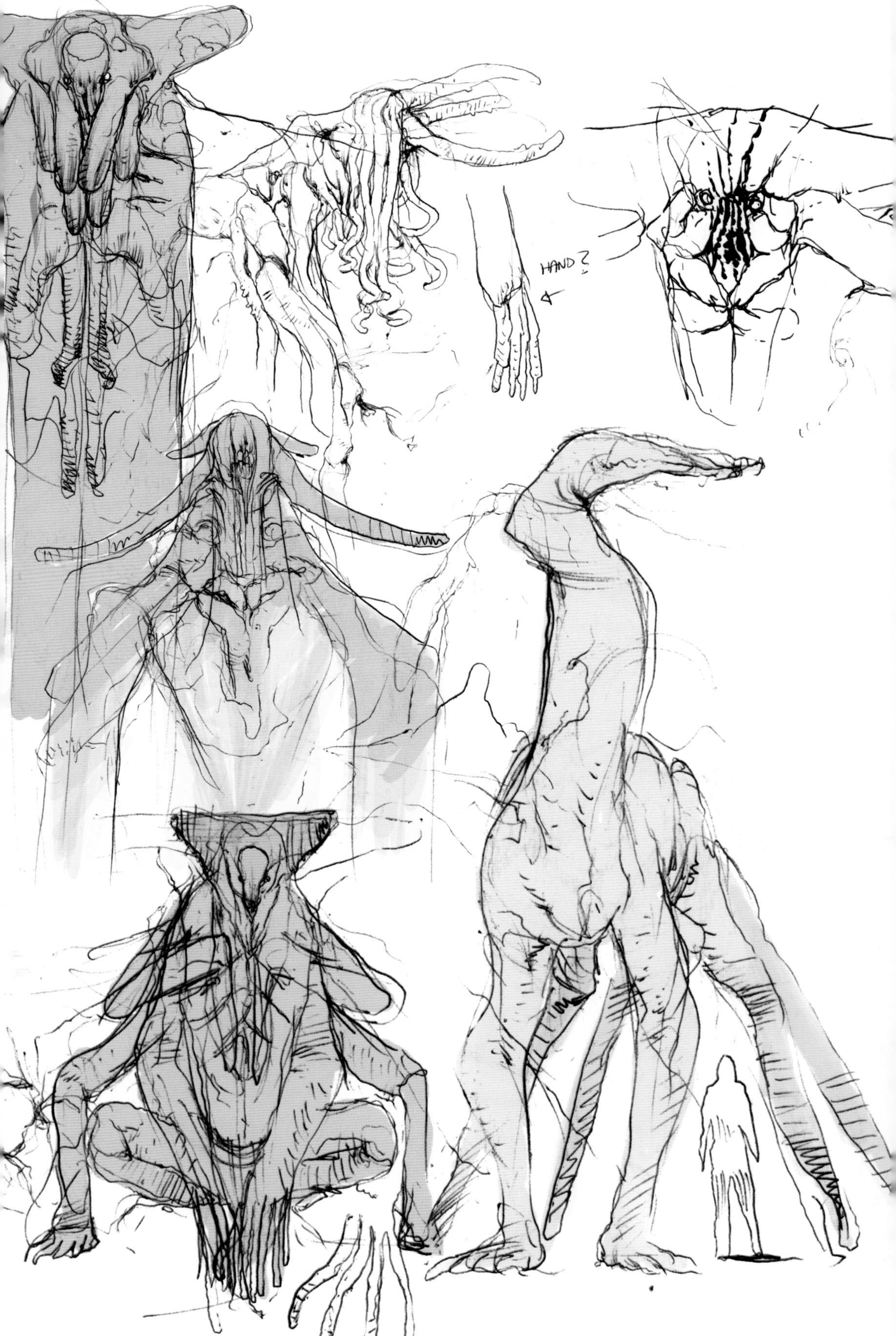
HAND ?

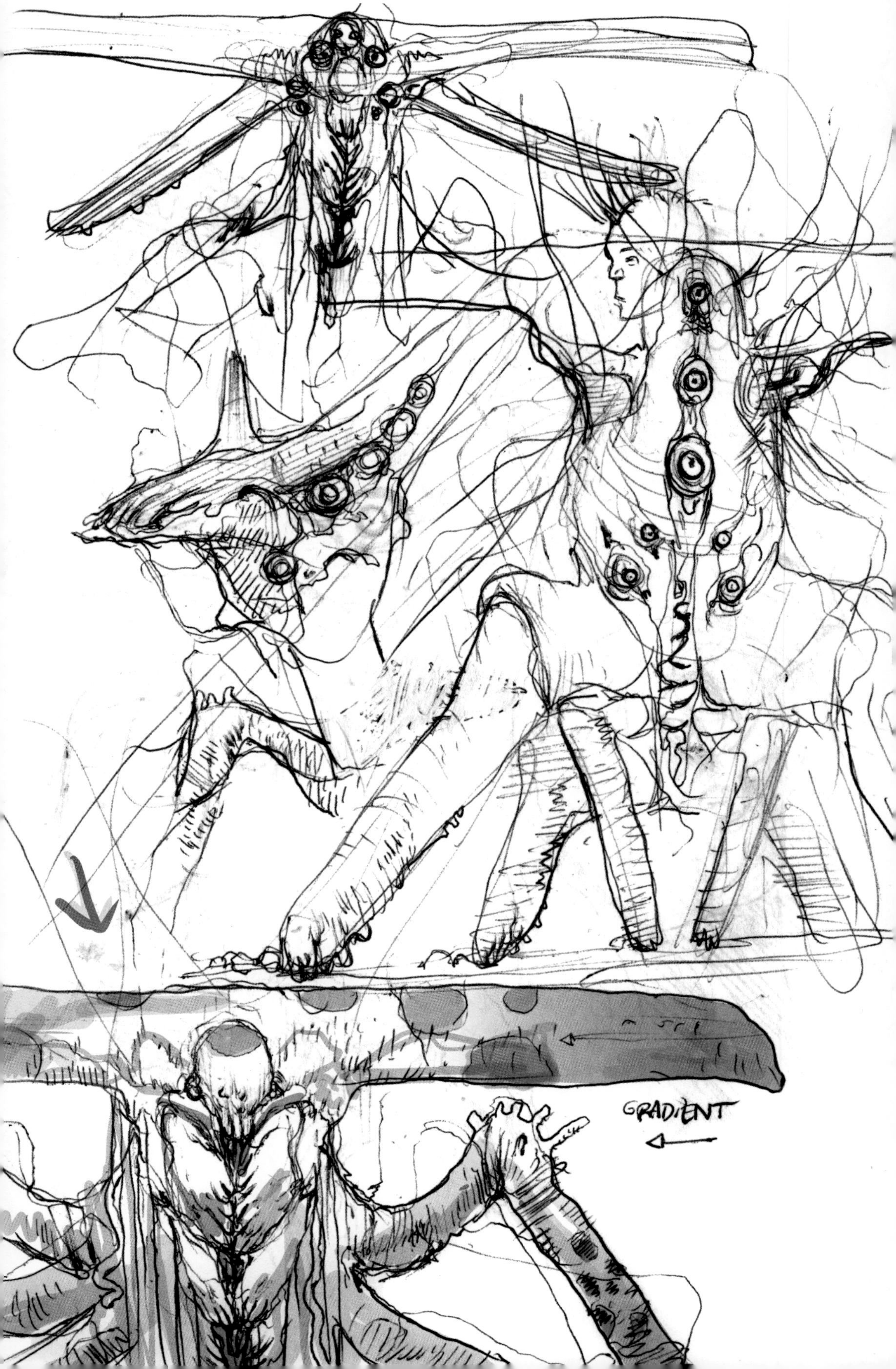
GRADIENT

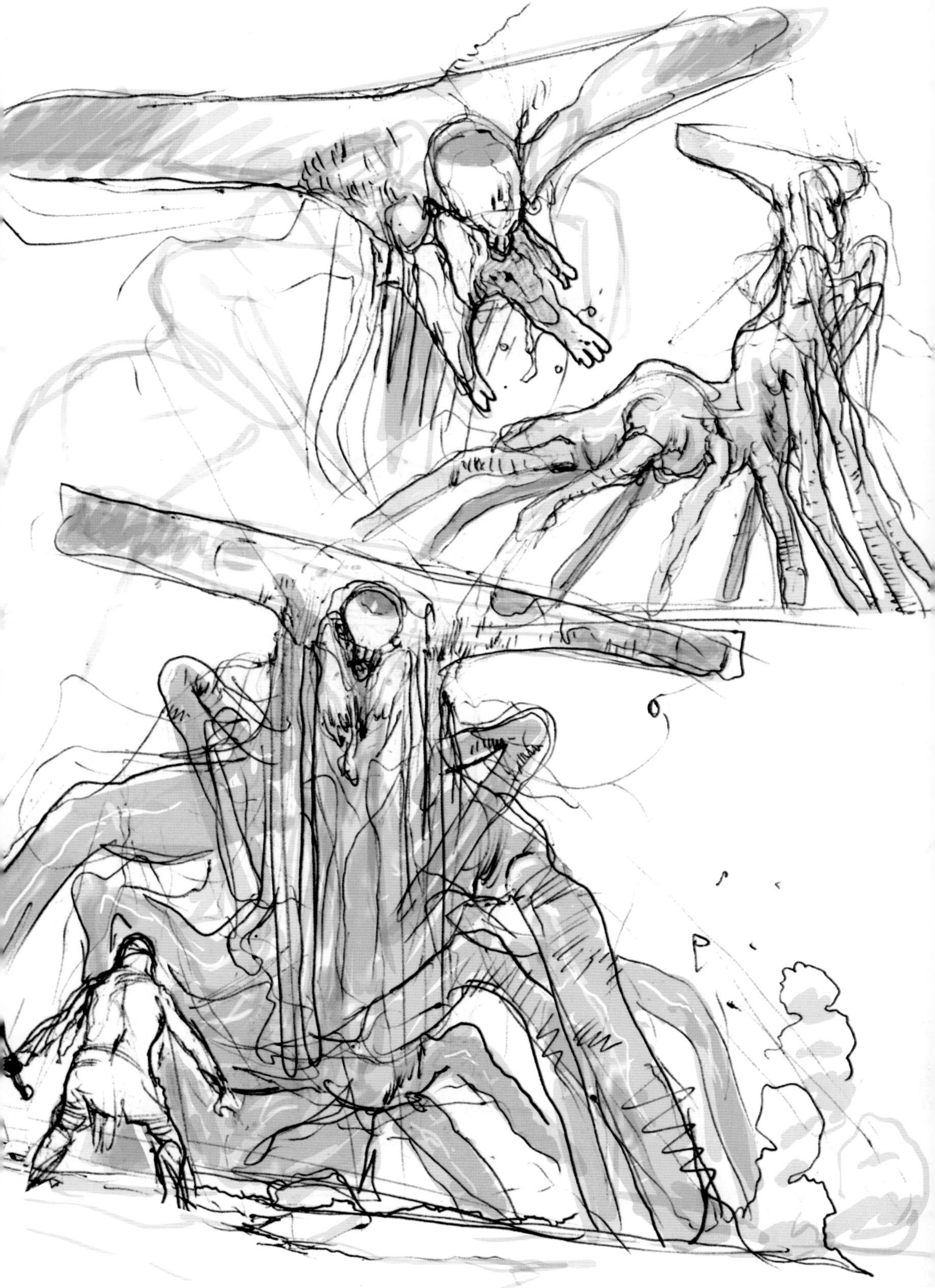

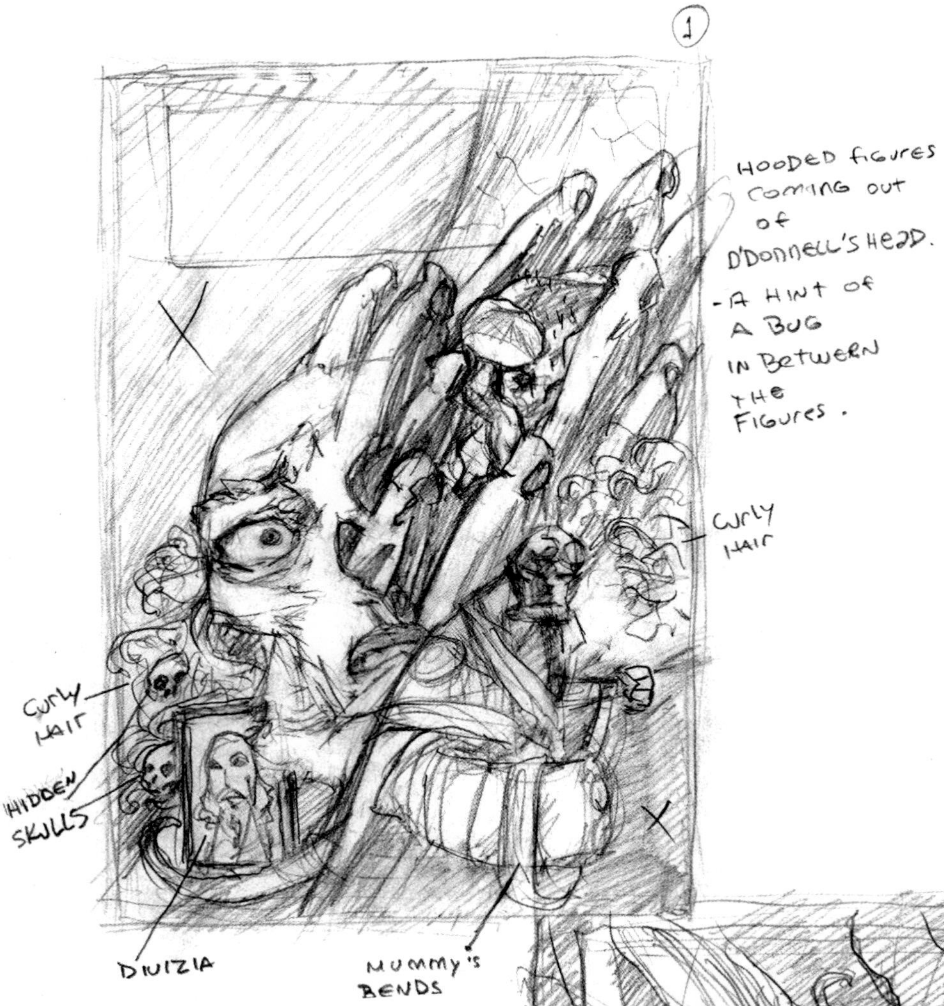
1
HOODED figures coming out of O'DONNELL'S HEAD.
- A HINT OF A BUG IN BETWEEN THE FIGURES.
CURLY HAIR
CURLY HAIR
HIDDEN SKULLS
DIVIZIA
MUMMY'S BENDS

Max's cover sketches for *The Transformation of J. H. O'Donnell*, and tight pencils. Compare to the final, on page 51.

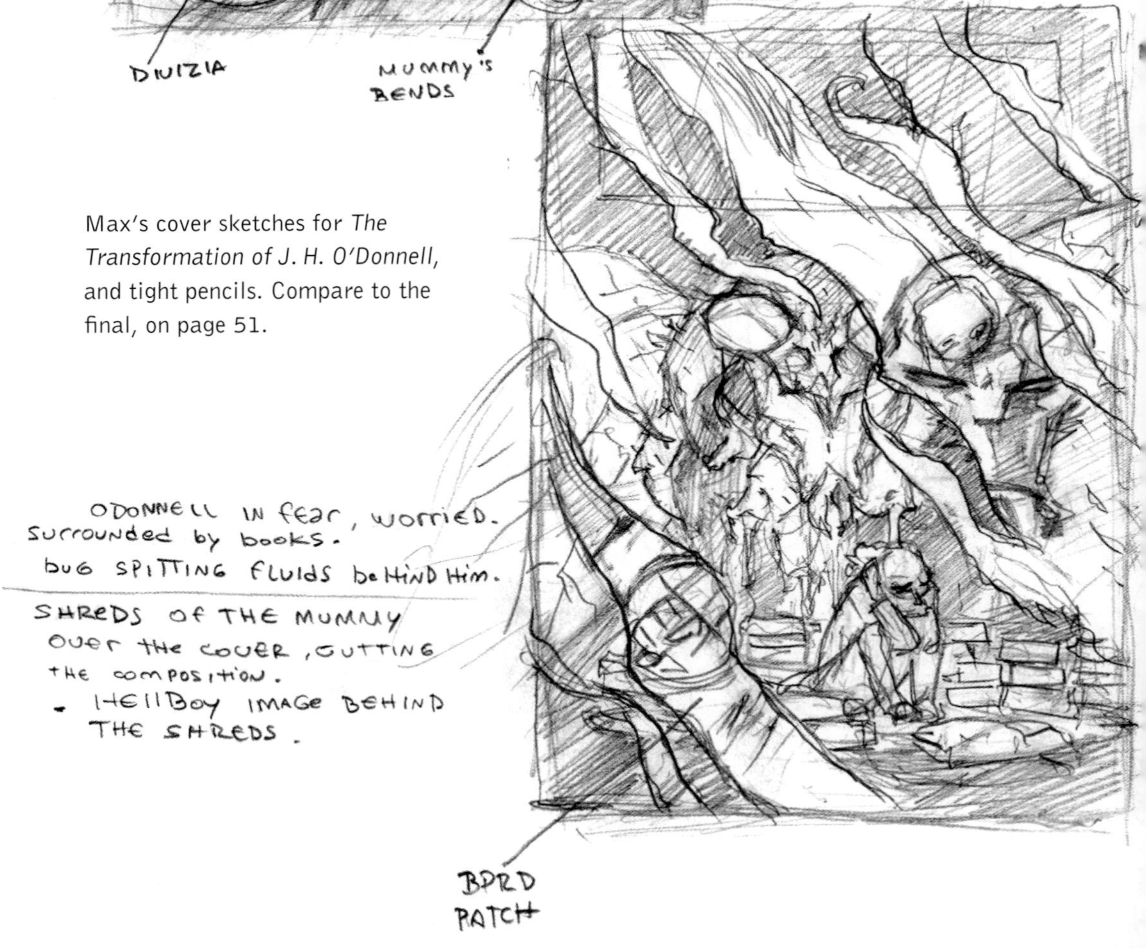
ODONNELL IN fear, worried. surrounded by books. bug SPITTING fluids behind Him.
SHREDS OF THE MUMMY OVER THE COVER, CUTTING THE COMPOSITION.
- HELLBOY IMAGE BEHIND THE SHREDS.
BPRD PATCH

ISSUE: ARTIST:

ALL "BLEED" ART MUST EXTEND TO THIS OUTERMOST DOTTED LINE.

TRIM MARKS INDICATE WHERE A PAGE IS CUT TO SIZE.

ALL LETTERING AND ESSENTIAL ART MUST FALL WITHIN THIS SOLID "LIVE AREA" BOX. THIS IS THE BORDER FOR A STANDARD, NON-BLEED COMIC BOOK PAGE.

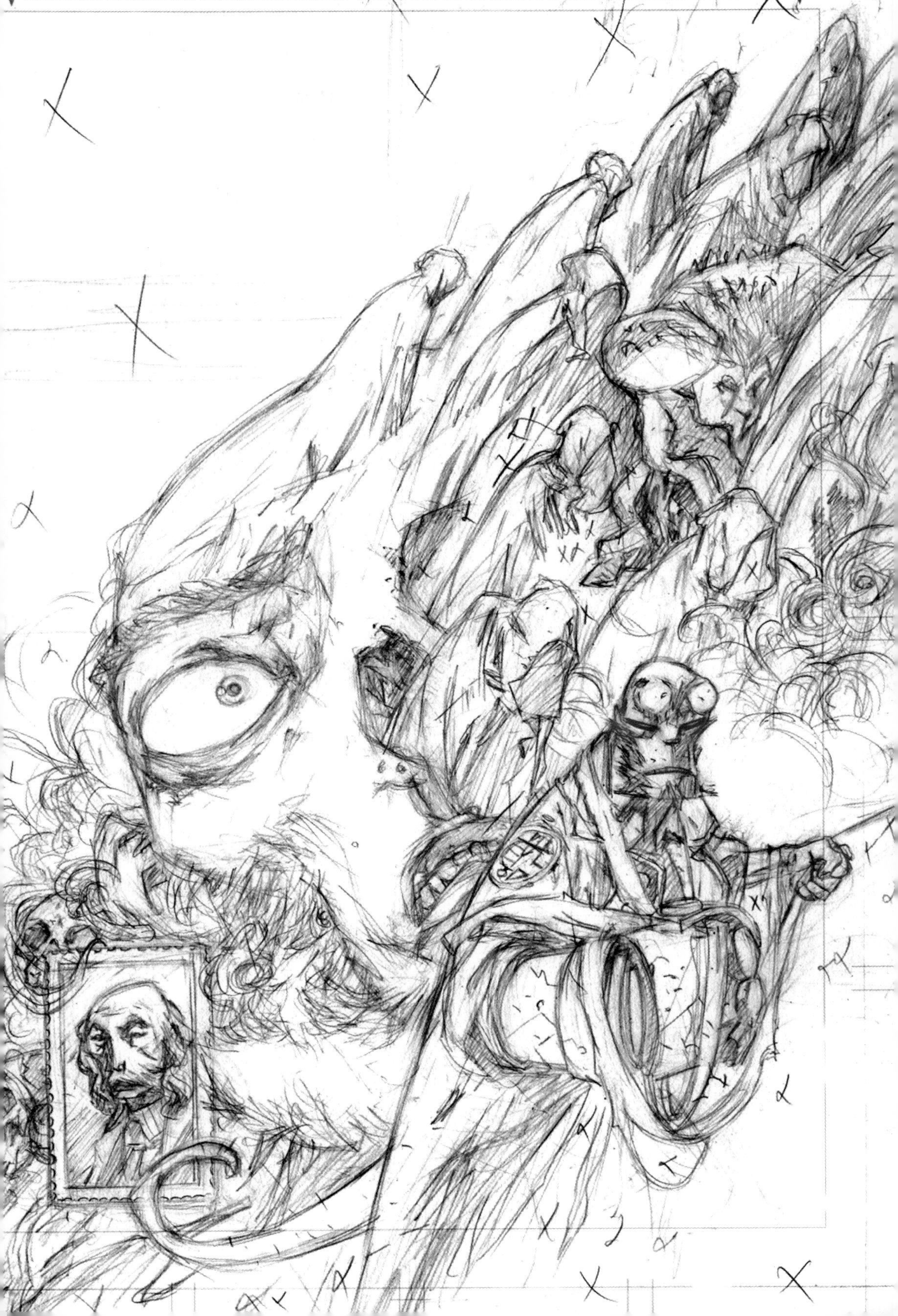

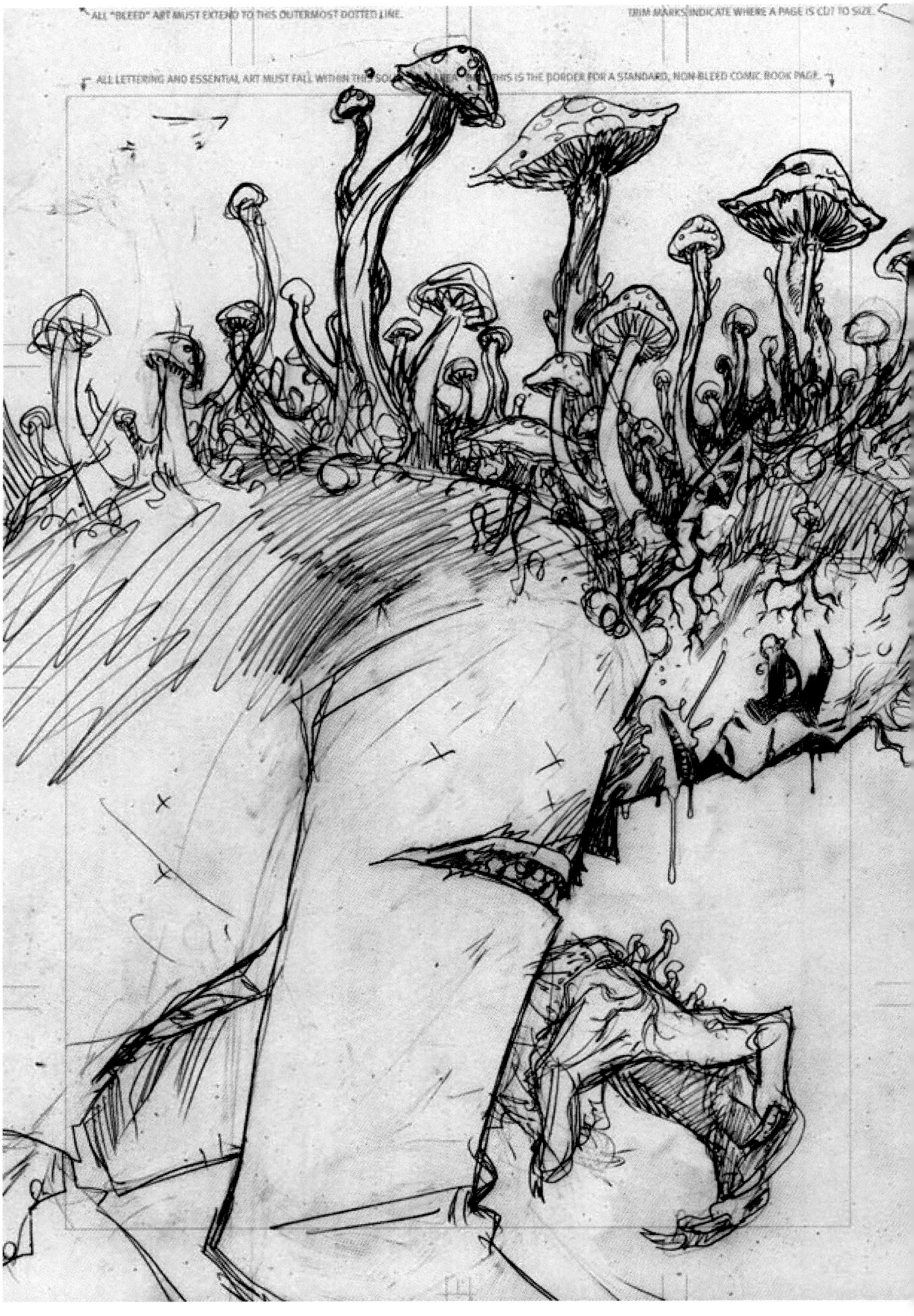
ALL "BLEED" ART MUST EXTEND TO THIS OUTERMOST DOTTED LINE.

Becky Cloonan's cover pencils for *The Pickens County Horror*, Part 2, and the final image. All covers are colored by Dave Stewart.

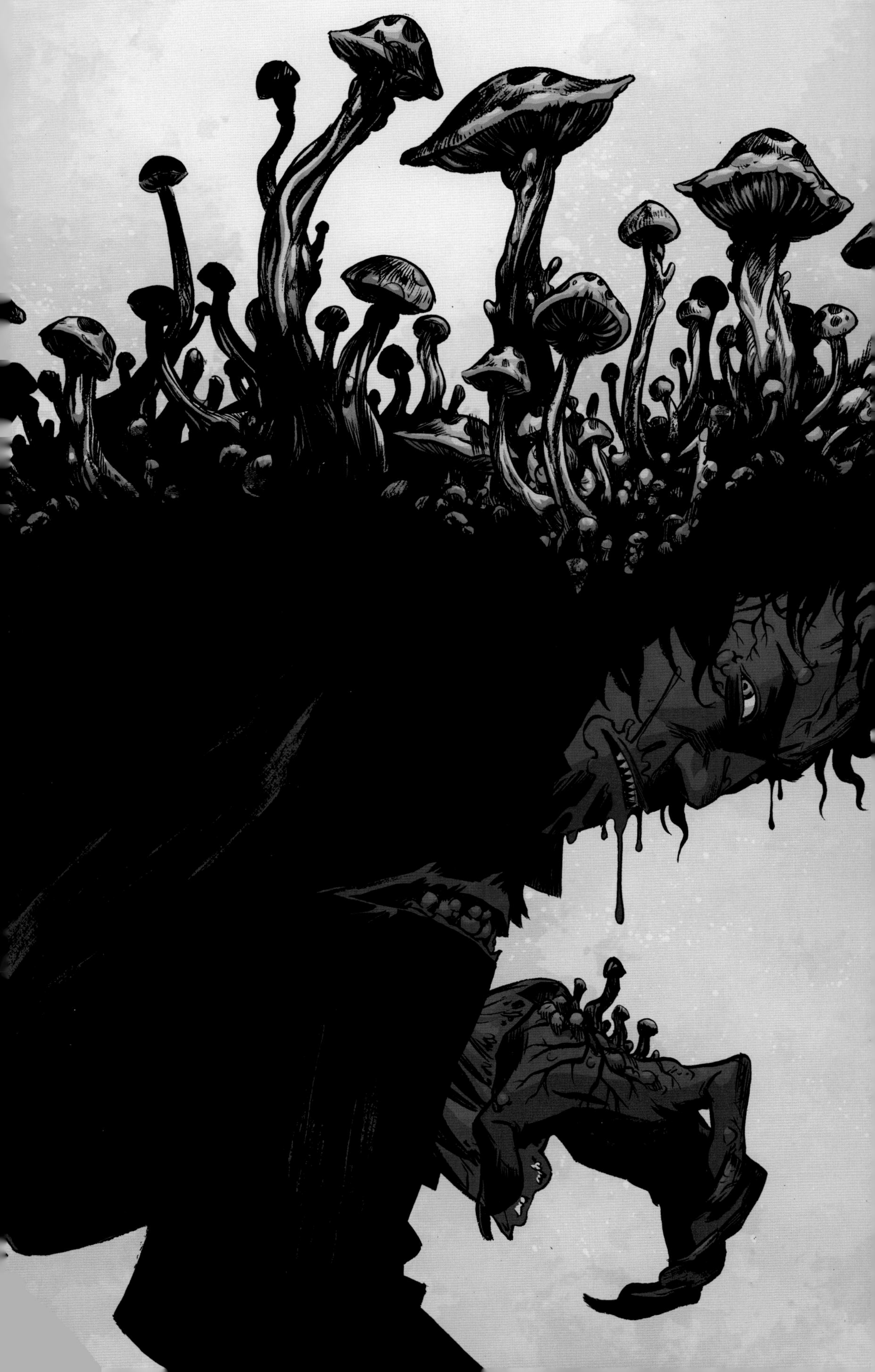

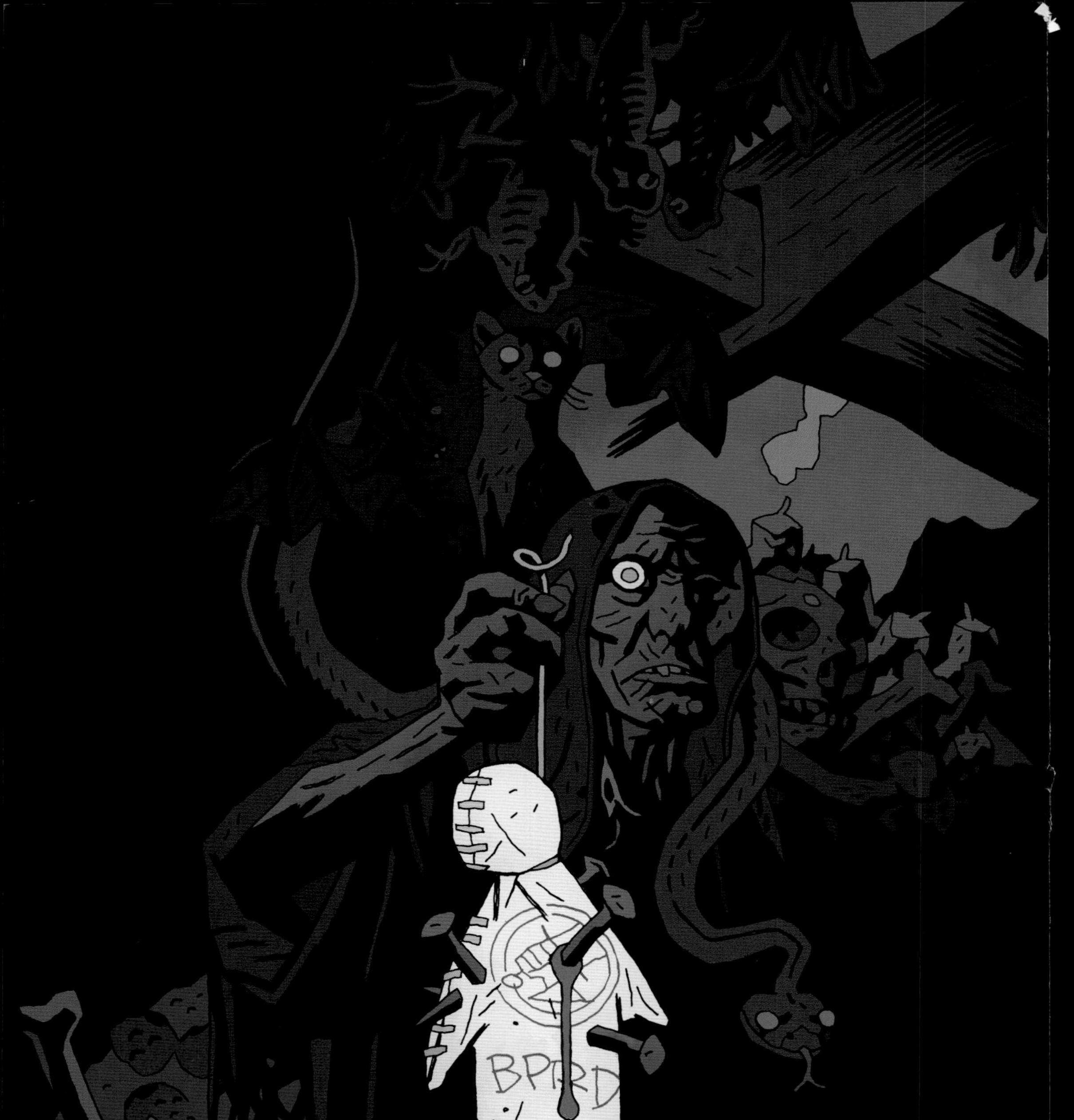
BPRD

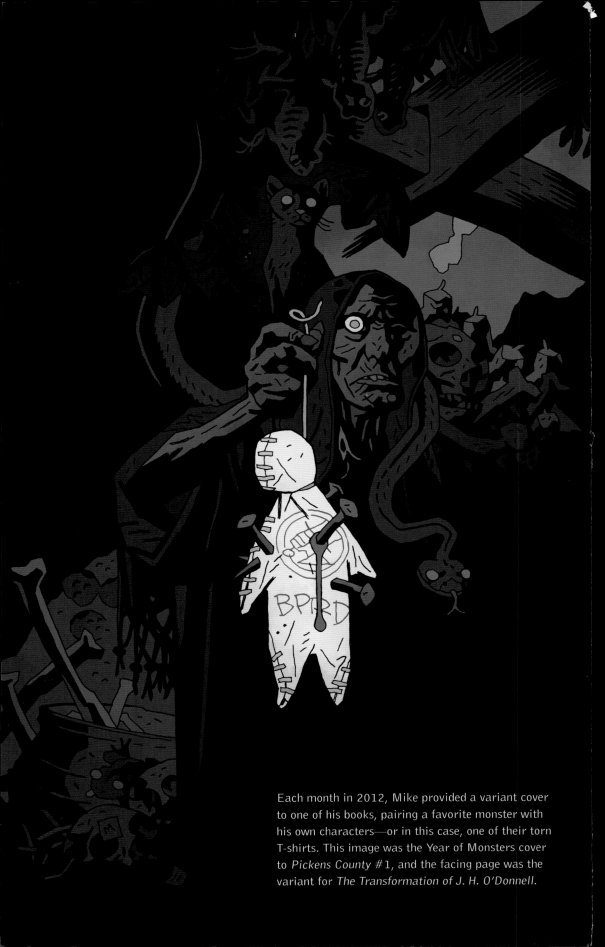

Each month in 2012, Mike provided a variant cover to one of his books, pairing a favorite monster with his own characters—or in this case, one of their torn T-shirts. This image was the Year of Monsters cover to *Pickens County #1*, and the facing page was the variant for *The Transformation of J. H. O'Donnell.*

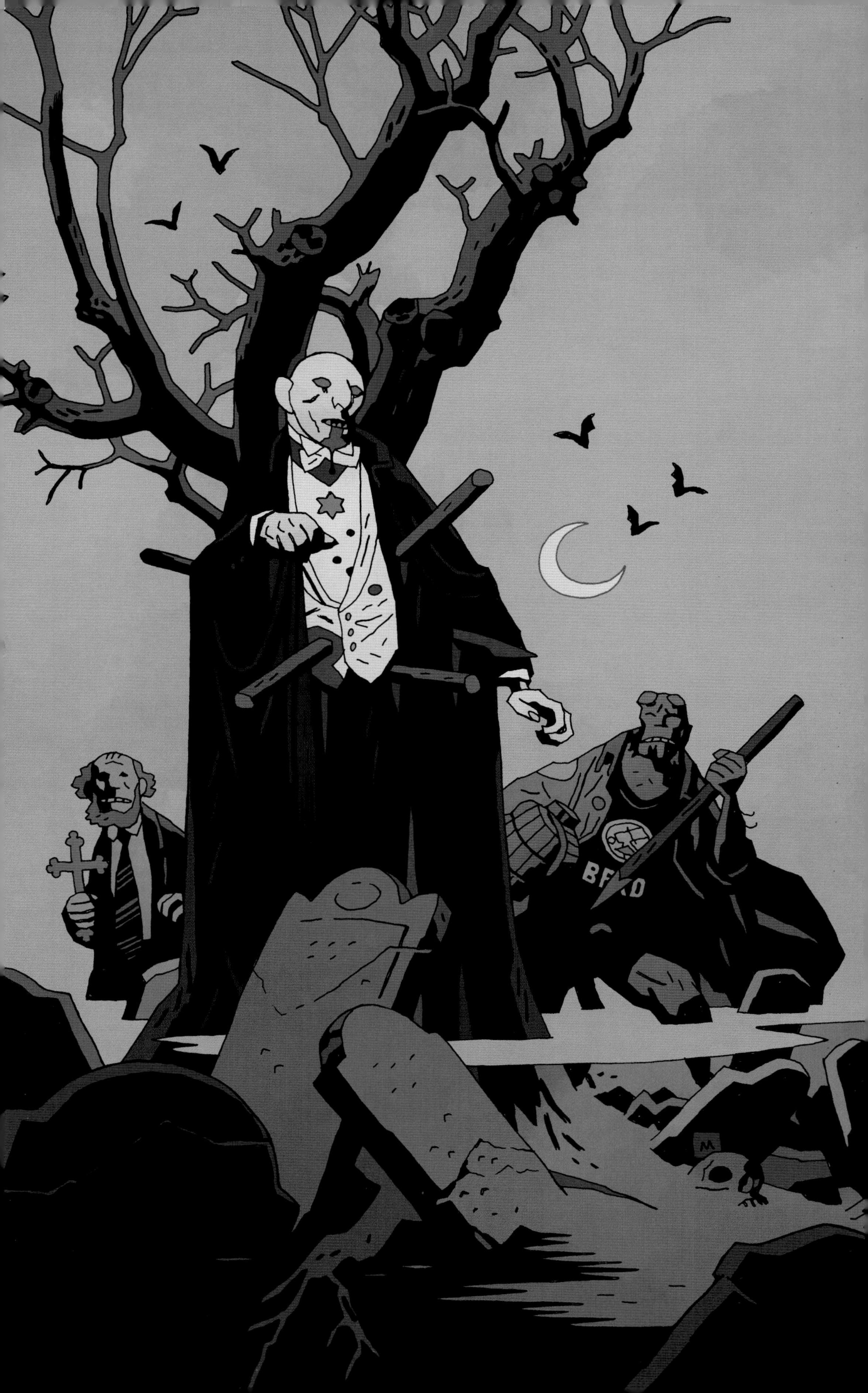

James Harren's cover to *The Abyss of Time* Part 2.

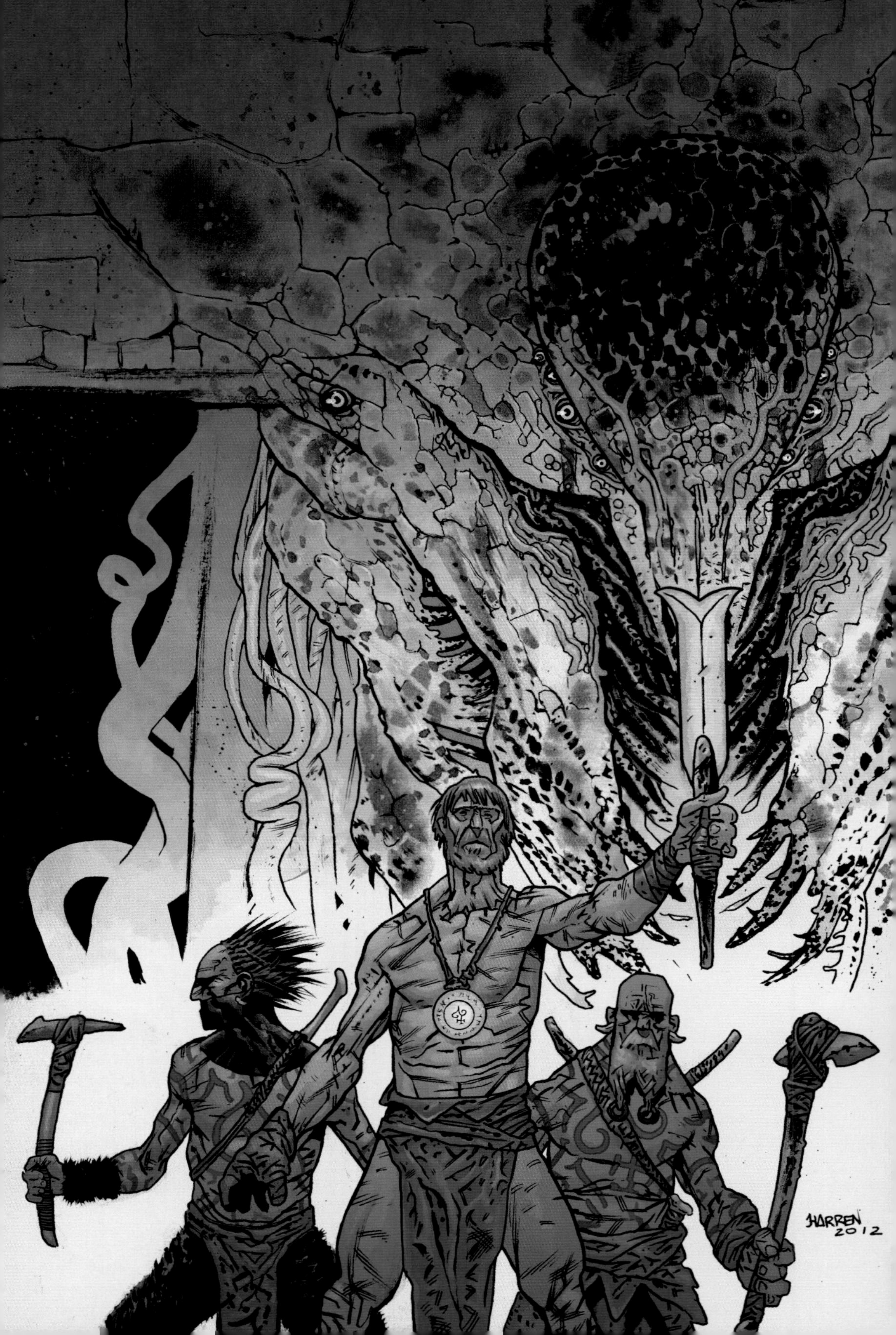
HARREN
2012

Also by MIKE MIGNOLA

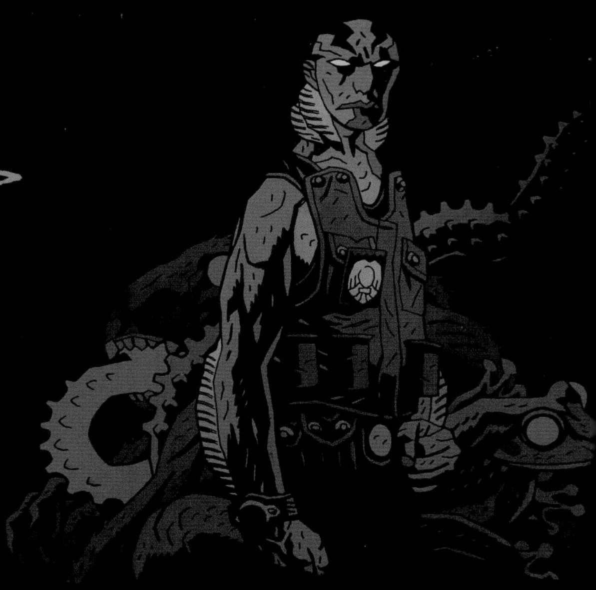

.P.R.D.: PLAGUE OF FROGS
ardcover Collection Volume 1
Mike Mignola, Chris Golden,
ıy Davis, and others
BN 978-1-59582-609-1 | $34.99

.P.R.D.: PLAGUE OF FROGS
ardcover Collection Volume 2
Mignola, John Arcudi,
avis, and others
BN 978-1-59582-672-5 | $34.99

.P.R.D.: PLAGUE OF FROGS
ardcover Collection Volume 3
Mignola, Arcudi, and Davis
BN 978-1-59582-860-6 | $34.99

.P.R.D.: PLAGUE OF FROGS
ardcover Collection Volume 4
Mignola, Arcudi, and Davis
BN 978-1-59582-974-0 | $34.99

.P.R.D.: THE WARNING
y Mignola, Arcudi, and Davis
BN 978-1-59582-304-5 | $17.99

.P.R.D.: THE BLACK GODDESS
y Mignola, Arcudi, and Davis
BN 978-1-59582-411-0 | $17.99

.P.R.D.: KING OF FEAR
y Mignola, Arcudi, and Davis
BN 978-1-59582-564-3 | $17.99

.P.R.D.: 1946
y Mignola, Joshua Dysart, and Paul Azaceta
BN 978-1-59582-191-1 | $17.99

.P.R.D.: 1947
y Mignola, Dysart, Fábio Moon,
nd Gabriel Bá
BN 978-1-59582-478-3 | $17.99

.P.R.D.: BEING HUMAN
y Mignola, Arcudi, Davis, and others
BN 978-1-59582-756-2 | $17.99

.P.R.D. HELL ON EARTH VOLUME 1:
EW WORLD
y Mignola, Arcudi, and Davis
BN 978-1-59582-707-4 | $19.99

B.P.R.D. HELL ON EARTH VOLUME 2:
GODS AND MONSTERS
By Mignola, Arcudi, Davis, and Crook
ISBN 978-1-59582-822-4 | $19.99

B.P.R.D. HELL ON EARTH VOLUME 3:
RUSSIA
By Mignola, Arcudi, Crook, and Duncan Fegredo
ISBN 978-1-59582-946-7 | $19.99

B.P.R.D. HELL ON EARTH VOLUME 4:
THE DEVIL'S ENGINE AND THE LONG DEATH
By Mignola, Arcudi, Crook, and James Harren
ISBN 978-1-59582-981-8 | $19.99

B.P.R.D. HELL ON EARTH VOLUME 5:
THE PICKENS COUNTY HORROR AND OTHERS
by Mignola, Scott Allie, Jason Latour, Harren,
Max Fiumara, and Becky Cloonan
ISBN 978-1-61655-140-7 | $19.99

LOBSTER JOHNSON VOLUME 2:
THE BURNING HAND
by Mignola, Arcudi, and Tonci Zonjic
ISBN 978-1-61655-031-8 | $17.99

ABE SAPIEN VOLUME 1:
THE DROWNING
By Mignola and Jason Shawn Alexander
ISBN 978-1-59582-185-0 | $17.99

ABE SAPIEN: VOLUME 2:
THE DEVIL DOES NOT JEST AND OTHER STORIES
By Mignola, Arcudi, Harren, and others
ISBN 978-1-59582-925-2 | $17.99

LOBSTER JOHNSON VOLUME 1:
THE IRON PROMETHEUS
By Mignola and Jason Armstrong
ISBN 978-1-59307-975-8 | $17.99

LOBSTER JOHNSON VOLUME 2:
THE BURNING HAND
By Mignola, Arcudi, and Tonci Zonjic
ISBN 978-1-61655-031-8 | $17.99

WITCHFINDER VOLUME 1:
IN THE SERVICE OF ANGELS
By Mignola and Ben Stenbeck
ISBN 978-1-59582-483-7 | $17.99

WITCHFINDER VOLUME 2:
LOST AND GONE FOREVER
By Mignola, Arcudi, and John Severin
ISBN 978-1-59582-794-4 | $17.99

THE AMAZING SCREW-ON HEAD AND OTHER CURIOUS OBJECTS
Hardcover Collection
By Mignola
ISBN 978-1-59582-501-8 | $17.99

BALTIMORE VOLUME 1:
THE PLAGUE SHIPS
By Mignola, Golden, and Stenbeck
ISBN 978-1-59582-677-0 | $24.99

BALTIMORE VOLUME 2:
THE CURSE BELLS
By Mignola, Golden, and Stenbeck
ISBN 978-1-59582-674-9 | $24.99

NOVELS

LOBSTER JOHNSON:
THE SATAN FACTORY
By Thomas E. Sniegoski
ISBN 978-1-59582-203-1 | $12.95

JOE GOLEM AND THE DROWNING CITY
Deluxe Hardcover
By Mignola and Golden
ISBN 978-1-59582-971-9 | $99.99

AVAILABLE AT YOUR LOCAL COMICS SHOP OR BOOKSTORE! • To find a comics shop in your area, call 1-888-266-4226
For more information or to order direct visit DarkHorse.com or call 1-800-862-0052 Mon.–Fri. 9 AM to 5 PM Pacific Time.
Prices and availability subject to change without notice.

DARK HORSE BOOKS

HELLBOY™

by MIKE MIGNOLA

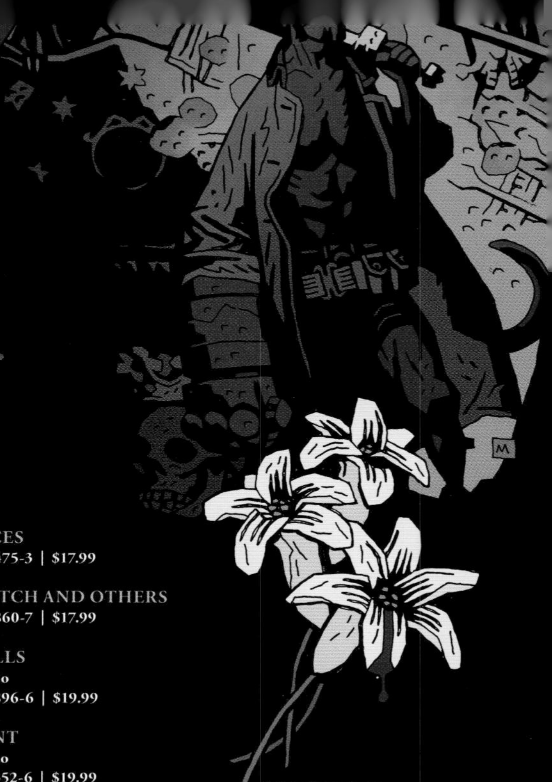

HELLBOY LIBRARY
EDITION VOLUME 1:
Seed of Destruction
and Wake the Devil
ISBN 978-1-59307-910-9 | $49.99

HELLBOY LIBRARY
EDITION VOLUME 2:
The Chained Coffin
and The Right Hand of Doom
ISBN 978-1-59307-989-5 | $49.99

HELLBOY LIBRARY
EDITION VOLUME 3:
Conqueror Worm
and Strange Places
ISBN 978-1-59582-352-6 | $49.99

HELLBOY LIBRARY
EDITION VOLUME 4:
The Crooked Man and The Troll Witch
with Richard Corben and others
ISBN 978-1-59582-658-9 | $49.99

HELLBOY LIBRARY
EDITION VOLUME 5:
Darkness Calls and the Wild Hunt
with Duncan Fegredo
ISBN 978-1-59582-886-6 | $49.99

HELLBOY LIBRARY
EDITION VOLUME 6:
The Storm and the Fury
and The Bride of Hell
with Duncan Fegredo, Richard Corben, Kevin
Nowlan, and Scott Hampton
ISBN 978-1-61655-133-9 | $49.99

SEED OF DESTRUCTION
with John Byrne
ISBN 978-1-59307-094-6 | $17.99

WAKE THE DEVIL
ISBN 978-1-59307-095-3 | $17.99

THE CHAINED COFFIN AND OTHERS
ISBN 978-1-59307-091-5 | $17.99

THE RIGHT HAND OF DOOM
ISBN 978-1-59307-093-9 | $17.99

CONQUEROR WORM
ISBN 978-1-59307-092-2 | $17.99

STRANGE PLACES
ISBN 978-1-59307-475-3 | $17.99

THE TROLL WITCH AND OTHERS
ISBN 978-1-59307-860-7 | $17.99

DARKNESS CALLS
with Duncan Fegredo
ISBN 978-1-59307-896-6 | $19.99

THE WILD HUNT
with Duncan Fegredo
ISBN 978-1-59582-352-6 | $19.99

THE CROOKED MAN
AND OTHERS
with Richard Corben
ISBN 978-1-59582-477-6 | $17.99

THE BRIDE OF HELL
AND OTHERS
with Richard Corben, Kevin Nowlan,
and Scott Hampton
ISBN 978-1-59582-740-1 | $19.99

THE STORM AND THE FURY
with Duncan Fegredo
ISBN 978-1-59582-827-9 | $19.99

HOUSE OF THE LIVING DEAD
with Richard Corben
ISBN 978-1-59582-757-9 | $14.99

THE ART OF HELLBOY
ISBN 978-1-59307-089-2 | $29.99

HELLBOY II:
THE ART OF THE MOVIE
ISBN 978-1-59307-964-2 | $24.99

HELLBOY: THE COMPANION
ISBN 978-1-59307-655-9 | $14.99

HELLBOY: WEIRD TALES
VOLUME 1
ISBN 978-1-56971-622-9 | $17.99
VOLUME 2
ISBN 978-1-56971-953-4 | $17.99

HELLBOY:
MASKS AND MONSTERS
with James Robinson and Scott Benefiel
ISBN 978-1-59582-567-4 | $17.99

NOVELS

HELLBOY: EMERALD HELL
By Tom Piccirilli
ISBN 978-1-59582-141-6 | $12.99

HELLBOY: THE ALL-SEEING EYE
By Mark Morris
ISBN 978-1-59582-141-6 | $12.99

HELLBOY: THE FIRE WOLVES
By Tim Lebbon
ISBN 978-1-59582-204-8 | $12.99

HELLBOY: THE ICE WOLVES
By Mark Chadbourn
ISBN 978-1-59582-205-5 | $12.99

SHORT STORIES

Illustrated by Mike Mignola

HELLBOY: ODD JOBS
By Poppy Z. Brite, Greg Rucka,
and others
ISBN 978-1-56971-440-9 | $14.99

HELLBOY: ODDER JOBS
By Frank Darabont, Guillermo del Toro,
and others
ISBN 978-1-59307-226-1 | $14.99

HELLBOY: ODDEST JOBS
By Joe R. Lansdale, China Miéville,
and others
ISBN 978-1-59307-944-4 | $14.99

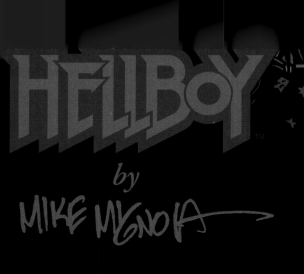